UP AGAINST THE WALL

BOOK THIRTY-FIVE
Louann Atkins Temple Women & Culture Series
Books about women and families, and their changing role in society

UP AGAINST THE WALL

Re-Imagining the U.S.-Mexico Border

EDWARD S. CASEY AND MARY WATKINS

University of Texas Press   Austin

The Louann Atkins Temple Women & Culture Series is supported by Allison, Doug, Taylor, and Andy Bacon; Margaret, Lawrence, Will, John, and Annie Temple; Larry Temple; the Temple-Inland Foundation; and the National Endowment for the Humanities.

Requests for permission to reproduce material from this work should be sent to:
  Permissions
  University of Texas Press
  P.O. Box 7819
  Austin, TX 78713-7819
  http://utpress.utexas.edu/index.php/rp-form

∞ The paper used in this book meets the minimum requirements of ANSI/NISO Z39.48-1992 (R1997) (Permanence of Paper).

Library of Congress Cataloging-in-Publication Data

Casey, Edward S., 1939–
  Up against the wall : re-imagining the U.S.-Mexico border / Edward S. Casey and Mary Watkins.
      pages   cm. — (Louann Atkins Temple women & culture series ; Book thirty-five)
  Includes bibliographical references and index.
  ISBN 978-0-292-75841-4 (cloth : alk. paper) — ISBN 978-0-292-75938-1 (pbk. : alk. paper)
  1. Mexican-American Border Region—Environmental conditions. 2. Mexican-American Border Region—Social conditions. 3. Mexicans—United States. 4. Mexican Americans. 5. United States—Social conditions—21st century. I. Watkins, Mary M. II. Title.
  GE160.M58C37   2014
  305.868'72073—dc23   2013048572
  doi:10.7560/758414

To *los ausentes*, the absent ones—those who had to leave home to find work in the United States and those who have died trying to cross the U.S.-Mexico border—and to their families.

Contents

Contents

Illustrations

Acknowledgments

The research for this book has required us to make multiple pilgrimages that have taken us far afield from our familiar homes and disciplinary pursuits. At every step, we have been blessed by the help of others—immensely so. Some have invited us into their homes and workplaces, sharing their perspectives on the issues pursued in this volume; others have shared their *testimonios* of crossing, living, or working at the border. Many who have been led to assist migrants and maquiladora workers helped us to speak with both migrants and workers and to more deeply understand the issues that make their lives precarious. Still others have read our work along the way, offering commentary and critique that have opened new vistas or led us to reconsider old ones. Given all the suffering occasioned by the border wall, it is striking how freely people we did not formerly know have warmly welcomed us into their worlds. We are grateful and hope that our words here can be received as an offering worthy of the time and life energies so graciously shared with us.

Three organizations helped us to immerse ourselves in U.S.-Mexico border issues: BorderLinks, in Tucson, Arizona, and Nogales, Mexico; the San Diego office of the American Friends Service Committee; and Global Exchange, in Berkeley, California. BorderLinks offers immersion experiences at and beyond the border to help participants raise their awareness about the impact of border and immigration policies, inspiring action for social change. They actively try to connect divided communities and "envision a world in which people, within and across social borders, respect and care for each other, value and celebrate differences, and build healthy and just communities where everyone has equal opportunity for a full and dignified life." These trips were invaluable for the contact they provided us with migrants, human-rights activists, U.S. Border Patrol officers, families divided because members now live in the United States, environmental and health experts, and the insights that grew from all this. We are grateful to Cecilia Guzman, of BorderLinks, who deeply and generously mentored us on conditions at the border in Ambos Nogales, and to Elsbeth Pollack, also of BorderLinks, who helped us create a daylong immersion experience in Santa Barbara to educate community members about the difficulties neighbors without documents are facing in the wake of the Secure Communities initiative of the Department of Homeland Security. Kiko Trujillo, director of BorderLinks in Mexico, shared incisive insights during two interviews.

The U.S.-Mexico Border Program of the American Friends Service Committee helped us to understand the history of the wall in the San Diego sector and its human costs. Its staff members also arranged the Quaker workcamp we participated in at Maclovio Rojas, which introduced us to communities at the border living in the shadows of multinational corporations' maquiladoras. In particular, we thank Christian Ramirez, the American Friends Service Committee's national coordinator for immigrant rights, whose knowledge about the wall catapulted our interest into the preoccupation necessary for this work.

We joined two human-rights delegations created by Global Exchange, one in Tijuana and the other in Chiapas, where we witnessed Zapatistas creating autonomous communities as an effort of alterglobalization. We are grateful to the artist and activist Carmela Castrejon for leading the Tijuana delegation and for helping us, on yet another occasion, to better understand the art on the south side of the wall in Tijuana.

In addition, we are moved to give special thanks to the following set of people whom we consulted closely on matters of the border and the border wall. First of all, Mike McCoy, environmental activist and leader of the efforts to restore the Tijuana Estuary after it had fallen into abuse and neglect over decades. He has not only dedicated himself to returning the estuary to a healthier state but also led many efforts to call the border wall into question and to suggest more constructive alternatives. For us, he has been a continual source of understanding and inspiration.

Second, we wish to thank heartily Bob Stone and Betsy Bowman, whose inspired educational work at the Center for Global Justice, in San Miguel de Allende, has effectively explored modes of resistance to corporate capitalism, particularly through the creation of cooperatives. Third, we are hugely indebted to Jay Johnson-Castro Sr., ingenious border activist; convener of the Border Wall Summit; instigator of RioFest; organizer against the T. Don Hutto Residential Center; founder of Border Ambassadors, Inc.; and organizer of the Regional Advisory Council of the Rio Grande/ Río Bravo watershed in 2010, which has become part of America's Great Waters Coalition. Jay listened to us describe our project and generously introduced us to people in the Lower Rio Grande Valley he knew we should learn from.

We were deeply instructed on the history of the wall in the Lower Rio Grande Valley by Scott Nicol, artist and border activist. Nick Braune, a colleague of Nicol at Texas Southmost College, was immensely helpful in discussing the deeper philosophical issues at stake in La Frontera. John A. Sproul Jr., the program coordinator and manager of the Rio Bosque Wetlands Park, El Paso, shared his knowledge of the fate of the Rio Grande in that area.

We also thank the Reverend John Fanestil, executive director of San Diego's Foundation for Change, for insight into the history of Friendship Park and the manner in which the wall fortification has affected it. He celebrates binational communion with participants on both sides of the border fence in Friendship Park. He exemplifies the kind of raw courage, ingenuity, and tenacity required to make progress in a desperate situation such as is found in the Tijuana area.

The work of several historians, philosophers, and cultural critics has been pivotal to the understanding we have reached regarding issues at the border wall; let us here name only Albert Camarillo, John McCafferty, Michelle Alexander, Rodolfo Acuña, Florence Krall Shepherd, Gloria Anzaldúa, Judith Butler, Gary Snyder, Wendy Brown, and Jacques Derrida.

The following individuals generously helped educate us about the border in south Texas: Beto O'Rourke, Blanca Villalpando, Antonio Zavaleta, Judy Ackerman, Eloisa Taméz, Chad Foster, Jodi Goodwin, Israel Reyna, Jaime Arizpe, Fred Morales, and volunteers at Annunciation House, El Paso.

In our effort to understand the transborder artistic partnerships that have arisen, we want to thank the artists Alfred Quiroz, Guadalupe Serrano (of Taller Yonke), and Carmela Castrejon (an early member of the Border Arts Workshop) for speaking with us—and, of course, for their art, which from our first viewing of it has inspired us to take the wall as a site for imagining, insight, and vision.

Along the way, we have been helped by many careful readers of chapters and sometimes of the whole manuscript. Our colleagues Nuria Ciofalo, Alicia Enciso, Drew Leder, Fred Evans, and John Protevi are to be singled out for their insights, their encouragement of this work, and their efforts far beyond the call of duty. We are grateful to Nina Falls and Jessica Sims for their generous help in the final stage of manuscript production. Jill Holslin located the source of an important photograph.

A veritable phalanx of graduate assistants from the State University of New York at Stony Brook have given close scrutiny to our manuscript at several critical stages while undertaking other research tasks along the way. Among these are Kriszta Sajber, Greg Wolfe, Jeff Epstein, Wesley Mattingly, and Stephen Bourque. We want to single out Andres Colapinto, Brady Heiner, Tim Johnston, Azucena Cruz-Pierre, and (again) Jessica Sims for their special contributions.

Special help and support came from Robert Crease and Eduardo Mendieta, respectively a recent and the current chairperson at Stony Brook.

We are grateful for opportunities to present our work at multiple points in order to receive feedback from various audiences, including the Radical Philosophy Association; the Committee on Asian and Asian-American Philosophers of the American Philosophical Association; the Society for Phenomenology and Existential Philosophy; the Ministry for Women at La Casa de Maria; the Centro para la Justícia Global; the Center for Interpretive and Qualitative Research at Duquesne University; the conference "Migration, Memory, and Place," organized by Sten Moslund for the Danish Network for Cultural Memory Studies and Network for Migration and Culture; the California Association of Marriage and Family Therapists; the Union Theological Seminary; Eastern Mennonite University; Berea College; Antioch University Seattle; the Konrad Adenauer Foundation in Dresden, Germany (especially Ed's host, Joachim Klose); Pacifica Graduate Institute; Cottage Hospital Grand Rounds; and a Malintzin Society conference. We want to express our gratitude to the conceivers and founders of Malintzin, Mónica del Valle and Themis de la Peña, for their vision of creating a bridge across Mexican and American cultures, a binational consortium that works against the winds of division that are chilling us and provides instead the warmth of creation and *communitas*.

As we attempted to understand the "border" in Santa Barbara, we were welcomed by PUEBLO, a Latino advocacy group working on a number of important fronts such as living wages, the seizure of immigrants' cars at DUI checkpoints, housing, and human-rights issues. From 2008 to 2010 Mary worked with members of the Immigration Committee at PUEBLO to create an oral history of Mexican migrants without documents in Santa Barbara, published as *In the Shadows of Paradise: Testimonies from the Undocumented Community in Santa Barbara*. These stories provided critical insights concerning the experience of neighbors without documents. Mary is grateful for the trust placed in her and the candor offered. In large part, the energy she has given to the writing in these pages is offered as a thank you and as a way to respond to what was shared with her.

On a more personal note, we are also grateful to our daughters—Ani Rosenthal, Lily Rosenthal, Rachel Rosenthal, and Danielle Granaroli—who have accompanied us on various trips to the border and to Mexico, sharing in our interest.

UP AGAINST THE WALL

Introduction

We live in an era of forced migration with unprecedented global dimensions. How are we to peaceably and justly coexist—those who must leave our homes forever to meet our human needs, and the rest of us, who often find our neighborhoods, towns, and cities changing as a result of these necessary migrations? In particular, how can we create a compassionate and just response to new neighbors who have come to the United States to find work or asylum? We offer this book as an invitation to a sustained reflection on these questions.

Migration is "forced" when people flee from ecological degradation and devastation, violence (as part of wars both international and civil, the drug trade, and genocide), severe governmental corruption, failing or inadequate infrastructure, and absolute destitution.[1] Desperate unfulfilled needs for adequate food, shelter, health care, education, and employment drive people to cross national borders, leaving their families, friends, home communities, and countries of origin. If all current international migrants on earth formed a single nation, it would be the fifth-most populous on the planet, roughly the population of Brazil. The number of migrants is growing daily.

Throughout the world, citizens of relatively more prosperous nation-states are grappling with their new migrant neighbors along a continuum from outright and often violent rejection to empathic hospitality and welcome: Israelis with Eritreans, for example, or the French with Gypsies, Spanish with Moroccans, Danes with Tunisians, Chinese with Vietnamese, Indians with Bangladeshis, Mexicans with Guatemalans, and Americans with Mexicans. Nations all over the earth are building separation barriers to literally wall out those attempting to enter under extreme duress, with examples of such walls visible worldwide: in Greece, against Turks; in India, against Bangladeshis and Burmese; in Iran, against Pakistanis; in Israel, against Palestinians; in South Korea, against North Koreans; in Saudi Arabia, against Yemenis and Iraqis; in Spain and other European

Union nations, against Africans; in Thailand, against Malaysians; and in the United States, against Mexicans and others from Latin America.

As climate change and global income disparities worsen, the number of environmental and economic refugees will further increase, making it imperative for us to re-imagine not only the character of international borders but also the human character we seek to cultivate, one that can guide us toward peaceful and just coexistence. As it turns out, these twin goals are inextricably linked and best pursued side by side, as we do in this volume.

In this book, we pursue the re-imagining that our present crisis of forced migration requires through a close consideration of the situation at the U.S.-Mexico border and the shadow this situation casts on Mexican and U.S. communities far from the literal border. The Chicana writer Gloria Anzaldúa describes the U.S.-Mexico border as an open wound, "*una herida abierta*, where the Third World grates against the first and bleeds" (1999, 25). Nowhere else is this wound between the First and Third Worlds as gaping as it is between the United States and Mexico. Here the self-proclaimed "leader" of the "First World" tries to close off its lands as if it were a gated community, locking out newcomers in need and ironically seeming to forget that most of its citizens' own ancestors were themselves newcomers to Native American and Mexican lands.

Approaching global forced migration through a stark confrontation with the formidable wall recently built at the U.S.-Mexico border, we will grapple philosophically with the nature of borders. We will bring you up to the wall itself, not neglecting its sheer physicality and varied design. We offer a view from the wall of the stark display of the vexed dynamics of forced migration. An international border such as that at La Frontera (the Spanish name for the U.S.-Mexico border) is a place where we can clearly see what pernicious forms of globalization produce, a vision that is critical if we are to re-imagine national borders and the relation between settled citizens and newcomers without prescribed documents.

We examine not only the literal separation wall at the U.S.-Mexico border but also the less literal yet no less real "walls" encountered between U.S. citizens and their Mexican neighbors now living in American cities and towns—barriers equally fateful in their consequences.[2] After migrants cross the death-dealing desert and mountains at La Frontera, the initial woundings at this international border are harshly repeated in the towns and cities where they try to settle, too often finding themselves once again locked out of basic human rights. Multiple forms of political, economic, and social exclusion, reinforced by racist projections, create daily "precarity" (Butler 2006), including the overhanging threats of detention and deportation.

We will move between a philosophical grasp of the nature of borders and boundaries as they reflect and affect issues of migration and a psychosocial understanding of the effects of social exclusion on both the newcomer and the citizen whose own family arrived earlier in history. To accomplish this task has required intertwining insights from a philosopher, Edward Casey, and a liberation psychologist, Mary Watkins.[3] We join forces in these pages to see through the multiple barriers that have arisen as the United States has sought to wall off its friendly neighbors to the south.

What began in 2002 as an attempt to educate ourselves personally about the relations between Mexico and the United States at the border itself, and between Mexicans and Anglos in our cities of residence (New York and Santa Barbara), drew us into a more than decade-long project. Circumstances at these borders have continuously worsened during this time, creating a humanitarian crisis not only at the border itself but also in many American towns and cities, as well as within hastily constructed immigrant detention centers throughout the United States. In the wake of 9/11 and a grim economic downturn, Americans are witnessing the criminalization of people who are poor and have left home to search for basic human rights of adequate shelter, food, health care, education, and security. The step of criminalization is an essential ingredient in the rapid rise of the detention and deportation industries in the United States, highly profitable adjuncts to the privatized prison system.

The dehumanizing tide of American racism has once again risen, singling out Mexicans who are indigent and lack proper documents. Citizens in neighborhoods, towns, cities, and entire states—despite being enlivened by Mexican culture and sustained by the hard labor of Mexican workers— are turning against those of Mexican descent. Some citizens have taken to hunting down, harassing, scaring, beating, and even killing Mexicans almost as pastimes. This decade strikes a tragically familiar chord in American history: after having given their labor for their "hosts'" convenience, often suffering abuse in the process, those who have labored are run out of town or country in violent and unjust ways.

For the last decade, we have moved back and forth across the border, studying the wall and meeting with border activists, Border Patrol authorities, migrants, and citizens. Closer to home, we have talked with Mexicans living in our cities about their struggles far from home. We have studied immigration legislation that has been passed by cities and towns—and legislation that has failed to be passed by the federal government. While we have written this book from our professional viewpoints, those of a philosopher and of a psychologist, we have encountered the rising tragedy primarily as neighbors. We are all neighbors to people who worry that immigrants will take their jobs, that their culture and language will fade, and that tax revenues will be exhausted in supporting too many newcomers, thus undermining their own security. But we are also all neighbors to the newly arrived, to those who had to leave their homes and families to survive, who find themselves misconstrued as lazy intruders when in fact they desperately desire to work and contribute to their communities.

We have both had to realize our own version of border crossing, moving away from the comfort and familiarity of our previous work into the arenas of immigration, detention, deportation, national security issues and myths in a post-9/11 world, and the history of the southwestern United States and Mexico. We have struggled with and enjoyed Spanish as we have taken part in bilingual conversations. Our field method has consisted of taking steady if somewhat irregular steps into places and relationships new to us. We walked the banks of the Rio Grande, talking to the Border Patrol agents we encountered, and we worked alongside Latino activists involved with local immigration issues.

The strengths and limitations of this book reflect our shared social location: Anglos who have become preoccupied with matters pertaining to La Frontera. Much of the literature about the border is by Latinos, and rightfully so. Little work that might fill gaps in Anglo understanding and particularly Anglo border psychology has been done. We began this project as an effort to address fellow Anglos who are ready to confront border issues in themselves and in our nation and world. However, our ideas have found a warm reception with Chicanos and Mexicans, many of whom feel deeply about the issues we take up in the following pages and welcome the ways we are pursuing them. International audiences have also welcomed our reflections, for their own countries are finding themselves either losing citizens through migration or "hosting" migrants, however ambivalently. We hope our efforts have led to insights that will be illuminating to those on both sides of the border, as well as on both sides of political divides over questions of immigration. We are convinced that all parties involved in border dynamics need to develop common cause if a more humane coexistence is to emerge at this historical moment.

Part 1 of this book, written by Ed Casey, focuses on the history and fate of the wall that the United States built at its border with Mexico, placing special emphasis on the role of the wall as a physical structure—its proposed justification, its actual construction, its location, and its varied effects on the local inhabitants and natural environment. Chapter 1 examines the relationship between the separation wall as a material entity and the U.S.-Mexico border qua border. However closely intertwined they may be, they are by no means equivalent. The wall purports to be the materialization of the border, but the border itself is a projected entity, the creature of a treaty signed in 1848. The elegant simplicity of the borderline as designated on official maps contrasts with the material ingredients of a wall that has been built of iron, steel, and concrete. Intended to be airtight and untrespassable, border and wall alike stand in contrast to boundaries, which are porous and open-ended forms of edge, giving breathing space to those who pass through them.

The first chapter closely examines the difference between boundaries and borders, defined here as two major forms of edge. Whereas borders in this account are rigid and unyielding, boundaries encourage (or at least permit) uninhibited movement across themselves: they are permeable. While the wall at La Frontera purports to be a physical embodiment of the U.S.-Mexico border, a closer look shows it to possess various boundary aspects that serve to complicate, and in certain cases to undermine, its status as a strict border. From another perspective, the U.S.-Mexico border has shifted from being a porous boundary in earlier times to becoming one of the most highly militarized borders in the world today. The wall, whose construction followed NAFTA in the mid-1990s and which was further fortified after 9/11, is one built against a wave of want, of unfulfilled needs, of people displaced by forces larger than themselves. Its purported purposes of immigration and drug control are only half the story. In cruel fact, the wall contributes directly to creating and supporting a world of low wages and high profits. It immobilizes many people just south of the border, many of whom work for low wages in the maquiladoras on the Mexican side. It also ensures that those who manage to cross into the United States must try to be as invisible as possible once there so as to avoid detention and deportation. Thus silenced, many are unable to fight effectively for fair and safe working and housing conditions and for access to health care and higher education. They are subject to identity checks at random moments, and if unable to show adequate documentation of citizenship, they are held in detention prisons and deported to their countries of origin in unprecedentedly large numbers.

The succeeding three chapters of Part 1 focus on particular locations of the wall, two cities in the western part of La Frontera and a region in the eastern portion of the wall's expanse. Its construction having begun in the mid-1990s, the massive wall continues to grow and to cast its baleful shadow over inhabitants on both sides.

Chapter 2 takes up the situation at the twin cities of Nogales, Sonora, and Nogales, Arizona. We show both symmetries and dissymmetries in the way the border wall affects these adjoining cities, which are linked by a long history of close association but are now severed by the border wall.

Characterizing the two towns as "incongruous counterparts," we delineate the fateful interaction of citizens of both communities, at once dependent on each other (and often related by ties of blood or marriage) and yet riven by the presence of the wall—sometimes driven literally underground into sewers and tunnels that connect the two cities and sometimes forced to the far edges of the wall in desperate efforts to cross the border. We also explore the emergence of hope in the face of despair: hope for a better future despite a discouraging current moment.

Tijuana, discussed in chapter 3, presents the very different situation of a town of recent origin that has mushroomed into a major city with all the growing pains of an adolescent metropolis. This chapter focuses particularly on the fate of the Tijuana Estuary, located on the American side but heavily polluted from the Mexican side; exacerbating the problem, the United States has begun building additional walls nearby, to the south, threatening to clog the already suffering wetlands. We pay special attention to the environmental dimensions of this vexed circumstance, dimensions that affect the whole region at this westernmost edge of the border—indeed, the entirety of La Frontera.

In Part 1's final chapter, we examine the differential impacts of the border wall throughout the Lower Rio Grande Valley, where the U.S government has seized land for its wall, expropriating citizens' backyards as well as portions of a college campus. We note the paradoxes generated by the many gaps in this purportedly continuous and impassable wall. The Rio Grande River forms the focus of this chapter because of its unique role as a naturally given basis of the border—but a basis that presents a significant quandary with respect to the exact location of the borderline between the United States and Mexico. The chapter closes with a cautionary tale illuminating the striking contrast between an artificially constructed wall and an earthbound river. A brief postlude concludes Part 1.

Concentrating on Nogales, Tijuana, and the Lower Rio Grande Valley enables us to enter more deeply into a detailed description of the border wall and its effects and thus to investigate how it has intervened in the daily lives of those who are directly affected by its presence. It also allows us to compare the differential effects of the wall's presence in terms of several factors that thread through the entire discussion, including the role of estuaries, rivers, and other natural phenomena; the environmental consequences of the wall's construction; modes of border crossing and surveillance by the Border Patrol; and issues of immigration and (to a lesser extent) drug trafficking. These various factors combine into a complex verbal palimpsest that amounts to a written portrait of La Frontera, one based on narratives of local citizens and our own experiences in its vicinity.

In each of the three case studies treated in Part 1, we bear witness to significant variations of the wall's divisive presence, a presence that is not only geographical and historical but also cultural, racial, and political. In this opening part of the book, we are concerned to show the many ways in which the wall is self-defeating, even as (and often to the very extent that) it is fiercely reinforced and surveilled by the U.S. Border Patrol. At the same time, certain basic themes sounded here will resonate through the remainder of the book—above all, the extensive and intensive suffering occasioned by the building of a single (and in some instances a double and triple) wall along the land portion of the southern U.S. border and the deeper human wounds that the wall's continuing existence causes.

Part 2, written by Mary Watkins, starts at the westernmost part of the border, at Friendship Park. We soon depart from the actual border and the material wall, however, looking instead at how we find their multiple echoes in the divisions in our neighborhoods, schools, and daily lives. The wall that now marks the U.S.-Mexico border concretizes the metaphorical walls that have been born of racism, fear, and avarice in many towns and cities throughout the United States. Part 2 examines how the border operates at psychological, interpersonal, and intercommunity levels.

As an opening example, chapter 5 traces how the project to radically redraw the U.S.-Mexico border in 1848 affected Santa Barbara, California, established as the primary Spanish outpost in Alta California. When the literal border moved southward as a result of the Mexican-American War, westward-moving Anglos rapidly gathered economic, social, and political power in towns and cities in the Southwest. Various kinds of walls were put into place between Anglos and those of Mexican descent, reducing many Mexicans' land ownership and shifting their predominant occupations to poorly paying wage labor. Pueblos and barrios became marked off from the increasing Anglo population. Segregation of schools, beaches, neighborhoods, and even movie theaters became commonplace. Such measures, which tended to relegate people of Mexican descent to internal colonies, ensured an easily available low-paid workforce while consigning U.S. citizens of Mexican descent and noncitizens of Mexican descent to an underclass caste status.

Chapter 6 reflects on the creation of a racial caste system in the United States, an arrangement that has consigned Mexicans to a low socioeconomic status, alongside Native Americans and African Americans. Several critical questions emerge here: How do we continue to construct and sustain racial caste in the United States? Whom and what does such a caste system serve? How does this system function with Mexican migrants, and how does it affect them? We examine how globalization creates internal colonies where people struggle with too few resources, condemned to assume a permanent position of low-wage labor and unemployment from which too few escape. We also take up the link between mass incarceration in the United States and the creation of multiple detention centers for migrants without documents. Following the work of Fanon and Memmi, we outline the psychological and interpersonal effects of such displacement on both those who are "colonized" and those who profit from such displacement.

In chapter 7, we look at the psychological and spiritual costs that the current immigration system imposes on Anglos. We focus here particularly on the price of social and historical amnesia, of "othering" and scapegoating, and of closing one's door in the face of others' need as these affect the psyches—the souls—of citizens. Turning to restorative shame, we investigate how an acknowledgment of historical injustices can help heal and reconcile damaged and divided communities.

In chapters 8 and 9, the final chapters of Part 2, we animate a prophetic imagination that can show us how to live our borders differently. What results when we refuse to accept an imposed limit, such as the U.S.-Mexico border wall, and not only contest it but create very different modes of being that resist and transfigure it? We move from the transgressive nature of border-wall art to varied examples of embodied prophetic imagination, examining cities where local citizens have worked out ways of living together that exemplify an emerging transborder ethics. Beginning with the United Nations International Convention on the Protection of the Rights of All Migrant Workers and Members of Their Families, we describe initiatives such as border peace parks, humanitarian initiatives at the border, sanctuary cities, provision of driver's licenses and identification cards, migrant-work centers, enfranchisement of migrants to allow political participation, living-wage initiatives, and education initiatives for nonmigrants that inform them about the challenges migrants face daily. We also consider forms of reconciliation between migrants and citizens in situations where people are willing to acknowledge the dark histories that shadow their communities and to imagine and forge together a future less burdened and stained by racism and injustice.

We hope that this mosaic of approaches—meant to be exemplary and suggestive rather than comprehensive and encyclopedic—will nourish readers' imaginations and provoke the desire *to live borders differently* at the levels of the individual psyche, neighborhoods, schools, towns and cities, and between nations. This is where we place our hope.

We are now witnessing the doors of a country with great resources closing against a people who are asking for an opportunity to work very hard in exchange for decent wages and basic human rights. Throughout the world, millions of people are far from home, searching for this same opportunity and set of rights. They are desperate and anxious as closed doors shut them out. How America works out its relationship to the U.S.-Mexico border in terms of the concrete relations between citizens and newcomers will set an example, for better or worse, for the rest of the relatively privileged world. How Americans answer the human address of the Mexican migrants among them will also determine whether American citizens can retrieve their souls from habits of fear, greed, neglect, derision, and unjust treatment.

The U.S.-Mexico border is a place where two historical-cultural tectonic plates are grinding against each other. A seismic change in national and personal attitudes toward forced migration is desperately needed in the United States, as in many other nations. To alter these general attitudes most effectively, we must begin with particular cases. There is no more revealing place to start than with the circumstance at La Frontera and its many repercussions in neighborhoods and cities, whether located next to the wall or far from it.

Part 1

RE-VIEWING LA FRONTERA

Borders versus Boundaries

CHAPTER 1

La Frontera as Border and Boundary

It is customary to think of La Frontera, the border between the United States and Mexico, in terms of troubled issues of immigration control and drug traffic, both of which have received increasing public attention in the last decade. The first part of our book offers a different, philosophically oriented, way of beginning to understand the situation in this vexed place. Before considering the injustices bred at La Frontera—on which emphasis will be placed in Part 2—we need to ask a few preliminary questions.

What, in effect, is a border? How did this division between two mostly friendly nations come to exist? How has its character as a border changed since its inception in 1848, especially since the construction of the massive wall built there beginning in the mid-1990s? By exploring these basic questions, we will be in a better position to discern not only what has been created at the border but also what the alternatives might have been—and still are.

EDGES AS BORDERS AND BOUNDARIES

Borders, along with boundaries, belong to the broad family of things we call "edges." Edges are where matter—be it the dense matter of solid things or the stretches of space that we call "regions" and "territories"—runs out or runs thin. Edges mark the place where things lose their dense consistency and land relinquishes its spread-out character. They are where material substance or physical landscape comes to a finish—where matter peters out.

At the same time, edges are where energies of many kinds—personal and political, demographic, geographic, and historical—collect and become concentrated. Edges are also where the contours and profiles of things come to full expression: where the impact and imprint of things take place. "Everything flourishes at the edge," says the philosopher Jacques Derrida (1987, 187). But edges are also often points of great vulnerability, where things fall apart and breakdown occurs. Noxious agents enter organisms at their edges, through their skins and orifices.

Whatever their virtues and vulnerabilities, *edges matter*. They make a decisive difference in how we distinguish one thing from another, one place from the next, one woman from her sister, one man from his son. Despite their abrupt or eventual vanishing, edges make it clear where one thing, place, or person begins and another ends. Edges matter to matter itself; they are a primary means by which differences between things and places, events and persons, get established and sorted out.

This is to conceive of edges in terms of what they *are not*: they are not merely parts of matter or space (if anything, they mark the moment when matter gives way to open space), and they have to do with the differentiation between things. But *what are they*, positively stated? They are the point where things exfoliate and enter into their surroundings. At least, this is so for the external edges of things, edges that we tend to take as exemplary of all edges. But there are also internal edges, in the form of folds and creases, cracks and crevices. Whereas external edges serve to terminate something, internal edges complicate and reveal it from within.[1] Each role for an edge is of positive, and often decisive, significance: things must end somewhere (or else they would no longer count as "things"), and it is valuable to know just where this happens; further, we need to know what inner structures are like, not just for purposes of medical diagnosis, but also, and more generally, for the perception of all complex objects. It follows that edges are not just peripheral presences; they have everything to do with how things *are* and not just with how they appear.

Edges thus understood come in a number of major forms: brinks, rims, margins, thresholds, frames—and the list goes on.[2] Borders and boundaries are edges that form a special pair. Both act to demarcate a given place or region; to set it off from other places or regions. In this capacity, each is decidedly two-sided; we talk of being "on this side" or "on the other side" of a given boundary or border. To straddle a border or boundary is to take up a precarious position; eventually, one must go one way or another—you can teeter on either kind of edge for only so long.

Despite this similarity, the members of this pair have diverse origins and modes of realization. A border is a clearly and crisply delineated entity established by conventional agreements, such as treaties or laws; even if animals of some species create distinctive edges (e.g., territorial markings), a border is primarily a product of human history and its vicissitudes. A boundary, too, can have cultural and historical aspects, but it is paradigmatically natural in status, as with the boundary of a forest, its outer edge. A boundary is rarely demarcated with exacting precision, varying in contour and extent depending on surrounding circumstances. Most important, it is porous, admitting the passage of various substances through it—not just for ritualistic reasons (as with a threshold), but also because of its very structure, as with human skin. A border is most often designed to be impervious. While a boundary lacks precise positioning (and hence is difficult to map), a border is located *just here* and nowhere else. It is at once securely fixed in place and unyielding in its form (thereby facilitating its mapped representation, as well as its measurement in miles and meters). Whatever the confusion between the usage of "borders" and "boundaries" may be in ordinary English parlance, we shall take them as quite different in kind. Each realizes a different destiny of the edge.

Border and Boundary at La Frontera

What do borders and boundaries have to do with La Frontera? In our view, just about everything—as can be seen if we focus on the ways in which La Frontera can be considered first as a border and then as a boundary.

The *border* aspect of La Frontera is massively evident, hence the common appellation "U.S.-Mexico border." Originally, "the border" was the result of the Treaty of Guadalupe Hidalgo in 1848, and it has never changed location except for the modifications introduced by the Gadsden Purchase of 1853 and one small sliver of land called "El Chamizal" just north of the Rio Grande in El Paso that was set aside in 1963. The original border was itself the conjoint creation of people bearing very different job descriptions: opposed armies that, though retreating from outright war of the kind that in the 1840s had been so devastating to the northern provinces of Mexico, were still on the ready; politicians, ranging from President James Polk to diplomats who carried out the treaty negotiations; special commissioners from the United States and Mexico; and surveyors and cartographers, who were charged with determining the precise location of the border and who, accompanied by astronomers and artists, spent many arduous months getting acquainted with the terrain on which the border was to be imposed. A little later, stonemasons arrived to lay down the marker stones that designated the border, along with wire-fence builders. These original creators of the border have now been joined by an army-like constellation of workers we shall later describe.

It has taken—and still takes—a veritable phalanx of specialists and workers of diverse descriptions to lay down, build, and maintain the border over a period of more than a century and a half. It is as if the very nature of La Frontera, in living up to its designation as a major international border, has called for strenuous effort and special vigilance at every stage of its history. A multidisciplinary task force was mandated from the start to ensure that this border be true to its essence as an exactly determined, tightly fitting edge, with durable markers and highly fortified means of enclosure positioned strategically to shore up its status as an artifact designed to contain efficiently and to keep out forcefully.

More pervasively, this entire enterprise has been an expression of state power on the part of the United States, which dictated the terms of the original Treaty of Guadalupe Hidalgo, thus bringing La Frontera into existence. This treaty was an unvarnished articulation of sovereign power that sought to expand itself—and claimed the right to determine the exact extent and shape of the border considered as property of the nation-state. What Michel Foucault (2004) held to obtain in circumstances of nationalist imperial power was true for La Frontera from the start: here, "sovereignty [was] exercised *within the borders of a territory*" (12).

Nevertheless, despite its origins in the naked assertion of national sovereignty, in the flush of a military victory that Mexico experienced as an invasion during the first century of its existence, La Frontera was a relatively relaxed place. Early photographs of the towns straddling the border on both sides show that a simple milestone or commemorative marker in the town square sufficed to remind people that this was indeed a "border town," as the phrase went. Citizens of both nationalities could wander back and forth freely and with nonchalance. One famous saloon prided itself on being located literally on the border, and painted a symbolic "border line" down the center of the bar to underline this geographical fact, serving different kinds of drinks on each side. Another such saloon, more cautious, sold liquor on the American side and cigars on the Mexican side (Ingram, Laney, and Gillilan 1995).

All this changed drastically after the North American Free Trade Agreement (NAFTA) and 9/11, the former highlighting issues of immigration control, the latter emphasizing questions of national security driven by the fear of a terrorist invasion. After NAFTA went into effect in 1994, Mexican farmers in large numbers were forced into dire poverty because NAFTA allowed the Mexican market to be flooded by U.S. pork and U.S. government-subsidized corn, which undercut Mexican prices. Millions of farmers have had to migrate off their land to Mexican cities and across the border to work in the United States in order to feed their families.

The wall at La Frontera was first conceived and constructed as a direct response to the forced migration caused by the first of these two developments, but its extent and associated reinforcements were modest compared to the considerable extensions that have been instituted since 9/11. At this point in history, the wall is found at all major, and many minor, towns along the border and at many points in between. With it comes a formidable array of those charged with its construction and upkeep and with the enforcement of rigorous strictures on rights of passage through its checkpoints. An entire industry—indeed, an entire culture—has grown up around the wall, to the point where the border itself is often identified with the wall in the popular imagination, even though for reasons of local topography the actual position of the wall sometimes deviates significantly from the original (and still officially recognized) borderline.

All the personnel employed at or near the wall on the U.S. side are expected to pursue certain goals in common, each of which bears directly on the reliability and strength of the wall as a safeguard for vested interests of the United States—interests that are commercial or military and (most especially) concerned with the flow of migrants (as we prefer to call those who attempt to enter the United States to find work, without "proper papers"). These goals include accurately demarcating the border; policing and surveilling the entire border region in the pursuit of increasing national security; preventing illegal drug importation and human trafficking; and, most prominently, controlling the flow of migrants without documents.

All these concerted aims converge in making the U.S.-Mexico border into something undeniably *there*, sufficiently consistent and sturdy to support these various objectives. The effect is to make La Frontera into a fetishized object—something like an ideal object, an asymptote or regulative ideal, a sheer limit—as well as a material entity. The brunt of the materiality is borne by the physical wall, but the border itself is projected as being untouchable and invisible.[3] In this light, a border is a constructed entity that acts to safeguard vested interests under the cloak of ideality. It is as if these interests were somehow legitimated by this very act of idealization, even though it is the interests themselves that seek the idealization as a protective shield. By the same token, precisely because of a border's projected status as ideal, concrete things like walls and border markers are required to put the border on the ground and in everyone's sight: walls and markers serve as material concretions, modes of surety, for what would otherwise remain an abstract entity. A wall is an especially effective way of embodying the very idea of border, a "pure border," by presenting a hard material edge, a physically realized limit,[4] for anyone confronting it (Byrd, Byrd, and Crosthwaite 2002).

Transgressing the Wall-as-Limit

The border that attempts to divide this region into an all-too-definite dyad of nationalities, ethnicities, languages, and classes is there to be crossed. It is *una línea divisoria* in the heart of a bioregion that was once one continuous area of inhabitation. The U.S.-Mexico border is a single, literally linear edge that defies the multiple edges and open intervals of a surrounding world in which there is a great deal of unconstrained movement. As such, it calls for transgression even as it forbids it, displaying the perverse logic of anything that purports to be a strict limit, whether as a law that permits no exceptions or as a wall that excludes all those without proper papers. It is perverse in the sense that it is a limit that invites the very action it is designed to foreclose. Michel Foucault has captured the perversity of this logic: "The limit and [the] transgression depend on each other . . . [;] a limit could not exist if it were absolutely uncrossable and, reciprocally, transgression would be pointless if it merely crossed a limit composed of illusions and shadows" (1998, 73). Moreover, as David Hoy underlines, "Resistance and freedom . . . are linked both conceptually and practically. To the extent that attempts to build freedom into the social structure miscarry, resistance will arise. The motivation for resistance comes from encountering constraints on freedom" (2004, 1).

Despite all the official rhetoric of excluding the illegitimate and the illegal, limits would not be limits if they were not transgressable, whether in fact or in fantasy. Recently, an artist constructed a mock ladder at Brownsville and placed it up against the wall, as if to invite its direct use by anyone wanting to cross from north to south.[5] Short of this sardonic action, there are many spontaneous transgressions of the wall at La Frontera: movements of the air, clouds, and weather over the wall; human voices that fly over the wall and can be heard on the other side; Internet communications between people in Tijuana and San Diego. Even the most fiercely constraining wall challenges those who have been kept from getting to the other side to cross it. Conversely, crossing a border of any kind, whether spatial or temporal, calls for a factor of resistance in that *across which* the movement is made. Otherwise, the crossing would lack motivation and point; it would be a crossing in thin air.

There is further irony, captured by Foucault, in another aspect of walls regarded as limits: "[The limit] serves as a glorification of what it excludes" (1998, 73). By rendering its trespass taboo, it makes it all the more attractive. In other contexts, limits that function as taboos effectively eroticize the act of their crossing, having previously rendered these limits the equivalent of prohibited sexual activity (T. Johnston, personal communication, August 12, 2010). In the current context, the wall-as-limit intensifies the attraction of crossing over it: crossing becomes an achievement of its own.[6] (For more discussion of "limit acts," see the end of chapter 7 and chapters 8 and 9.)

Indeed, it is as if the hope and despair of those wishing to cross were literally incorporated into the materiality of the wall, into its very substance. Regarded from the American side, however, the same wall embodies the fear of terrorists and "illegal immigrants" that led to its construction in the first place. From both sides, powerful feelings merge with the rigor of the real, material substance of the wall. Designed to be impenetrable, this substance receives as much as it repels. It takes in by keeping out, keeps out by taking in. As is emphasized in chapter 2, the wall-as-limit is held up by the efforts of people who prop it up from both sides, whether by pushing or pulling, excluding or entering, defending or breaching.

Transgression's role, adds Foucault, "is to measure the excessive distance that it opens at the heart of the limit and to trace the flashing line that causes the limit to arise" (1998, 74). Considered not just as a mass of materials but as a "flashing line," the border wall takes on a life of its own; it is a zone of challenge that calls border crossers to transgress it; it "opens this zone to existence for the first time" (ibid.). In this sense, every border crossing is a first-time crossing: migrants from Mexico describe repeated efforts at crossing as feeling new every time, fraught with unanticipated risks.[7] Even though the distance they must traverse is finite, sometimes just a matter of a dozen yards or less, at the time of crossing it seems infinite. The line they must cross announces itself as if it were a line burning brighter than the unforgiving sun as it is experienced in this part of the world.

Despite its rigid foreclosure, "no limit can possibly restrict [the will to transgress]" (Foucault 1998, 74). As one Border Patrol agent said to us in a moment of candor, migrants will find a way over or around *any* wall the United States erects, including a series of several walls built in parallel. This holds for all walls—not just the one at La Frontera, but also the Berlin Wall a few decades ago and, more recently, the Separation Wall between Israel and Palestine. But before this happens, much human suffering and a great deal of environmental damage will have happened, thanks to the indifference of borders to such suffering and damage.

LA FRONTERA AS BOUNDARY

The *boundary* aspect of La Frontera is less conspicuous than its border-like character, especially since the mid-1990s, but it cannot be overlooked in any full assessment. To begin with, despite its pretension to imperviousness in recent times, La Frontera has proven to be chock-full of holes and openings, not only at the official checkpoints (where bribery is far from unknown), but also in the wide spaces between parts of the constructed wall, where the only obstacles are easy-to-climb fences and natural obstacles such as gullies, precipitous hills, and desert areas. Many migrants opt to pass through these desert areas, with great peril to themselves and their families because of the intense heat and lack of water. Land animals are better adapted to these open regions, but they are stopped short by the wall, which chokes off their migratory paths and precipitates sudden confusion. Can you imagine a bobcat coming up against the wall and staring at it in disbelief? How can it know how to go around the end of the wall, which may be many miles away? Indeed, how can it know that the wall *has* an end? Only birds fly free over the wall, an action mimicked by protesters at Tijuana a few years ago when a human being was shot over the wall from an improvised cannon, as if to say that this was as close to being a bird as humans could come in the circumstances. In other performance art, birds have been set free on one side of the wall to fly freely, unlike humans, to the other side.

Undeniably, La Frontera has become obstructive of easy, open entry and traversal by human beings, whether drug traffickers or Mexican and Central American migrants who wish to find work in the United States. Still, despite its stated purpose of prohibiting and excluding, La Frontera is not unyielding to modes of passage. However fiercely defended or surveilled it may be, in the end many creatures, human and non-human, make their way across the border, often with considerable effort and ingenuity and always with definite danger.[8]

Despite such acts of transgression, intrinsic boundary features of La Frontera are not prominent; one must search the situation to locate them. Where they do occur, however, they allow the border to breathe, opening it to flows of several kinds. It would certainly be too much to proclaim of this situation that in it, *panta rhei* ("everything flows": Heraclitus). But *some things do move* here: they move under, over, and through an enclosure designed to be impenetrable.

The truth is that we cannot think of La Frontera as a single, simple kind of edge, for it is both border and boundary, making it literally ambiguous. This minimal realization is important if we are to fend off the inveterate tendency to reduce what is in fact a very complex situation to an oversimplified image or interpretation of it.

Complicating things further, neither aspect of La Frontera is to be confused with the *borderline* between the United States and Mexico. A borderline is a cartographic entity, a linear representation of a limit established by political negotiation.

This suggests that a border, considered in the way we have proposed, is situated between a boundary and a borderline in a series of terms that serve to specify an edge like La Frontera. As an airtight posited entity, a border lacks the permeability of a genuine boundary; yet it is not reducible to anything strictly linear either. Its ideality floats free of linear representation as well as of material embodiment.[9]

Another term that also belongs in this same series is *borderland*, made famous by the writings of Gloria Anzaldúa (2007) but having an extensive history of its own. A borderland is the area that flanks a recognized international border, usually on both sides. It is an area, a region, in the form of a band or strip that cannot be measured in so many meters or miles. In its indeterminacy of exact extent, a borderland resembles a boundary, but a borderland is bound, conceptually and concretely, to the border it surrounds. A borderland, like the land alongside a stream, draws energy from the border it flanks. The borderland at La Frontera is remarkable for its profusion of culture and its distinctive hybridity of custom and language.

GAMUT OF RELATED TERMS

The foregoing analysis suggests a series of five terms that can be arranged in a series that will help us to understand the situation at the U.S.-Mexico border: boundary, borderland, border, walls and fences, and borderline.

At the left end of this spectrum, we encounter porous and malleable edges for which the paradigm case is that of boundaries, with a borderland providing an intermediary case. On the right end, closure and exactitude are prized. Here the exemplary instance is the borderline, which is highly determinable in terms of both actual measurement and cartographic representation. Walls and fences mark and reinforce the border, even if not with the precision of a borderline.

In the very middle of this series is the *border*, which is closer to a borderline in terms of its putative precision but also integral to the very idea of a borderland. The Treaty of Guadalupe Hidalgo speaks of "the U.S.-Mexico border" (which it established by means of its literal discourse) *as if it were something altogether definite* or at least definite enough to be counted on in future political discussions, historical accounts, land surveys, and maps. And necessarily so: each of these four latter forms of representation, to be effective on its own terms, requires a constant point of reference. This suggests that the very notion and term *border* is as much a discursive entity (dependent on words and their meanings) as anything materially "real"; that is, something one can see or touch or walk over.

If this is so, it helps to explain the paradox that, powerful as the idea of an international border is—not just at La Frontera but also in other comparable cases, such as the border between East and West Berlin, the one between the occupied Palestinian territories and Israel at the current moment, and indeed that between any two or more states or territories—a border is *never a visible phenomenon*. Has anyone ever *seen* the U.S.-Mexico border, whether on the ground or anywhere else? Of course not![10] Its real force is "the force of law," which is to say, something set up by international treaties, continually reinforced by border guards and border patrols, and (increasingly often since 1994) rooted and reified by the building of high walls. Such walls introduce a factor of sheer physicality that is lacking in the very notion of "border" itself. This helps to explain the strong temptation to construct them whenever the political will and the funding exist to do so—and then to confuse such walls, once built, with the border they materialize. Quite apart from issues of national security and the enforcement of treaties, much less of so-called "illegal immigration," it seems as if something like a wall or its equivalent is called for by the very idea of borders; alternatively, we could say that the counterpart of the rhetorical and theoretical power of an international border, which is considerable in historical and political domains, is a wall or some other such physical entity (including marker stones or fences), which acts to transmute what is discursively projected into concrete material thinghood. As we shall see, to resist engaging in such materialization of an international border often proves more difficult than to construct a brute wall itself. Indeed, a different kind of thinking is involved in creating a peace park at an international border; such a park is in effect a borderland that breathes and manifests a different politics that has its own visionary aspirations (see chapter 9).

Borders, then, are rather strange hybrid entities: they are not physically real as formulated in words or represented in images (they are "irreal" in Husserl's term), but they can be materialized in real things such as walls. In contrast with boundaries and borderlands, borders are abstract, ideal entities; they are constituted and projected by words (typically written words, though these are often based on prior negotiations conducted orally), or by images (as with borderlines considered as drawn features in the maps that depict them).[11]

At the same time, borders are conventional and historical—and just as much economic and political, social and ethnic—and, in all these various respects, reflective of human beliefs and actions; thus, they could well have turned out differently. As with the discourse that set them up in the first place, or with the images that depict them, their meaning is something intentional: the expression of human needs, desires, and resolutions. This meaning is a product not just of words and images at a reflective level but also of such prereflective forces as economic factors and class differences, political struggles, and racist attitudes. The meaning of a border is something that is made, posited, or sustained (however tacitly) by a group of speakers who are also political actors, not something discovered or found in material reality. In this respect, a border is a supervening variable that does not belong to the order of the physically real—an order that contains the animals and people who try to pass over a border, actual local environments, and the materiality of markers chosen to designate the border (marker stones, barbed-wire fences, or metallic and concrete walls). Yet in their very lack of concrete reality, borders as cultural constructs are powerfully determinative forces in regional and international history and politics. They shape many things that belong properly to the realm of human action and material construction.

THE MUTABILITY OF BORDERS VERSUS THE STABILITY OF BOUNDARIES

What does the bivalency of irreal and real, meaning and matter, image and thing, portend for understanding the situation at La Frontera (and, by extension, at any comparable border circumstance)? One straightforward thing it portends is that borders, despite their discursive and geographical ideality, evolve and are subject to birth and decay. Borders have a life and death of their own, and their history can be traced in exquisite (and sometimes excruciating) detail. The mutability of borders, then, reflects their status as cultural constructions endowed with meaning. It is important to underline such mutability, given certain political discussions that all too often assume that a particular border, such as that at La Frontera, is here to stay, that it is somehow "natural" or "right" in its exact current avatar— that it is something we can count on into the indefinite future.

Yet this is simply not so. The factor of drug-war violence, for example, has altered the public perception of the fact and function of the border at La Frontera. The public mind has been captured by the widespread violence that has recently plagued border towns such as Juárez and Tijuana. The walls built near these places show themselves to be woefully inadequate for coping with the illicit drug traffic that manages to get through, if not by way of ruses and bribes at the checkpoints, then by extensive underground tunnels that are built by the drug cartels under the existing wall (Archibold 2009). With respect to the drug traffic, the U.S.-Mexico border has always been more like a boundary—a highly permeable edge that offers little resistance to being crossed in one direction or another. This is still the case—indeed, increasingly so in recent years. Drugs flow into the United States from the south at various points, while illicit arms flow south into Mexico from gun dealers in Arizona and Texas. As a result, the very meaning of "security," including that at stake in the much-vaunted "homeland security," is contingent and ever changing.[12] The daunting metallic wall with a thick and deep concrete base that has now cost upward of seven billion dollars is in fact a leaking vessel (Emmott 2009).[13] Nor does the high-tech surveillance equipment (klieg lights, 24/7 panoramic cameras, ground sensors, patrol cars on the ground, and drones) make a decisive difference in stopping the flow of people, drugs, and money (McKinley and Lacey 2009). New ways around, over, and under the wall continue to be devised. Cell phones carried by "coyotes," who guide groups of migrants over the border, are now being used to alert the crossers as to the exact location of nearby Border Patrol officers (Lacey 2011).

The situation now in effect returns matters to the state of affairs before the wall began to be built in the mid-1990s, exhibiting a vulnerability not unlike the string of fences that used to stretch out between the original marker stones—fences that were never a serious deterrence to the movements of humans. Only cattle were held back. The fences and marker stones constituted what Julie Mostov (2008, 56) terms a "soft border" and resemble nothing more than a boundary. Here we see that the formal differences between the two sorts of edge are becoming ever more slim in practice. The effort to produce a rigid barricade in the form of a wall made of reinforced steel set in concrete is foundering. Far from making people more secure, La Frontera increasingly casts its shadow on a scene of lawless behavior, from the state-sponsored corruption of Border Patrol agents who engage in bribery and human rights violations to the criminality perpetrated by gangs of unruly and desperate youth who cluster on the southern side of the wall in cities such as Nogales and Tijuana (Rosas 2012). The harder a border becomes or purports to be, the more violently transgressive people must be to subvert its intention. Mexican border cities are now occupied by the Mexican military. Mexican citizens live in terror of drug violence brought to the front doors of their homes. U.S. ranchers contend with the effects of unlawful intruders onto their properties, sometimes tragically taking their lives, even though the intruders are most often migrants on their way to cities where they can find employment.

Even if the wall has proven ineffective for a kind of traffic not foreseen by those who planned it in the first place, it has been at least partially successful in stemming the flow of migrants who sought jobs in the United States following the institution of NAFTA in the Clinton presidency.[14] I say "partially successful," since determined migrants continue to use ladders to scale the wall late at night from the Mexican side, and a few have tunneled under (though not on the elaborate scale realized by the drug cartels). Many more have gone around the end of the wall, all too often to then meet their death on the burning desert or freezing mountains that open before them. Despite the many physical and legal obstacles at the wall itself, undocumented workers continue to flow across the border near, if not actually *at*, the wall itself. The wall, in short, has fallen far short of its intended purpose: the prevention of immigration that is declared "illegal." Even if the net flow of migrants diminishes sometimes—for example, as a reflection of the U.S. economy's recent downturn and the large number of deportations carried out over the last few years[15]—the highly fortified wall has failed to contain the influx, which is likely to increase once the American economy picks up fully.

We cite these facts of recent history at La Frontera not just to make the point that the U.S.-Mexico border has been subject to vicissitudes that were never fully foreseen but also, and more important, to indicate that borders can very quickly lose their purportedly protective function and thereby remit their essence—their very raison d'être. If La Frontera is any indication, borders seem to contain the seeds of their own undoing.

The putative tightness of the U.S.-Mexico border—based on the all too tempting belief that border walls can achieve genuine security for the homeland—is unraveling and will probably continue to do so. Security walls offer belated and imperfect solutions to problems that are more often than not intractable and uncontainable. Once built, they invite transgression on the one hand and increased militarized surveillance on the other. This is not just to say that they engender "resistance" in Foucault's sense of the effect of any strict institutional limit but also to suggest that they bring about their own demise, as if by a subtle form of self-undermining—not only from without (that is, from a failure to hold back overt invasions), but also from within, on their own terms. This suggests that *borders are always already in the process of becoming boundaries.*

We are talking not only about the physical frailty of constructed things such as fences and walls but also, and more especially, about the striking way in which such limiting and protective entities end by being ineffective at the very thing they were originally designed to do. They are subject not just to penetration and eventual ruination in historical time but also to a process of self-undoing by which they render themselves unable to perform the very tasks for which they were designed and constructed in the first place. To this exact extent, they lose their being as strict borders and more closely approximate open-ended boundaries.

Boundaries, though not permanent either, are more perduring than borders. This is so even though their detailed configuration changes continually—indeed, more rapidly and easily than with borders, especially in view of the heavy institutional investment (and resulting inertia) inherent in the latter. For the underlying contour or profile of boundaries, being more closely attuned to the layout of their landscape setting, is comparatively stable, reflecting a circumambience that is slow to change: think of the way in which rivers, as natural boundaries, retain their overall shape despite vicissitudes of drought and flooding. Many boundaries are integral members of entire life-worlds, cultural as well as natural, rather than being artificial intrusions into them, as so many borders manifestly are. Moreover, their perduringness occurs not despite their fluidity and porosity but *because of it.* The basic resilience of boundaries allows them to retain a fundamental gestalt, a lasting identity, over long periods of human history and through considerable climatological and geological change.

Borders, in contrast, have more contingent origins (La Frontera would have been a very different reality had the U.S.-Mexican War turned out in Mexico's favor) and a greater need for support once established. They can be altered at any moment—for example, if the international balance of power shifts or a new technology of constructing walls arises. Between these moments of major political or technological change, borders such as that at La Frontera have to be controlled and patrolled intensively, day and night, with guards and police hired for just these tasks. Such surveillance shows the fragile nature of the fortified border, always at risk of failure of purpose despite their show of force.

Ultimately, once it has outlived its political, economic, or symbolic usefulness, every border is destined to become a boundary, returning to an abiding state of nature. This happened, for instance, to the Great Wall of China, which, many centuries after its military significance had faded, rejoined the open landscape of western China, crumbling into the earth that underlay and surrounded it. Animals and tourists now move over it at their ease.

This will be the fate of La Frontera as well—even if, from today's perspective, such an outcome seems a long way off. Its mode of materializing the U.S.-Mexico border in the form of a border wall is so starkly salient at this moment that we can barely imagine the day of its demise—the day when La Frontera will have become much more of an overt boundary than a policed border, once again, and this time (it may be hoped), lastingly. By then, the dark edge the border wall imposes so ominously on city and desert alike will be more of a phantom than a reality.

Meanwhile, much suffering is occurring at and in the immediate vicinity of the wall. It behooves us to become more fully acquainted with the concrete forms this suffering takes. In the remainder of Part 1, we shall acquire such acquaintanceship by studying life close to the wall in Nogales, Tijuana, and the Lower Rio Grande Valley. Each of these locales will teach us a significant lesson about the effects of the border wall in their midst, whether these effects are felt in city life or in the surrounding natural environment.

CHAPTER 2

Ambos Nogales

A Tale of Two Cities

In the minds of faraway policymakers, a fortified, floodlit steel wall separates Nogales, Arizona, from Nogales, Sonora. Real places, though, never
begin and end quite where they're supposed to.

Gregory McNamee, as cited on the back cover of
Ambos Nogales: Intimate Portraits of the U.S.-Mexico Border

The minimum number, strictly speaking, is two.

Aristotle, *Physics*

STARTING WITH TWO

It is not accidental that we begin with a circumstance in which *two* cities
are at stake. On the one hand, this reflects the historical-geographical fact
that all along the U.S.-Mexico border there are such paired cities, large and
small: besides Ambos Nogales (*ambos* means "both" in Spanish), there are
at least twelve other such pairs.[1] Taken together, these sister cities, along
with their suburbs and outlying villages, establish a border zone that can
be as much as 100 kilometers wide and that punctuates the entire length
of La Frontera from Brownsville/Matamoros on the Gulf of Mexico to San
Diego/Tijuana on the Pacific Ocean (Ingram, Laney, and Gillilan 1995). No
comparable set of paired cities exists on the U.S.-Canadian border—and
rarely elsewhere.[2] Common to all the pairs found at La Frontera is the co-
evolution of urban complexes that are linked together by many ties of family, personal experience, shared history, culture, language, climate, animals,
and environment yet at the same time are driven by distinctive differences
of economic reality and political practices.

In these bilocal circumstances, cities on both sides of the same international edge share a single line of demarcation that runs between them:
"the borderline." But the exact means of designating the border itself can
take many forms. In an earlier day, the mere presence of marker stones was
considered adequate. In the case of Nogales, a single open street running

Figure 1. The U.S.-Mexico border at Ambos Nogales, circa 1898–1899. Photo by W. I. Neumann, courtesy of the National Archives.

between the two towns sufficed, as we see in figure 1. A broad street here serves as a boundary rather than a border—given that it is inherently permeable and traversable. So much so, in fact, that photographers sometimes had to *draw in*, literally, the borderline in the development phase of the photograph after the shot was taken, since it was not otherwise evident. In the same spirit, the Nogales railroad depot straddled both sides of the border, with no distinction made between the American and Mexican sides of the building.

It was only at later stages of history and politics that the demarcation became so massively materialized that no single building could span the two countries (as happened at the Berlin Wall), nor were superimposed lines any longer called for in official photographs. The wall that came to be built in the mid-1990s speaks volumes in and of itself: for all practical purposes, it *is* the line, and its unmistakable presence effects the division between the two Nogaleses before our very eyes. The stark reality of a concrete-and-metal structure took the place of open stretches of shared space, reducing and condensing this space into a single razor-sharp site (fig. 2). The border wall's construction, beginning some twenty years ago, established an especially fierce form of edge. Its sheer imperviousness (the sheet metal was largely steel) and formidable height (fourteen feet at Nogales, with current projec-

Figure 2. U.S.
border wall at
Ambos Nogales,
2008. Photo by
"Elnogalense," ©
2008 Wikipedia
Commons.

Figure 3. U.S.
Border Patrol
surveillance tower,
viewed from
Nogales, Mexico.
Photo by Mary
Watkins, 2006.

tions of an even higher new wall to replace the first), not to mention the constant surveillance by cameras mounted high over the wall (fig. 3), brought about a very different border circumstance than had existed previously.

In the sequence of situations just sketched from the history of La Frontera, we move from one extreme to the other. Contemporaries who are as young as thirty years old today recall the ready accessibility of the other city, which they could reach simply by strolling over, unimpeded by anyone checking their identities.[3] By now, however, the situation has changed drastically, particularly at the official checkpoint station in Nogales that dominates cross-border traffic and makes coming and going between the two cities into a major venture—if it is allowed to happen at all. What had been genuine two-way movement has become virtually one-way; passage from the United States to Mexico is usually unimpeded, with drivers and pedestrians being waved on, while those entering from the other way are burdened with lengthy waits of several hours, insistent searches of cars and of individuals (often with search animals trained to detect drugs), and, above all, a close examination of identification papers. Ease of traversal has been replaced by the prohibition on any unauthorized movement, to such an extent that one local resident remarked, "The only crossing that requires no inspection is that of cattle who walk over fences that have blown down in remote areas" (A. Enciso, personal communication, June 18, 2008). The result of this prohibition has been such that the contemporary border now keeps people apart from one another, starting with family members and extending to friends and associates (Ingram, Laney, and Gillilan 1995).[4]

What was unthinkable earlier—the segregation of human beings who belonged to a single city complex—has become a painful daily reality. Tensions have mounted as the impact of the wall, whose construction and reconstruction continue to the present day, has come to be more fully felt. Nevertheless, the circumstance cannot be reduced to a set of simple oppositions such as exclusion versus inclusion, free versus impeded movement, American versus Mexican, English versus Spanish, north versus south, and so on. In the very midst of these dichotomies—despite, or better, *across* them—various bridging actions have emerged. These only rarely take the form of overt political demonstrations against the wall, much less anything coordinated on both sides. More often, constructive connections between the two sides of the wall have assumed the shape of focused conversations among U.S. and Mexican citizens, alliances between those with environmentalist concerns, and concerted collaborations between Mexican and American artists in the creation of art on the border wall itself (see chapter 8).

The very existence of the wall as a divisive force has called forth an array of imaginative possibilities that emerge from thinking differently about the present and future of the border. These possibilities are all political in the deepest sense. "Political" here draws from the Greek term *polis*: the city-state. A major issue raised by the particular stretch of La Frontera at stake in this chapter is that of the recombination of two separate cities, each of which exists as a distinct, historically and legally delimited entity: Los *Ambos* Nogales. Aristotle remarks in his *Politics* that a *polis* must be nei-ther too small nor too large and that one should be able to view it as a com-pact whole from a neighboring *polis*. This is precisely the case with the two Nogaleses. Accessible to each other perceptually, and literally contiguous geographically, these two cities conjoin bilaterally across the border. This suggests that the wall that acts to separate so forcibly can also be reappro-priated and transfigured so as to offer opportunities for bringing together the different cultures, languages, and peoples that its sheer brute presence sets apart.

The very same physical wall that represses and segregates can thus, by imaginative forays and intentional efforts to create connection in the face of division, become an occasion for meaningful continuity. Rather than a source of dissension and difference alone, we can reconceive it as something that links rather than severs, thereby becoming a place for the expression and appreciation of similarities as well as differences. This can occur for-mally in artworks and expressions of solidarity and in less formal actions undertaken by the Nogalesians on both sides (such as daily conversations, cross-border shopping, or simply going out to dinner on the other side) (Theroux 2012). The *polis* is rooted in the poles of differential culture and history, and the task is to span the poles rather than keep them so far apart as to allow no significant interactions to occur.[5] The creation of transitional actions and spaces serves to leaven what is otherwise a scene of sheer sepa-ration, constituting "zones of encounter" between ordinary citizens who link up spontaneously on diverse fronts in the practices of their daily lives (Faier 2009). Brady Heiner remarks, "Certainly a border or prison wall *as such* cannot 'act' as a force of cultural conjunction. When it does so, as is the case here (partially, of course), it is being transformed into something else; it is being reformed by alternative intentionalities and so is made to function (again, partially) as a force of cultural conjunction *despite itself*" (personal communication, 2009; his emphasis).

If it is true that the current border wall at La Frontera unites individuals and spaces even as it divides them—a theme that we shall develop in this and subsequent chapters—its alienating effects are nevertheless much more forcefully experienced than are the possibilities for unification among those it holds apart.

Traveling to Ambos Nogales with BorderLinks

Doubtless, our very descriptions of the border situation in these chapters display our own political preferences concerning issues that arise there—in particular, issues bearing on immigration policies and practices. There is no entirely neutral description of these complex conflictual circumstances, which effectively pit those who would seek employment (and, more rarely, permanent residence) in the United States against those who are actively charged with regulating the border or seek to protect their privately owned land.

This deep divergence of positions and views must be acknowledged if one is determined not to adopt a model whose simplicity fails to reflect what is happening on the ground and if one wishes to avoid a repressive regimentation of political thought and practical action. For the same reasons, any claim to offer a simple solution for the current impasse at the border must be regarded with suspicion, given that the situation at La Frontera is continually changing and that the forces behind it are staggering in their complexity. Indeed, given this complexity, it is naive to believe that one could ever understand the situation fully enough to ensure right action.

In view of this impasse, the better part of wisdom is to pause before offering final assessments of this circumstance. The pause we take in this chapter will provide us with an opportunity to explore a concrete instance of life on the border in its multiple layering: geographical, historical, environmental, economic, political, and artistic. The very particularity of this instance will reflect the way the border is experienced at close quarters: how a given person takes in the border from her or his own point of view. Accordingly, before returning to a more public, third-person account, we shall offer a brief narrative stemming from two visits to the border region in Ambos Nogales, the first undertaken by Ed Casey and the second, by both of us.

Setting out south from Tucson with the program director of Border-Links (a Tucson organization that sponsors firsthand experiences of the U.S.-Mexico border so as to foster a better understanding of its recent history and contribute to its improved future), we drive past the debris of a vast copper mine, debris that has been bulldozed to a certain level, giving the outward appearance of a long and low mesa. That this is not a natural formation is manifest from the garish color of the earth that has been amassed and from the absolute absence of vegetation from the slopes of this artificial mound. Only a few miles down the road, we pass a golf course whose brilliant green bespeaks continual watering and tellingly signals the wealth of those whose houses ring the course itself. (Later, I was to learn that a number of the American managers of the factories just over the border in Mexico live in the sumptuous homes of this exclusive enclave.) An hour later, the otherwise unbending freeway gives way to a winding road that descends gradually amid intense hills, depositing us in Nogales, Arizona, on the American side of La Frontera. Seemingly an unremarkable town of little visible life—at least at first glance—*this* Nogales looks out toward the other Nogales just across the border.[6]

As I look southward, my vision is arrested by the stark profile of a dark, winding structure cutting across the hills to the south. I am unable to make out what this is, as I've never seen anything like it before. Suddenly, I realize that it is an outsized wall that cuts its way aggressively through the hills, crudely squatting on the earth. A vast metallic structure has been imposed on the gently sloping hills: one might have imagined it having been sculpted by Christo and Jeanne-Claude had it not conveyed such a deadly seriousness. Already, I am struck by the indifference that the wall exhibits toward the natural environment, even as it is forced to follow its contours: it appears as a dark belt, a steel serpent, that winds its way over the landscape, as if by arbitrary will (but in fact following the borderline wherever possible).

Consternated by the sinister silhouette of the serpentine wall, I cease to pay attention to the first (i.e., the American) Nogales through which we are driving. I do not even focus on the checkpoint at the border itself, through which we are waved nonchalantly by a Mexican border officer. Indeed, he likely recognizes my driver as a trustworthy figure from BorderLinks, and anyway, he does not concern himself much with traffic coming from the north—that is, the "safe direction."

Precipitated into Nogales, Sonora, Mexico, we soon find ourselves in a highly commercial world of small shops and other businesses, with many shoppers and tourists in evidence. This busy scene is occasionally punctuated by public spaces, in the form of small parks, all in evident steep decline. A ruined band shell appears on the left, the only remnant of a former plaza that in more settled times had been the center of town life. I find myself in a city that appears to have lost its heart, its center.

Proceeding through town to its western edge, the BorderLinks guide takes us straight to the maquiladoras—immense factories built in the immediate wake of NAFTA, when the inducements of cheap labor, low tariffs, lack of environmental regulations, and low taxes led many U.S. and other foreign companies to establish plants here. By the time of this visit (2008), some of the companies that had moved in so quickly in the mid- to late 1990s had already moved out, many relocating to China, where the same enticements (especially low-cost labor) are to be found in still more abundant supply.

Figure 4. U.S. border wall outside Ambos Nogales. Photo by Mary Watkins, 2006.

Driving through the vast industrial parks, which took the place of the public lands where the natives of Nogales used to go for picnics on Sundays,
I see sleek late-modern buildings whose empty enormity I feel intensely. I
also feel the duress of those laboring in these same buildings under constant
surveillance. Our group will be turned away twice from planned visits to
several of these same buildings—visits requested by BorderLinks and scheduled for particular times; upon arrival, we will be told that there is no one
to show us around that day. A likely story! Evidently, the managers are not
anxious to reveal working conditions to inquiring eyes. In one case, the
aroma of chlorine permeated the office that was located next to the working
space, where (we were told independently) a number of pregnant women
work at very demanding tasks (most maquiladoras are assembly plants that
call for very precise piecework). The impression is that of businesses that
are open yet closed. Those employed there are paid at a level of compensation that is better than elsewhere in Mexico yet still not a living wage.

As if to prove this last point, a foray into a nearby supermarket reveals
the high cost of living in Nogales, Sonora, much higher than the average salaries in the maquiladoras could ever support. "The big problem,"

remarks our guide, "is having the money to be here—here on the border. Everything costs much more here. Food, clothing, everything." The result is a contradictory picture of apparent prosperity (compared, that is, with the nonborder rural areas) combined with extensive penury and real-life suffering. Contributing to the misery is the prohibition of unionization for many workers, along with numerous human-rights violations on the part of employers.[7] The combination of low wages and an inflated market effectively coerces these workers to remain on the job for extremely long hours, which both negatively impacts their health and separates them from their families.

On the west and the north, the maquiladoras frame Nogales, Sonora. Oppressive as these factories are, they prove irresistible to many workers, mostly from impoverished regions farther south in Mexico and Central America, who have swollen the population of Nogales tenfold in the last decade. These workers cluster just south of the U.S.-Mexico border, where they often seek employment in a local plant. Many of these migrants are tempted to risk crossing the border to seek work and better wages in the United States, if work is not to be found at the maquiladoras; this act of desperation is of course risky in itself because crossing the border at this point (especially after 9/11) often results in eventual deportation back to Mexico—or to prison for a felony, which is the fate of anyone caught on a second effort to enter the United States "illegally."

Those who are fortunate enough to find some form of ongoing work—if not in the factories, then in public transportation, restaurants, and private households in Nogales—live in the densely populated areas called colonias, in which human beings are herded together like cattle. A current resident observes wryly, "Nogales, no es un rancho, es un corral!" ("Nogales is not an open farm, it is a corral!") Indeed, he makes it clear that this corral is ultimately surrounded by a single fence, the border. Beyond simply fencing people in, Nogales is corral-like in another sense: it is a trap into which willing workers are lured, only to find that there are few ways out.

Each colonia is a jumble of dirt streets (often without designated names, much less street signs) that link hundreds, and sometimes thousands, of ramshackle dwellings, many of which are huts with nothing more than dirt floors, enclosed by cardboard walls and roofs with somewhat random openings punched out to serve as doors and windows. Some of the houses in the colonias, however, have poured concrete floors and wooden walls with asbestos-shingled roofs. In view of the deeply impoverished conditions in which they have been built, the dwellings in a given colonia are all the more remarkable for their sheer variety.

On a second trip to Nogales, the two of us spend two nights in one such house in Colonia Flores Magón as part of BorderLinks' border-immersion experience. It is a relatively well-furbished dwelling, with doors in place and fitted screened windows. Being the senior guests, we are invited to sleep on a bed, whereas younger members of our group make do with sleeping bags on dirt floors. Our host is a woman from Chiapas who immigrated to Nogales with her husband and three children several years ago. Her daughter of twelve, who speaks no English at all, helps me find the TelMex public phone a few blocks away on unlit streets. As the two of us walk in the dark of night, lively recorded music arises from surrounding houses. It is as if the music fills a void in long-suffering lives and allows local residents to dream of those things that better-off people so casually possess: health care, adequate salaries, leisure time to spend with one's family.

This impoverished but lively scene is to be compared with the wealthy neighborhoods of Nogales, where we witness a plethora of luxury homes, each with a wall and a gate, as well as garages sheltering several new cars. These are the homes of high-level managers of the maquiladoras—or at least of those who have chosen not to live in the fancy area in Arizona that we noticed when driving south. Each of these houses has its own yard and carefully demarcated property lines, unlike the shantytown colonia of Flores Magón, where squatting on an ill-defined piece of land is the first act of inhabitation (and where, nevertheless, one has to make monthly payments to the titular "owner" of the colonia).[8]

In between these extremes of opulence and squalor are intermediate modes of housing, rows of duplexes that are subsidized by the local maquiladoras. These lower-middle-class dwellings are brightly painted, even if bars on the lower windows signal that they are targets of frequent break-ins, most likely by drug users (Nogales is a major center of the narcotics trade).

Beyond these contrasting forms of housing, a very different world is found at the Casa de la Misericordia, the headquarters for the Mexican operations of BorderLinks. The Casa, renamed "Hogar de Esperanza y Paz" (House of Hope and Peace), sits atop a high hill overlooking all of Nogales, Sonora, at the opposite end of the city from the colonias and maquiladoras. It serves as a community resource center, offering educational and social services to those who live in the older part of Nogales. ("Misericordia" signifies "mercy" or "compassion" in Spanish, but English speakers who recognize its Latin roots cannot help but hear "misery of the heart" in this word.) It is clear that the activities of the Casa are undertaken with an eye to helping those who live locally; for example, it contains a free day-care program for the children of working parents, including art and language classes and a nutritious lunch. Beyond offering these services, the Casa also sponsors consultations and lectures by experts on environmental degradation in the region.

Francisco Trujillo, known as "Kiko," heads this remarkable institution. At the time of our visit, Trujillo was training local political leaders in the colonias by meeting with them to discuss how they could make a substantive difference to their constituents. His conviction was that the lack of such leadership had contributed substantially to the disadvantaged circumstances of the colonias. Residents of the latter have never been represented on the city council, much less in regional or national legislative bodies. With so much energy taken up with day-to-day survival, local residents have had precious little opportunity to devise effective plans for improving their living conditions. Trujillo's efforts were attempts at addressing this problem.

Standing in the open courtyard of the Casa de la Misericordia, we look out over a panoply of life in Nogales, Sonora: the colonias, the maquiladoras, the well-to-do neighborhoods, the downtown shops—and the border wall, whose sinuous shape can be seen stretching over the back of the entire landscape. The variegated parts of this scene come together only in the inspired vision of someone like Trujillo: "If there is to be any hope for this damaged city," he remarks in his impeccable English, "it will have to come from a creative coalition of the most diverse forces—the wealthy, the poor, the politicians, the artists, and the teachers."

Soon after this memorable visit to the Casa de la Misericordia we are back at the central Nogales checkpoint, this time heading back north to Tucson, where we will debrief at the BorderLinks headquarters, comparing notes and observations with others who have taken the same journey.

GOING BIVALVE

To exist in a life-world is to confront a continually changing congeries of edges that keep human beings (and other denizens of the earth) apart even as they also serve to unite them. Everywhere, animate beings find themselves involved in a dense tangle of rims and frames, brinks and verges, margins and thresholds. This is a world of edges that are sensed as such in incisive experiences of pain at the edge (think of the dentist's drill as it reaches the edge of your ailing molar), of exclusion (as in locked gates that keep out those declared "undesirable"), of difference (as when we move from one ecosystem to another). The world we inhabit is a world of places and things and events, each of which has its own characteristic edges as one experience in that world gives way to the next, whether in sensed reality or at the level of representation, and whether our experience bears upon what is perceived, or imagined, or thought.

The dual world of Ambos Nogales is crisscrossed with edges of many varieties. The leading edge is doubtless that of the U.S.-Mexico border as it runs between the two cities. The border is an edge that is at once incisive and decisive: incisive as cutting across otherwise continuous land like a knife, decisive in altering and controlling the lives of millions of people who live in the circumambience of "Nogales," a single name for two urban entities.

Building on the border/boundary distinction described in chapter 1, we shall here single out several other edge-formations that are specific to the Nogales area. Beyond creases and folds, two in particular will be emphasized: the *bivalve* and *incongruous counterparts*. A bivalve structure is formed from two surfaces that fold out from a central edge acting as a hinge for these same surfaces. Such is the topological character of the two Nogaleses, which spread out from La Frontera, considered as a hinge connecting them. Incongruous counterparts occur when two figures are reverse images of each other. We shall find this structure at play in an area east of Nogales, where two kinds of landscape (and two groups of people) converge at the border. In both of these two major formations, the borderline, acting as its own distinctive kind of edge, provides the common axis for what is found on either side.

The purpose of our analysis is not to focus on geomorphic or topological shapes for their own sake but to employ them as a basis for better discerning an underlying order in what presents itself at first as dense and unconfigured in first-person experiences of local landscapes.

Many cities are constructed from polar oppositions and involve various zones of encounter or transition (e.g., between two or more neighborhoods). Ambos Nogales is special in that its overall shape—that of the two cities considered as one urban region—resembles that of a bivalve clam whose two shells are laid out flat, linked by a single common hinge: the artificial edge provided by the U.S.-Mexico border. This structure is subjacent to the *both* that this city's paired name puts in play. It makes manifest the way in which the border acts as the critical pivot of the two cities it severs as well as connects.

Every edge can be thought of as formed from the convergence of two lines that intersect at a single point—or, in three-dimensional space, as the intersection of two planes that meet at a single line (Gibson 1986). This linear axis serves as a hinge or pivot for the two surfaces it connects. The material mode of this axis differs from case to case; it can vary from being a sheer line, such as a borderline (i.e., a cartographic construct situated at the very limit of materiality), to something that is made from physical materials. In this way, two sides, surfaces, or planes are linked together. Their conjunction constitutes a *fold*, which we take to indicate a doubling both in the common notion of a "fold in a fabric" and also in the Deleuzian sense of a "continuous labyrinth" of self-touching material substance (Deleuze 1992, 6). This newly formed double surface is a fold insofar as its sides, or planes, can be seen (or imagined) as forming part of a single surface folded out from a single axis, much like the two shells of a clam that has been pried open.

Ambos Nogales can be imagined as an exemplary bivalve fold, given that its twin cities occupy surfaces that fan out from the border at La Frontera. This border acts as an axis that connects the cities of Nogales, Arizona, and Nogales, Sonora. The resulting urban complex is in effect a duplex: it consists in two cities linked by the U.S.-Mexico border taken as their common spine. Both cities spread out from this spine even as they also flow into it. Given that they share the border, each city is an integral part of the same folding structure; they are co-implicated despite their disparities. The fact that the outer limits and the inner contents of the two contiguous cities are ever-changing does not detract from their confluent flowing into each other in close proximity; the geopolitical character of the folding—at once out from the border and back into it—retains the formidable power to determine the fates of those who live within its embrace.

This pattern obtains even though none of the edges of the tandem cities, internal or external, is neatly or precisely delimited. Each is notably amorphous. Technically speaking, official city limits do exist, but the sprawl of a city such as Nogales, Sonora, spills right over them. Indeed, formal determinations such as city limits fail to capture the feel of any multiply configured cityscape. Almost all of Nogales, Sonora's, edges (and most of those in its sister city) are inherently vague. These edges are curvilinear and continuous, and often blunted, in ways that are irregular and intensely informative. This is evident in the manner by which the various maquiladoras have spread out to the north and west of the city on the Mexican side. The irregularity of Nogales' internal edges is not confined to this area alone. The irregularity extends to the peripheries of the constituent parts of these cities—to the wealthy tracts, the lower middle-class housing areas, the downtown shopping streets, the boulevards and streets, even the most humble piece of "property" in a dusty colonia in Nogales, Sonora.[9]

At the same time, the border itself, the axis or hinge of the fold that holds the two Nogaleses together even as it divides them, is a line that acts as a potent force in this urban scene: potent enough to call for marker stones and barbed-wire fences in an earlier era and now checkpoints and the massive wall that turns the hinge into a locked joint. Stones, fences, and wall constitute the materialized axes for the bivalve situation that obtains for Ambos Nogales.

CAMPING IN A LANDSCAPE OF INCONGRUOUS COUNTERPARTS

Let us contrast the situation at Ambos Nogales with a camp for migrants that is located outside the small town of Agua Prieta, just south of the border and approximately forty miles east of the Nogales cities. Tommy Bassett, a former maquiladora manager, conceived the idea of this camp and oversees its ongoing operation with significant help from recovering alcoholics and drug addicts. The camp itself constitutes its own exceptional state—this one for the benefit of migrants in their attempted border crossings. In this instance, aspiring migrants are outside not just the law but also the immediate presence of the border wall that concretizes it (the wall at Agua Prieta had not yet been extended to the area encompassing this camp). Despite the absence of the physical wall, the dangers inherent in border crossings remain considerable; many migrants (estimated at more than six thousand) have lost their lives in taking to the desert that looms before and beyond the border.

The casual composition of this extraordinary camp—consisting of diverse items such as blankets, bread, lunch meat, cheese, soft drinks, and so on, all placed on the earth under several sheltering trees—sets it apart from the high technology employed by the Border Patrol only one or two miles to the north. On the one side is equipment for migrant detection costing many millions of dollars; on the other side, an expenditure of less than several hundred dollars weekly to provide basic food and shelter. The first amount is drawn from the Department of Homeland Security budget; the second, from religious organizations and private donations. The former funds are dedicated to a culture of defense and surveillance; the latter, to opening up a world of expanded opportunity for those who have been deprived of any viable path to such a world.[10]

Bassett's camp is situated directly across from the formidable presence of the Border Patrol, as well as a group of armed vigilantes, or self-styled "Minutemen," who are pursuing their own form of policing operation. Looking out from the camp, especially from the railroad tracks just to the north, we can see the cars of the Border Patrol and the vans of the vigilantes, as well as both groups' binoculars glinting in the unrelenting sun. Standing on the tracks, we find ourselves looking into the very face of a fierce inhospitality, embodied by two groups that, despite the difference of their official status, act in concert. Each posse is devoted to *vigilance*, creating an entire landscape of supervision—a veritable panopticon in the remote reaches of desert and mountains. To evade detection by either group, migrants must move in the dark of night, picking their way across treacherous arroyos and open patches of desert populated by spiny cactus and venomous snakes. Vigilance calls for countervigilance.

Assembled here are two groups of people and materials confronting each other—the fragile forces gathered in Bassett's transient camp against the aggressive counterforces of Border Patrol and vigilantes amassed across the railroad tracks, with the border as the invisible but fateful dividing line between them. These groups constitute two parts of a single massive fold— a fold set in the open landscape rather than in a city scene. In both cases, La Frontera serves as the central hinge around which are clustered two worlds characterized by distinctive differences of culture, language, and landscape, even as these same two worlds harbor certain common aspirations and hopes.

Let us imagine the migrant camp as occupying the southern flange of a continuous folded surface whose northern flange is made up of mountains and desert. Each flange is a landscape formation capable of displaying various contents on its surface (e.g., bushes, arroyos, grass, a few trees, and very little water on one side; pickup trucks and miscellaneous food supplies on the other). Both of these flange areas open out from a common construct, that of the border, an indiscernible edge from which an intense energy radiates into the two landscapes that diverge from it, to the north and to the south, respectively.

In this way, the border links two encompassing landscapes. The outer edges of these landscapes are quite different, being scalloped with an apparent irregularity that recalls fractal geometry. To the north stands the notched profile of mountains, while the ragged edges of the low desert stretch out beneath the mountains indefinitely to the south.

Two very disparate groups of people here meet and clash within a single bioregional world. This world, in this place, consists of two distinct parts that are, for all their manifest differences, continuous along their edge of intersection, arranged on two sides of a shared axis provided by an intangible border. This axis unites these groups in a common landscape, but it also serves to hold them apart from each other, setting them into conflict when migrants cross *la línea divisoria*.

This complex and telling scene represents the conjunction of two incongruent counterparts. Such counterparts form a topological figure (formally designated as "enantiomorphs") in which two spatial extents, alike in various regards, nevertheless do not occupy space in the same way. The classical example is that of right- and left-handed gloves, which possess the same internal relations but cannot be used interchangeably (e.g., a right-handed glove cannot fit onto my left hand without being turned inside out). So, too, the two stretches of landscape west of Agua Prieta are deeply similar to each other inasmuch as each falls distinctly on one side or the other of the same definitive line, bearing the same relation to it, yet they are incongruous with respect to the concrete landscape features that each possesses—the steaming desert on the south side giving way to the rapidly rising mountain terrain on the north.

Similarly, those who occupy the two territories are counterparts; they are members of the same human species, yet they are sharply incongruent in aim and tactic, intention and body movement, being driven by motives of defense and expulsion on one side and of border crossing and its support on the other. Further, the standing or seated postures of the vigilantes and the officers of the Border Patrol contrast strikingly to the walking, running, and crawling motions of the migrants who seek to reach American soil.

As joint members of the same incongruent structure, each set of landscape features and human beings rejoins the other across their very differences. All are members of a dyad composed of like and unlike, odd and even, same and other, self and other, American and Mexican, U.S. citizen and migrant, not to mention opposing cardinal directions: north and south, one direction leading to imagined prosperity for migrants and the other to the extreme poverty from which the same migrants are trying to escape.

The complementary coexistence of the two Nogaleses—two cityscapes, or rather, two versions of one city, despite all their economic and cultural differences—departs from the overtly contrastive character of landscape and humans to be found outside Agua Prieta, where two very different kinds of landscape conjoin. The deep congruency of one situation is set against the manifest incongruency of the other, a more or less symmetrical bivalve structure giving way to an asymmetric formation. Nonetheless, both configurations of landscape/cityscape fold over and out from the single constitutive axis of the U.S.-Mexico border.

In other parts of the same region, we encounter *creases*: these are folds that cluster around an entirely natural axis in the form of a folding into the earth. This happens literally with Nogales Wash, a local river that runs north and south, crossing La Frontera in the very center of Ambos Nogales. This north-south axis runs perpendicular to the wall in the same setting, and it goes literally under the wall at one dramatic point. While a hinge is a product of human history, a crease is an expression of natural history. Despite marked differences in character and genesis, creases and hinges alike effectively conjoin that which they also divide. Further, like artificially constructed hinges, a natural crease such as Nogales Wash possesses certain positive attributes: it channels life-sustaining water from the nearby Santa Cruz River to both Nogaleses, and it has served as a conduit for migrants (Rosas 2012). This remains the case even if the wash is subject to considerable pollution and to periodic flooding. As a fold in the earth, it is an instance of *natura naturans* ("nature naturing"), Spinoza's term for a self-generative natural process (Spinoza 2000, 100).

Restricting Movement across Striated Space

In stark contrast to the creases of natural landscapes are walls constructed to protect and exclude. Entirely artificial instances of *natura naturata* ("nature natured"), such structures rise straight from the earth and extend across whole landscapes. They create a striated landscape of order and control. "Striated space" is the aptly chosen term Deleuze and Guattari use to designate space organized in keeping with an assumed master plan whose purpose is to map movement across that space's extent, often with the aim of controlling this movement. A security wall contributes directly to the creation of a striated space in which human movement, with all its intention and volition, is made subject to control. The wall at Nogales is an exemplary instance of a structure that reinforces the highly organized, constrictive space under its supervision. Its express purpose is to place human traffic into gridlock.

Yet even as this wall forbids free movement across the border it materializes, it invites its own transgression. In fact, as emphasized earlier, no wall can altogether foreclose such transgression, whether pursued by digging underneath it, or sneaking around its edges, or using rope ladders to scale it when no one is noticing (or seems to be noticing).[11] For this reason, its contribution to the creation of a prohibitive striated space is delimited: it is literally full of holes.

Such space stands in contrast with areas of "smooth space," places of spontaneous action that charts its own course by actions of spontaneous "legwork" occurring in uncharted traversals. The striation of space at La Frontera, set up by the simultaneous horizontal and vertical thrust of the wall, challenges migrants to discover the equivalent of smooth space in their efforts to find paths of unsanctioned crossing—paths that are contingent insofar as their trajectory offers room for improvisation and change of direction to those who dare to forge or follow them. When such improvisation succeeds, striated space gives way to smooth space—the space of open movement across an uneven landscape.[12] In this way, what had been a border becomes a boundary, and the presumably impervious becomes permeable, at least for the time being and in certain circumscribed ways.

What was designed to be an impervious obstacle to the free flow of migrants and drugs ends by being undermined by adroit actions that out-maneuver the wall at its own game. At La Frontera, the wall was installed to mark and materialize a border, yet no sooner was it built than it was per-ceived by migrants and drug traffickers as there to be breached (B. Heiner, personal communication, July 1, 2009). Just because it acts so fiercely to preclude certain movements, it invites the creation of others that open up its locked-in spatiality; its fixed immobility begets creative legwork as a transgressive response of resistance.

However much traversal happens in the very face of its prohibition, the wall and its immediate environs constitute a physical and cultural *no-man's-land*. Even if subject to transgression, an international border is inimical to inhabitation, not just because it is too narrow (especially when construed as a literal border*line* on a map or in an aerial photograph, as well as when taken as a literal wall), but also because it is a space under duress that is not meant for residence of any significant sort, any more than is a flagpole. However, just as a flagpole can become, at least temporarily, the seat of an acrobat, an anchorite, or a pole dancer, so a certain officially sanctioned kind of occupancy is permitted on the border. We refer to the offices of the Department of Homeland Security. Members of the aptly named "Border Patrol" certainly *work* on or near the literal borderline in these offices, even if they do not live there.[13] Their offices constitute an artificial and state-imposed strip or band that is a site of law enforcement, not inhabitation. At Nogales, these offices are found in a plain rectangular building that is located a few paces north of the official borderline.

This building is appropriately *gray*, and in its deliberate dullness, it contrasts with the fanciful white arch affixed to the Sonoran side of the main checkpoint. Where the arch (whose curvature suggests an eagle's open wings) can be read as a welcoming gesture, the squat rectilinear building of the Border Patrol is distinctly unwelcoming. The undersized windows seem to squint from the facade, like mechanical eyes looking blindly into the daz-zling sun. Within, the building conceals its secrets inside thick cinderblock walls, leaving much to the imagination; the more curious or suspicious that imagination is, the more the interior will be thought to contain secrets of various kinds (technological, informational, military). As it stands there in mute silence, this building seems to pose the question, *Quién sabe?* Who knows? Or more exactly, who is permitted or authorized to know? And what is there to be known, what is archived, deeply buried within this encrypted structure?

Like the wall itself, this building not only exists in striated space (i.e., at a determinate location on a cartographically determined grid) but is itself an embodiment of striation thanks to its cubic rectilinearity. In contrast to the arch just south of it—through which pedestrians and automobiles pass when allowed to do so—it does not invite active movement. Literally self-enclosed, it permits only two motions: entry and exit through doors that stay locked at all other times. Migrants quite understandably steer clear of this building. It is a mute monument of surveillance that morphs the one-dimensionality of the borderline into a built three-dimensionality. Its squat squareness resists conversion into a boundary. Not itself a border, but set next to one and integral to its full-scale operation, it arrogates to itself the right and the power of reconnaissance over the entire U.S.-Mexico border in this geographical region.

Both the wall and the Border Patrol building stand in stark contrast with the bivalve structure formed by the two cities of Nogales. Their stern striation is a matter not merely of human construction but also of a pronounced effort to organize the local landscape in ways that disfigure it. Folded as they are, the twin cities and the migrant camp, as well as the land to the north, follow the contours of the landscape, but the border is an artificial addition to this landscape and thus stands indifferent to its exact configuration.

The border *adds a line to the landscape.* Its one-dimensionality is less conspicuous than the two-dimensional surface of a wall or a three-dimensional building. At the most, the border regarded as *la grande línea* (as it is referred to in Mexico) acts as a hinge for the varying surfaces, urban and rural, that ripple out from it. In the end, however, the linearity of the border disappears into the very landscape onto which it is imposed.

BORDER DYNAMICS: TAKING SIDES

The wall at Nogales—so densely material in its constitution, so defiantly exclusionary in its intended effect—fails to be self-sufficient in another regard. Its very functioning depends on the activities of the Border Patrol and of the migrants they are charged to control. Each group, in its own way, animates the physicality of the wall and its insistent striation. This wall would not be such an effective force without their convergent, albeit conflicting, interests. The situation is not unlike that of creation as construed by Descartes, who speculated that God, for all his omnipotence, creates the world not once and for all but continually and at each successive moment (Descartes 1998). So too, the wall is constantly propped up by all those who are engaged with it—whether they are there to police it or to transgress it, to affirm it or to contest it.

In this scene of bilateral support, any contestation of the wall amounts to its affirmation; its traversal is a reassertion of its presence. This holds true both for those who are officially sanctioned to work at or near the wall—that is, the border agents and their support system—and for those who try to scale it, dig under it, or do an end run around it. Despite their opposite interests, each of these groups is required for the existence of the wall, since it would not have been built in the first place had the U.S. Congress not mandated the control and restriction of migrants, nor would it continue to exist were the flow of concerted crossers (and now increasingly drug traffickers) to dwindle away. The result is a rather special form of "border dynamics" in which one-way hegemony (e.g., of economic and military power) is replaced by a two-way dependency.[14] Without the movement of migrants northward, the border guards and patrol officers would lose their raison d'être and thus their jobs—as would, ironically, the *polleros* or coyotes, Mexican guides who are paid for smuggling migrants across the border and into the United States. Conversely, without the wall and its policing, the migrants would no longer need to devise elaborate strategies for negotiating the wall, nor would they need to rely on expensive and often unreliable advice regarding how to get past it. The chagrin that those in the first category might feel at being out of work as well as the migrants' delight at their new ease of passage cannot obscure the fact that both sides would lose the focus, the *punctum*, that the sheer existence of the wall brings with it.

Others have pointed to comparable situations, wherein a structure built and fortified by the superior power of one side depends on the ingenuity and wiliness of those it is intended to confine to the other side. An international wall in particular depends on the ongoing existence—in effect, the very resistance—of two (or more) approximately equal but opposing forces. James Clifford says, "There are always smugglers, as well as border police. And often the smugglers and the border police depend on each other for their jobs, for the value of what they do" (2003, 59). In any concerted conflict, something like a conspiracy of enemies often operates: think of World War I, Vietnam, or Iraq. The wall at La Frontera is peculiar in that the site of the two-way interaction is embodied in a single object, a wall whose construction is justified on the basis of a policy of immigration and drug containment and control, as well as of a naked nationalism. Peculiar, I say, but not unique: the Berlin Wall likewise materialized the oppositional energies of the conflict between East and West Germany during the Cold War; after its construction in 1961, both sides contributed forcefully to its formidable presence—with a tragic result in terms of lives needlessly lost in its direct vicinity, as is now happening at La Frontera. The erection of such a structure is at once polarizing *and* interanimating, the latter because of the former. It is as if a separation wall engendered diverse directionalities that include nonseparative countertendencies that are connective, albeit in a conflictual mode, achieving a far from peaceful equipoise.

This is not to deny that one side must plan and construct the forbidding structure—putting up a fence, building a wall—and that this is done from a motive of containment or defense on the part of the initiating agency: in the case before us, the U.S. government. *The wall is put up*: this is an undeniable fact that arises unilaterally, almost always on the part of a state or nation that asserts its sovereign right to enclose itself in such a strictly structured way as to exclude others whom it deems inadmissible (Brown 2010). The reciprocity to which I have just been pointing evolves in the wake of this initial situation; it is a response to the wall's existence once it has been put in place (T. Johnston, personal communication, May 31, 2011).

Despite coming to depend on each other in a variety of ways, those on either side of this stressed situation nevertheless experience their own side with a special acuity—not just from greater familiarity but from a sense of its being "my side" of the vexed circumstance. All too often, that side is felt acutely and directly as *the side of suffering*—suffering of one's own as well as the suffering of loved ones. Such suffering takes the form of being excluded (in the case of migrants who come to the wall out of economic deprivation) or of being invaded (as with the American ranchers whose property is being overrun by migrants)—even (and sometimes especially) if one lives on the side opposite to one's place of origin (e.g., the many Mexicans who live in Nogales, Arizona). However different the suffering may be, both in quality and intensity, and whatever respective ethical merit one may wish to accord to it, the two situations are nonetheless internally related; without the extreme poverty that exists in many parts of Mexico and Central America, the migrants would not take such concerted steps to reach the United States at almost any cost and thus to "trespass" upon the open ranch lands and open highways lying on the other side of the border.[15] The ranchers along the border experience the "immigration issue" with an intimacy that most other Americans do not feel. For them, the "breaking into" the country that migrants pose is conflated with having one's own personal land, and sometimes one's home, broken into. Fear for the safety of one's family members and neighbors, as well as for one's own safety, is intense and increasingly so as sophisticated and hardened criminals traffic drugs and human beings in ranchers' backyards.

Further, members of each such group—ranchers and migrants—may take themselves to be not just on their own, more familiar side of the wall but on *the side of right itself*. Many on both sides thus tend to feel quite justified in their attitudes and actions, whether these take the form of risk-laden efforts to cross the border or the armed patrolling of one's personal property. Each group, not surprisingly, regards its own stance as fully justified by its particular suffering and therefore as morally and politically correct.[16] In this respect, those on one side can be said to represent the inversion of those on the other side, not unlike mirror images, despite manifest differences in overt positions on a given issue. Indeed, Azucena Cruz (personal communication, July 1, 2007) comments, "Each side depends on the other for their own identity . . . , defining themselves quite often if not always in relation to the other . . . , not the other as they *are* but the other as they are perceived [to be] since the other is held at a distance by the presence of the border." Here we see that the mirror effect of the border holds at a distance and therefore distorts each side in the face of the other, leading many to feel justified in their resentment of those on the other side.

The fact remains, however, that a significant leeway of voluntary action, as well as of open thought, exists on both sides of the wall: some ranchers do not react angrily or defensively toward the presence of migrants but instead, empathizing with their plight, offer food and water to help them along the way. A waitress to whom we spoke in Duncan, Arizona, was glad to feed migrants passing through her property and would even leave food out when she was away from her house. Most migrants steer clear of all violence and intentionally do not intrude into the personal lives of ranchers. Still, even though freedom of action and thought largely prevails on both sides of the border, the migrants indisputably enjoy far less freedom than the ranchers do. Indeed, whereas ranchers may or may not offer hospitality—they are in a position to do this or to refuse—migrants are focused on finding safe passage into the United States, often against formidable odds. Their freedom consists in making microdecisions that are concerned with the precise place to cross the border, how much risk each step involves, and how to cope with the challenges of the climate and weather. Each of these particular actions is a single phase in one overarching yet basic movement: that of crossing the border by whatever means possible.

Despite its brute materiality, the barrier wall that marks a border such as La Frontera reflects and condenses differences of many kinds: economic and ethnic, racial and linguistic, ideological and cultural, regional and national, and even (as we shall see in subsequent chapters) environmental and urban—or rather, it is because of its being as a sheer material thing that a structure like a wall is able to bear these differences and to act as a mute foil onto which they are projected. At the same time, it intensifies them; it puts them to work.

In this way, a border wall serves as a consolidating presence in striated space. Such consolidation may be experienced with a certain relief, given that human beings by and large seek certainty, yet it incurs the danger of premature definiteness of action and thought as well as emotion. Ambivalence splits into outright hatred or love, envy or admiration, just as it converts openness of mind into settled opinion and rightful hesitation into precipitous action. When this happens, rigidity sets in, and a destructive antagonism replaces a more sensitive multilateralism of approach; alternatively, a projected exoticism or nostalgia concerning *el otro lado* replaces the flexibility of mind that such a complex circumstance requires. What had seemed to be a gain at first—the securing of definite location, the grounding of difference—then becomes loss, whether of attitudinal openness or of dialogic proclivity. Instead of admitting the intrinsic ambiguity of the border, a descent into dogmatic self-righteousness looms.[17]

INSTITUTIONAL ARROGANCE AND THE STATE OF EXCEPTION

Contrasting with the acceptance of ambiguity is the sheer institutional arrogance that is so often evident at the border. One form of such arrogance arises in the discrepancy between the official borderline, as determined by treaties and maps, and the placement of the recently constructed wall. Borderline and wall often coincide, but at other points they diverge. The divergence can be quite considerable in certain stretches—they run separately for up to two miles in some areas of the Rio Grande Valley—while in other locations it is slight. Either way, this divergence is important for what it implies: by defying an exact literalism of location (i.e., as determined by the original land surveys agreed to by Mexico and the United States), the wall claims the right to determine its own location. This imperious gesture is evident in figure 5, which shows an original boundary marker juxtaposed against the high wall looming over it at a distance of approximately ten feet. The wall's authoritative presence bespeaks an attitude of arrogant sovereignty that feels no need to pay homage to the exact history of La Frontera, in which both the U.S. and Mexico are implicated, however lopsidedly.

Another sign of institutional arrogance is manifest in the fact that police and Border Patrol power is everywhere in evidence in the Nogales area. This power is especially conspicuous in the U.S. Border Patrol's claim to complete jurisdiction over the twenty-five-mile band of land just north of the border. In that strip of land, any suspect can be arrested and detained without court orders, as we witnessed dramatically when two squad cars of Border Patrol officers set upon a small group of migrants less than two hundred yards north of the main Nogales checkpoint, frisking them, handcuffing them, and putting them in a van. They were doubtless going to be deported back to Mexico or else held in a local jail or detention center.

Figure 5. Stone border marker below the U.S. wall, Nogales, Mexico. Photo by Mary Watkins, 2006.

After Arizona's passage of SB 1070, and before limits were placed on it, such scenes were increasingly frequent and could occur anywhere in the state, which effectively extended the effective border far beyond the narrow limits established by the Treaty of Guadalupe Hidalgo. Not only is the original borderline buttressed by a wall, but the wall itself, considered as an embodiment of the force of law, can worm its way into the very heart of the state.[18]

The kind of episode just reported not only points to the existence of a legal limbo north of the border but also instantiates the "state of exception" that Giorgio Agamben has aptly described: "This [is the] no-man's land between public law and political fact, and between the juridical order and [human] life. . . . Only if the veil covering this ambiguous zone is lifted will we be able to approach an understanding of the stakes involved in the difference—or the supposed difference—between the political and the juridical, and between law and the living being" (Agamben 2005, 1–2). Such a state of exception, exemplified in the claim to have the right to apprehend and incarcerate certain people without any regard to their rights as human beings, is intensified in border incidents all along La Frontera. The migrants we saw being seized by the Border Patrol in Nogales, Arizona, were first singled out and ethnically profiled by their somewhat disheveled dress and anxious looks. So far as we could tell, they had not committed any specifiable crime, such as theft or assault. Instead, they were perceived as border crossers by their untidy manner of dress and furtive ways of looking around—and doubtless by their racial identities. Without any warrant for search being produced, they were considered already guilty once they could not produce the "proper" immigration papers.

Even though this was only a passing incident, it is a telling illustration of the state of exception presumed by the U.S. government in the wake of 9/11, which claims the power to arrange the fate of any persons not fitting an ideal type of the normative American citizen. We see here the long arm of the proclaimed "Global War on Terrorism" extending into issues of national immigration, with which this war is often semideliberately confused: the panic generated by 9/11 serving as cover for the abusive handling of "illegal immigrants," who cannot be considered terrorists by any coherent criterion.[19]

Ambos Nogales as a Scene of Suffering

Despite their shared geography and history and their topological complementarity, the two Nogaleses differ from one another in almost every imaginable way: demographically, economically, politically, and environmentally. With its local Walmart, Home Depot, and major movie theater, as well as its greater overall prosperity (but also a more limited population, currently estimated at one-tenth or less than that of its neighbor to the south), Nogales, Arizona, stands in stark contrast to Nogales, Sonora, with its manifest poverty, overt drug culture, and amassment of migrants. Yet the two cities also belong together; they share a great deal of history and culture, much of it predominantly Mexican in origin (Ingram, Laney, and Gillilan 1995).[20]

The cities are epicenters in a bivalve life-world located on two sides of the same border. Indeed, at this point in time, one city is not conceivable without the other, nor is one *livable* without the other. The city to the north needs the cheap labor of migrants in homes and stores and restaurants, and its counterpart on the south looks to the north as a place with affordable markets and as a source of possible employment beyond the maquiladoras. We know a couple who, to get to their house-cleaning and gardening jobs, commute almost every day to the United States from Magdalena, more than twenty-one kilometers south of the border. On a larger scale, the south side of the border is home to a number of highly successful agricultural businesses, including firms that grow and ship tomatoes to places all over the United States. Those migrants who do make it across the border and find employment in the United States send a large part of their earnings to their families back in Mexico: billions of dollars each year, the second largest inflow of capital (after oil revenues) to Mexico.

Despite such intimate interdependence, life in the two cities is often fraught with pitched tensions and unappeasable antagonisms. Unlike twin cities such as Minneapolis and Saint Paul or Kansas City, Missouri, and Kansas City, Kansas, where each city benefits considerably from a proximity to its twin and inequality never exceeds tolerable limits, the two Nogaleses suffer acutely from their very contiguity. The primary cause is the competition for goods and services that occurs in the midst of an utterly impersonal international flow of capital. This competition results in conspicuous and problematic income inequalities. Not surprisingly, many of those (mainly on the Mexican side) who earn much less than their northern neighbors experience an intense resentment. Those residing on the American side inflict further suffering on their southern neighbors by deploying massive police surveillance (including both the Border Patrol and the National Guard) and using abusive language. While many Americans in lower Arizona harbor derisive and racist attitudes toward Mexicans in general, many Mexicans regard the borderlands of northern Mexico as "uncivilized" because it has been permanently tainted by the influence of the United States. The antagonism between the two sides is further exacerbated by stereotypes of race, misunderstandings of cultural difference, and ignorance of history, amounting to a veritable vortex of distrust, racism, and recrimination (to be further explored in chapters 6 and 7).

The differences between the two cities are only rarely natural (the surrounding landscape is often quite continuous on both sides of the border; that at Agua Prieta is exceptional in this regard). For the most part, the differences are cultural and historical, as well as economic and social. Such differences originate from one-sided treaties and maps and are often carried forward on the shoulders of ethnic, linguistic, and national disparities and power differentials between the two countries. These disparities are further intensified by contemporary preoccupations with immigration, drug trafficking, and international terrorism. The result of all of this is the creation of an ever-widening, and seemingly unbridgeable, disparity between Anglo and Latino life-worlds. It is as if the wall were the contemporary equivalent of the serpent in the Garden of Eden, presenting choices not between innocence and knowledge but between two nations, two races, two languages, and two ways of life—and all too often between individual members of the same family who are forced to decide between gaining employment and staying close to the heart of familial life.

Such separatism and strife stem above all from that sort of edge we have been calling a "border"—in particular, from its exclusionist character, its recalcitrance to change, and its comparative impenetrability. Moreover, a powerful political statement is made when a wall is erected in order not just to mark the position of the border but also specifically to exclude the members of one nation from admission to the other. The wall erected at the U.S.-Mexico border beginning in the 1990s exemplifies the lengths to which one nation will go in order to prevent certain people from entering its sovereign territory. Such a wall cannot help but divide and polarize, as we see so graphically in the circumstance that obtains in and around Ambos Nogales.[21]

Where Is Hope?

What is to be done? Is there any hope remaining in the increasingly desperate circumstance of Ambos Nogales? We believe that there is. For one thing, any border can in principle become a boundary; even heavily guarded borders can be traversed, given sufficient intentions and agility of movement. This particular border can be traversed either by swimming across it or by following escape routes into the desert—the wet and the dry here providing elemental bases for enabling willing bodies to accomplish border crossings. As we have noted at several points, even the most formidable border walls can be climbed over or dug under, conquered by motion through open air or dense earth. The terms of the crossing itself are set by the material makeup of the border, a makeup with which the moving bodies of migrants must cope (e.g., a river, a barbed-wire fence, a sheet-metal wall). Human beings may not be able to move mountains, but they can do things that eclipse the imagination of those who design walls to keep them out. As one senior Border Patrol agent candidly said to us, "There is no wall we can build that will not be traversed sooner or later."

Instead of rising to the physical challenges of border crossing, however, one may seek to constructively alter the border circumstance itself. This is a matter of changing the border's character, transforming its very identity. Yet examples of such alteration are relatively difficult to find. In addition to the cross-wall dialogues and artistic collaborations that we have mentioned (and will treat in detail in chapters 8 and 9), a very different instance of resourceful transformation of the circumstance is found in a commercial venture such as Just Coffee, a coffee-roasting business in Agua Prieta that buys beans from independent growers in Chiapas and roasts the beans to sell on both sides of La Frontera. The restrictive and prohibitive character of the border at Agua Prieta, which has its own separate checkpoint for automobile and pedestrian traffic, here contrasts with an effort to do cross-border business that benefits both farmers and roasters, without the usual middlemen. Just Coffee and hundreds of other cooperatives have been created in Mexico to encourage young people to stay and work in their home country rather than risk the perilous passage to the United States.

Another excellent example of the transborder creation of cooperatives is the work done by Bob Stone, Betsy Bowman, Clifford DuRand and others at the Centro para la Justicia Global/Center for Global Justice, in San Miguel de Allende, Mexico. This nonprofit helps to educate local people about the economic and social benefits of cooperatives and, more generally, about the creation of a solidarity economy. The center offers a variety of forms of assistance that help to initiate and sustain local cooperatives: "referrals to legal, technical, agricultural and financial help; help in creating linkages and networks between communities with cooperatives—local, regional, and international; [and] help in forming productive democratic relationships among the communities themselves, individuals[,] and the groups who may be able to provide the direct services such as technical knowledge, training, credit and/or other resources that they need" (Center for Global Justice 2011).

Despite these promising moves, the tragedy continues to play itself out on a daily basis. It motivates increasingly significant demonstrations and processions that protest the deaths of the thousands who have died in desert crossings since the inception of Operation Gatekeeper.

Still other ways of transforming a tightly patrolled border circumstance into a permeable boundary will doubtless be devised in times ahead. Such transformations will contribute to the creation of a common frame for an emerging matrix of places and populations that is less divisive and destructive than the contemporary circumstance presents. Were this to happen, the hinge of the paired cities of Ambos Nogales will no longer be a rigidly reinforced line; it will have become an open band of spontaneous actions and interactions, a zone where leeway is allowed and new initiatives are encouraged. At that time, the two cities will come to form a new, revitalized region where people can flourish in diverse ways not now permitted or even envisioned. On that day, Ambos Nogales will no longer be confined to its cruelly disruptive current fate; its two populations will be able to join forces in ways more constructive and imaginative than those now followed, and a shared experience of what it is like to move freely back and forth across a line of strict separation will emerge.

If and when this happens—however long it may take—Nogales will have become a single, albeit complex, city. In certain respects, this will be to return to a much earlier historical moment when there was only one town through which the border ran lightly: a border that was little more than a point of reference, punctuated by occasional marker stones. These marker stones announced the border to the world, a border that would otherwise have gone unnoticed except in history books—unnoticed not just because the borderline itself was invisible but also because it was not enforced by border guards, much less reinforced by technologies that bring about a circumstance of hypervigilance.

That was a different world; it will not return in anything like its original form. But in the current impasse, it can at least be hoped that some semblance of the former freedom of passage can be reinstated. Such an opening can be realized by the relaxation of current exclusionary policies so as to permit easier visitations by family members and friends who live on different sides of La Frontera and (still more important) to make it possible for workers to move from one country to the other with comparative ease and impunity. In this new stage of its history, the border will become a boundary once more; it will facilitate its own traversal—and that will be significant progress.

In the case of Ambos Nogales, sibling cities will be folded over onto each other so as to become co-imbricated in every facet of their existence: they will become more fully congruent with each other, not just in a topological sense, but in many other respects as well. These cities will certainly retain many cultural and historical differences, but beyond these, they will merge more completely into a continuous urban complex within which people will breathe more easily and talk more openly, having been freed from the fear of apprehension and recrimination.

In other words, "Ambos Nogales" will give way to "Nogales," this one toponym sufficing to signify a reunited city. The two cities will become a shared smooth space no longer bisected by a stark border wall that severs one body of people from another.

CHAPTER 3

Tijuana

The Wall and the Estuary

A people who would begin by burning the fences and let the forest stand! I saw the fences half consumed, their ends lost in the middle of the prairie.

Henry David Thoreau, "Walking" (1991)

The world is as sharp as the edge of a knife.

Northwest Coastal Indian saying

THE CITY AND ITS HISTORY

Tijuana: here is a city that is not just located at the U.S.-Mexico border but *born from this border itself*. As a city, Tijuana did not arise for the usual historical reasons (because it was, e.g., a stopping place on a larger indigenous trail system, a trading post, near the site of a battle, or the place of origin of a given tribe or group of people) or because of its fit with the local landscape (e.g., being linked to other places by a local stream, as is Nogales, or lying at the foot of a mountain range or in a cooler zone, such as a valley). Instead, it emerged because of what the border made possible for it. In its origin, and still today, Tijuana is a creature of the border, a child of La Frontera.[1]

In this chapter, we continue to trace the effects of the border and the border wall on life in its immediate vicinity. But in this case, we pay special attention to the dialectic between Tijuana and the extensive estuary that lies just to the north of it, on the American side. In particular, we focus on certain environmental consequences of the border circumstance, an emphasis that is also to be found, though in lesser degree, in our treatment in chapter 4 of the environmental impact of the border wall in the Lower Rio Grande Valley.

In contrast to Nogales, Tijuana is a city of comparatively recent vintage. It does not exist on standard nineteenth-century maps. It first flourished in the 1920s, when Prohibition drove Americans to seek alcohol across the border. The rough-and-tumble town that grew up to quench this thirst resembled a frontier town in the Old West, with heavy drinking, gambling, prostitution, and cockfighting all much in evidence. By the time of World War II, it was commonly said—not just in the southwestern American states but throughout North America—that one could go to Tijuana for a "blast," "the time of your life."[2] A large naval base and marine camp at San Diego, just to the north, meant that many enlisted servicemen went over the border—at that time easy to pass through in either direction—for binges of drinking, often ending up AWOL. This scene, coupled with the arrival of the maquiladoras, caused Tijuana to grow to a population of 1.8 million today.

Despite the presence of mesas and various other natural outcroppings, Tijuana itself is set on mostly flat land. This land can be described only as desperately dry; indeed, no water flows between the banks of the Tijuana River for most of the year. The Mexican government—in the hopes of collecting what little rainwater does fall there—has fully paved over the bed and banks of this river. In theory, this concrete is supposed to prevent runoff rainwater from sinking into the ground, but the actual effect of this "channelizing" has been a steady flow of trash and sewage into the United States (Rainoff 2010).[3] The contemporary city of Tijuana is located to the west and south of this paved-over river and is rapidly expanding into suburban developments along both these directions. Reflecting the earlier division of rural lands into sheer rectangles, an unremitting grid pattern structures the streets, allowing little inconsistency except where the grid intersects with the river, forcing an alteration of its regular patterning.

To the immediate north of the city, just over the U.S.-Mexico border, lies the Tijuana Estuary, a scene of abundant water, newly cleansed and replenished each day by the ocean tides that course in and out of the estuary. No paving over is to be found here, much less any grid pattern. The only obvious incursions of civilization are the raised walking paths that have been built within the estuary and the small nature museum at the northern edge. The estuary, once on the verge of destruction, has been restored, thanks in large part to the extraordinary efforts of Mike McCoy. But it has been threatened by the construction of the original border wall and, more recently, by the newer outlying walls.

Beyond its effects on this estuary—to which we shall return below—the presence of the border and the border wall enters intimately into every sphere of life in Tijuana. It is part of every daily transaction, large or small, finding its way into every pore of the human bodies that inhabit the downtown area, and even the nearby villages. By their effects, the border and the wall also insinuate themselves into animal and plant life, into the very air breathed by humans and nonhumans alike, extending even into the open and desolate landscape that surrounds this city, and finally into the entire province of Baja California Norte. The pervasive presence of the border and its wall reveals itself concretely in the highly polluted atmosphere in and around Tijuana, which is heavily laden with carcinogenic substances, much of it stemming from the maquiladoras that operate in the vicinity of Tijuana. Adding to the problem, American companies dispose of waste from the United States in Mexico so as to avoid high landfill costs (M. McCoy, personal communication, June 21, 2007).

The wanton spilling of chemicals is strikingly visible. In one particularly alarming case, that of the Metales y Derivados company, leaking barrels of industrial sludge, containing lethal chemicals such as lead, sulfuric acid, cadmium, and arsenic, were still in the firm's yard. Meanwhile, just below the mesa on which this company was located lies Chilpancingo, a colonia constructed on the edge of a stream filled with the runoff of the company's chemicals. Here children routinely played in the polluted streams, oblivious to the danger that surrounded and invaded them, until community activists began a concerted public education program.

Earlier in this part, we discussed the kinds of transborder dialogue that have arisen in the face of the wall. This is very much the case with regard to common environmental concerns that have grown graver as a result of NAFTA's failure to protect the environment around the border and Mexico's reluctance to pass environmental legislation or to monitor the few laws the country did enact. Metales y Derivados itself has been forced to close because of protests and legal actions taken by the *Colectivo Chilpancingo Pro Justicia Ambiental* (Chilpancingo Pro-Environmental Justice Collective), an organization formed by women whose families were affected by the chemicals that had tainted their water. This collective worked together with the Environmental Health Coalition in San Diego in a transborder partnership for the sake of their common bioregion. The case has been a groundbreaking one for transborder environmental partnerships in the face of NAFTA's disregard for the environment.

BEING AT THE BORDER IN THE FLESH

The strictly enforced, and continually reinforced, border wall in the Tijuana region has affected people's lives there at the deepest levels, to the point that this wall has gone right under their skin, becoming, as it were, subcutaneous. The wall is in a sense both outside and inside people's bodies at once. It has also entered into the life of the estuary, compromising its future. What has enabled such a deep and extensive penetration of human bodies and a major body of water alike?

The standing wall is an aggressive external edge, especially at Tijuana, where it has been rebuilt several times and supplemented by additional parallel walls. In its assertive vertical thrust, it lifts itself off the ground and seems to mock the earth on which it is built. Its fiercely inanimate verticality ultimately reflects the verticality of human bodies confronting it in their own, organic, upright posture. Just by standing there so defiantly, it thwarts migrants who are eager to get past it by any means possible. Its concrete and metallic body contrasts with their fleshed bodies, challenging them and often humiliating them unless—somehow—they manage to find their way over it. (Or unless they decide not to try this time, given the grave consequences of being apprehended and deported back to Mexico.) Nothing on earth could be more external to these bodies—more alien, more other, more coercive, more prohibitive. The wall acts like a vast shield that literally repels these "foreign" bodies, whose arrival in the United States is felt like an invasion by those Americans who wish to keep their home country racially and linguistically pure. Thus, unlike walls that accommodate and welcome—such as the walls of one's own home—this wall repels unauthorized entry in an unmistakable gesture of concerted inhospitality.

This wall does not, however, simply stand over and against those who come into contact with it as something radically external. This same wall also insinuates itself inside these bodies. It becomes *part* of them. Not as a mere image or memory—a mental representation—or as an emotional *imago*. Rather, it is a matter of the wall's *incorporation* into the very muscles and sinews of those bodies that have to deal with it. This includes not only the bodies of those who are anxious to cross over the wall but also the bodies of all those who live in and around Tijuana, even those who are simply passing through the city or its environs. Everyone there—from cooks to street cleaners, merchants to artists—*embodies the wall in her or his own way, in the very corporeal practices of daily life.* Psychological aspects of incorporation are further pursued in chapters 6 and 7; here our question bears on the sense of "body" relevant to these matters. Is it the physiological body only—the body that ingests corporate wastes?

The physiological body is critical and is deeply vulnerable at La Frontera, but we must here consider another sense of body: that of the body *as lived*. The lived body refuses reduction to the status of an object (e.g., in the form of the body as posited by medical science), nor can it be understood solely in terms of what pure consciousness says about it or as a mere composite of physical and mental properties. Rather, the lived body is an absorptive entity whose very indeterminacy allows it to take on many attributes, including those that characterize a border wall. These qualities are so diverse (some are perceptual, some physical, some psychological, some social, some historical) that they would be experienced as incompatible by a judging mind—and certainly challenging for any machine whose task is just to register them mechanically (say, a camera or recording machine). Only a lived body is sufficiently pliable and porous to take in such a wide variety of attributes—to hold them together in one complex commixture and to express them by means of its actions. These actions inevitably take the form of habitual movements that reflect this manifold of immanent influences as they interact. For the lived body is best described as a *receptive matrix* that is open to the incursion of very different things, where "things" includes not only physical objects but also qualities and events, persons and groups, words and thoughts.

For example, James G., a middle-aged Tijuanan, said to us that "the border is in me—I can feel its presence there" (personal communication, July 10, 2007). Here we can invoke Husserl's idea of *Leib* ("live body") and Merleau-Ponty's notion of *le corps vécu* ("the lived body") as the vehicle of such an act of incorporation. Whether as borderline or as material wall, the border becomes lodged in James G.'s flesh as an intertangled mass of sensibilities. The porosity that characterizes the flesh of the lived body allows this flesh to contain something that is starkly external—to experience it as being at one with this body, as *part of it*, or as a foreign body intruded on or into it. In the case of the border, it is a matter of taking into the lived body a fateful edge in the form of a borderline or a wall that has been inserted into one's somatic matrix. Such forced incorporation does not require the denial of the line's geometric status, or the wall's physical externality—the line and the wall retain their own identity as drawn or built—but it does mean acknowledging that they also can attain a lasting presence in the lived bodily experience of human subjects. From being a separated and separative line or wall outside this subject, it becomes an integral part of one's ongoing bodily experience. The subject to whom this body belongs becomes thereby a *being of the border*—not just marked by it, or obsessed over it, but effectively living it from within, oriented by it day in and night out: literally preoccupied by it.[4]

To this it must be added that the body-subject need not be an individual person. It can very well be a collective subject, a group of human beings who are related as members of a community that has the same or comparable experiences. Thus, lived bodies may *together* embody a sense of the border, sharing in the experience not by partitioning it out among themselves as individuals but by participating jointly in an experience of the border. Such shared experience is a matter not just of emotional empathy with others but of a deep continuity and connection with them, consciously recognized or not. In the case of many who live near the border at Tijuana, such an experience most often manifests itself as a sense of being oppressed; of being hindered, held back, set back, or burdened by the border if not crushed by it; and above all, of being alienated by it.

In such "intercorporeity" (to use Merleau-Ponty's word), we are in effect dealing with *flesh*—a term that, in English, captures better than any other the ambiguity of the lived body. Flesh is not limited to the bodily surface (the "skin") but extends both beneath it into an indefinite interior and outward into an equally definite exterior. It connotes what is most sensitive and sensible about the lived body, what is at once eminently porous yet also intact and integral, all the while remaining essentially indeterminate as felt. Flesh is the boundary of the body mass, not just in one or two places, but throughout its existence. From flesh, we can go straight inside the lived subject, or else we can go outward into the environing world. Flesh is itself a very special kind of edge, that of the lived body as a whole; it is thus an amorphous edge that is closer to a band than to a line. It is special above all in possessing the peculiar power of taking in the edges of many other sorts of things, from other people and automobiles, buildings and streets, and walruses and walls.

Flesh connotes the way in which the lived body is continuous with the surrounding world: the *Lebenswelt*, or "life-world"—or better still, the "place-world." In this capacity, it is a matter of "the flesh of the world," as Merleau-Ponty has posited in *The Visible and the Invisible*: "My body is made of the same flesh as the world . . . [;] this flesh of my body is shared by the world, the world *reflects* it, encroaches upon it and it encroaches upon the world" (1968, 248). The flesh of the world signifies the massive—albeit often denied or repressed—fact that the lived body flows into the particular place-world in which it finds itself. Such cosmic flesh is a more expansive notion than that of incorporation; whereas the latter implies a one-way movement from thing or world *into* the lived body, the flesh of the world suggests that body and world are coeval in status, paired from the start. Each permeates the other; the energy flows both ways at once, in from out, out from in. In this way, body and world energize each other. And the opposite obtains as well: each can enervate the other. Indeed, the wall at La Frontera can become a literally exhausting presence. Thanks to the vulnerability of the flesh, a rebarbative thing like a border wall is not simply an obstructive presence but instead becomes a troubling presence felt from within. Indeed, it is acutely felt by everyone in places like Nogales or Tijuana—by businessperson or migrant, family member or artist, tourist or relative.

Beyond helping to explain how a border wall pervades the lives of those living near it, the flesh of the world has a very particular application, namely, to the natural environment. The very word *environment* literally signifies what *surrounds* the body-subject, "environing" it. It is effectively another name for the flesh of the world in its immediately impinging presence. The natural environment has everything to do with the flow between the lived body and the experienced world. It is the very medium between the two, ensuring that what affects the body will also affect its world, and vice versa.

A Matrix of Edges

The current precarious state of natural species in the Tijuana Estuary region reflects the massive facticity of the flesh of the world. The flesh of the world is an encompassing state that binds natural entities, human and nonhuman alike, to one another in very intimate ways, and yet this very intimacy can also be said to render these entities acutely vulnerable to one another's incursions and excesses. One way to conceive of this interspecies vulnerability is as a circumstance within which edges intermesh in diverse and numerous ways, some mutually enhancing, some noxious in their effects. Ways that enhance are found in the edges of the estuarine channels that direct tidal waters in their daily course. These edges possess an inherent "shapefulness," a material directionality that itself reflects many years of inflow and outflow of the tides. The characteristic curvature of the channels allows tidal waters to be efficiently flushed by being brought into contact with more cordgrass (*Spartina foliosa*) than would be the case if the channels were simply straight. Indeed, nature favors a serpentine flow in any river, creek, or stream, so as to distribute nutrients and modulate the flow of energy within the system.

This smoothly flowing estuarine circumstance is to be contrasted with the concrete-clad bed and banks of the nearby Tijuana River on the Mexican side, straightened out with artificial embankments, poured-concrete surfaces that destroy the natural flow pattern of water. In earlier days, when it was unobstructed, this river moved nutrients and sediments, distributing them throughout the estuary region with seasonal regularity. Now the paved-over riverbed and banks increase periodic flooding, thereby putting people, animals, and plants at risk in ways that never occurred in the original circumstance. It is difficult to imagine a more striking contrast between naturally occurring and humanly engineered waterways.[5]

Not that nature does not benefit from assistance from time to time. When a reconstruction of part of the Tijuana Estuary was undertaken in the winter of 2000, 135,000 cubic yards of excavated soil were imported to create a marsh plain with a set of tidal channels to replace earlier channels that had become clogged by soil erosion in the Tijuana watershed region. The designers of this project had to imagine channels anew and at first created patterns with acute or right angles, reflecting a human penchant for the measurable and the regular. But these rigid edges were softened by natural forces over time, producing less abrupt channeling that yielded a gentle flow supportive of the whole renewed marsh area, benefiting various grasses transplanted there and having salubrious effects on the surrounding areas. Throughout the restoration process, marshland edges played a powerfully formative role.[6] We might imagine such edges as interactive parts of the flesh of the world—parts that touch each other, much as my right hand touches my left hand. No wonder that a disturbance in one part of the marshland affects other parts with which it is in touch, directly or indirectly (T. Johnston, personal communication, August 3, 2010).

The Tijuana Estuary exemplifies how the flesh of the world can be seen as engaged in a reciprocal relation among its parts. This type of literally symbiotic relation can be contrasted with what has been created at the border less than a mile south. There the controlling edges belong to the border wall, whose recent redoubling (and even tripling, at certain points) risks ruining earlier efforts to rescue the Tijuana Estuary, including that of the model marsh.[7] These edges are not only fiercely artificial, but they are also remorselessly rectilinear, being composed of regular panels of discarded military metal. The panels march right into the ocean, as though oblivious to their submersion.[8]

The edges in this part of the border world are also dangerous: there is barbed wire on top of the chain-mesh fence that fills in gaps between sections of the wall proper. These are not edges with which one wants to tangle, however desperately one may wish to scale the fence. The world overall may not be "as sharp as the edge of a knife" (to quote the Northwest Coastal Indian epigraph to this chapter), but certainly this particular part of it is too sharp to allow for the kind of spontaneous interfusion of elements that makes life in the marshlands possible.

Two kinds of edge collide here: edges belonging to the sharply etched border wall at Tijuana and edges inherent in the Tijuana Estuary and in the ocean that embraces them both. From an elevated position on the Tijuana side of the wall, one perceives a scene of soft edges spreading to the north, those of Border Field State Park and, just beyond, the estuary, while toward the west a spectacle of swelling edges of breaking waves introduces another order of edge morphology and temporal rhythm.

In such a view of the estuary and ocean, the natural world seems to resemble one's own body, with its permeable skin and gentle edges. It is

Figure 6. Tijuana Estuary seen from the south. Photo by Ben McCue, courtesy of WiLDCOAST.

in effect "the world's body" (to borrow John Crowe Ransom's phrase) as grasped in vistas whose flesh is provided by the marshlands, beaches, and ocean waves (fig. 6). The flesh of my viewing body here becomes continuous with the world's flesh. But the fact that I can glimpse parts of such natural spectacles through the dense mesh of a border fence does not mitigate the rigor of the fence's gridded, wiry surface, stratified with fiercely nonnegotiable metallic edges. And if I walk to the right or left and face the opaque wall that frames this surviving stretch of fence, I am abruptly confronted with still stricter edges, those of the ridges on its steely surface and those that make up its acutely angular top parts.

Figure 7.
Tijuana
Estuary seen
from the
north, with
Imperial
Beach,
California.
Photo by Mike
McCoy.

From all this, we are able to see that the kind of hard edges and striated space that define the wall and fence at this point along La Frontera stand starkly contrasted with the multiplicity of soft edges that comprise the natural environment to the north. The estuary region is composed of a dynamic mosaic of edges, whether natural or reconstructed, constituting its own smooth space. This becomes especially clear in figure 7.

In this second aerial photograph, we can see the curvilinear gestalt of the estuary as it coils forth from the ocean and enters the landmass, branching into several sinuous arms before disappearing into a myriad of smaller channels. The fanning-out estuary is distinguished from the rectilinear mass of apartment buildings on the right, which are bordered by clearly demarcated streets. Quite different are the shapes of the waves coming from the ocean onto the beach; we have no exact name for these forms as they occur in nature, since, in their dynamic movement, they fall outside the bounds of any formal geometry. In this single image, we are presented with a schizoid edge-world—a world in which many edges are soft and sinuous, while others are intensely organized and striated.

BORDER VERSUS BOUNDARY IN THE NATURAL ENVIRONMENT

"The environment is something that doesn't have borders," says Mike McCoy, who has been working to save and restore the Tijuana Estuary for more than forty years (McCoy and Roma 2008).[9] Here is a statement whose basic truth seems evident, but how is it to be understood more precisely? In order to address this issue, we shall again draw on the critical difference made previously between borders and boundaries. Borders show their sharply defined edges, either materially (in physical reality) or formally (e.g., in terms of formal shapes); they differentiate one area from another, to the point that, in certain concerted constructions, they keep people or animals out of a given area for economic, social, or political reasons. Sometimes borders are circumstantially useful, as in raising children, for whom parents feel they must "set limits." Sometimes they are wholly arbitrary, as when someone wants to keep a certain distance from someone else for no justifiable reason. Overall, borders are paradoxical, if not deceptive: on the one hand, they often present themselves as more or less innocuous—for instance, the edges of curbs on an active street, where it is important to distinguish between pedestrian and automobile traffic; on the other hand, in certain contexts they can be anything but innocent, as we know from the wall that has been built at La Frontera, a massive construction that channels and controls the lives of millions of people. In themselves, borders may usefully help to delimit and shape regions; they become problematic, however, when they are used as material barriers that separate people (and animals) from one another.

Boundaries, by contrast, are intrinsically permeable; they are osmotic in their capacity to facilitate flow-through of many sorts—for instance, the migration paths of nomadic animals. The natural world abounds in boundaries, including transitional zones where flora and fauna, or water and air currents, intermingle. When saltwater meets freshwater, a subtle boundary between two bodies of water occurs. Such a boundary is highly porous. When a salt marsh and inland vegetation conjoin, a boundary emerges, even if the exact edge is difficult to delineate precisely. Thanks to the facilitation of movement they effect at many levels (from tissue membranes to the edges of melting glaciers), porous boundaries are essential to the evolutionary potential and physical fate of the many things they act to draw together. It follows that the imposition of a strict border, one that blocks or inhibits natural flow patterns, inevitably carries with it the risk of devolution, even biological death, including the loss of local species.[10]

Boundaries do more than simply facilitate the intermingling of animal or plant bodies with the surrounding environment; they can also serve as the ground for psychical forces and forceful ideas. In Martin Heidegger's formulation of their pervasive range, "A boundary is not that at which something stops but . . . that from which something *begins its presencing*" (1971, 154). The gerund *presencing* (as *Anwesen* is here translated) refers to the dynamics of becoming as an event. In the broadest sense, then, the presencing arising at the boundary at La Frontera includes activities such as plant growth and animal movement, as well as the concerted actions of migrants as they seek to cross the border wall. The presencing occasioned by boundaries includes all the ways in which these various edges contribute to the emergence of new directions, patterns, and, on occasion, new forms of life. A boundary, by its very plasticity and porosity, supports the realization of these various potentialities, acting as the place of their emergence. Nor need the presencing be of something new: it can be of the regular and repetitive, as in a tidal inlet or in the inner channels of the estuary, right down to the most minute level of the marsh grasses, where microbial cleansing occurs in channels that form natural boundaries. In this instance, we are able to witness how boundaries represent a material condition for the health of a finite part of the earth.

One main effect of boundaries of every kind is that they *leave open* spaces that would, in a border regime, be constricted or closed up altogether. This is true both of naturally occurring boundaries and of humanly constructed ones. The aptly named "boundary markers" (or "boundary stones," as they were also called) first set out along the U.S.-Mexico border left open the land in between, thereby providing significant gaps through which animals and humans could move more or less freely. The open-ended nature of these boundaries stands in stark contrast to the closed character of constructed borders, which aim at gapless continuity and a form of physical presence that actively thwarts passage from one side to the other. Figure 8 shows the original boundary marker at Tijuana. Notice that this curiously shaped obelisk-like marker, whose original purpose was to mark the westernmost segment of the boundary between the United States and Mexico, has by now become *part of the wall*, literally situated on both sides of the mesh fence that here serves as the wall. Its historical significance has been fully absorbed into its current function: legitimating an untraversable border.

From these considerations, we may more fully appreciate the significance of McCoy's contention that the environment has no borders. Borders do not belong integrally to the natural world in its aboriginal, or wild, state. They fail to preserve locales wherein animals and plants and people have tangible histories or, more generally, a basic orientation or an identity as denizens of a given place. *To places thus construed, boundaries accrue*, because only this type of edge can bestow shape on a place, indicating where it begins and ends while leaving open the possibility of multiple ingressions into its midst.[11]

Borders, by contrast, belong to *sites*, not to places. Sites in our construal are homogeneous and isotropic sectors of space, affording what Whitehead

Figure 8. Westernmost U.S.-Mexico border marker at Tijuana/San Diego. Photo by Edward S. Casey.

(1953) calls "simple location." This location is a particular position on an explicit or implicit spatial grid of striated space, and with rare exceptions, it is constructed and not found—planned and projected, demarcated with special instruments and built from artificial materials (Casey 2009). We see a number of such sites on the right side of figure 7. It is hardly accidental that these shapes stand out when seen from the objectifying distance of a vantage point far above a given landscape. Nor is it accidental that such shapes belong to humanly constructed roads that are designed to direct and regulate traffic—to channel automobiles and trucks. Such rectangles and squares reflect the modernist conviction that world-space should be divided into strictly measurable units such as blocks, counties, and even whole states (Casey 2002). The result is the "sitification" of such space—a process of disciplined normalization in which borders delimit inflow and outflow with the purpose of controlling it, keeping it within the strictly determined perimeters of discrete units of space.

The reinforced sitification of Tijuana in its city plan and nearby wall artificializes the local landscape by imposing on it structures that pile one border on top of another. The recent construction of additional border walls has in effect created a no-man's-land between the walls, given that no humans, animals, or even plants are to be found there. The U.S. government here indulges in the fantasy of perfect control and complete supervision through the construction of the border wall and its reinforcements. This concretization of imperial power has come at the expense of the land as a region of naturally given boundaries that help to define the smooth places of an unsitified region.

Secretary of Homeland Security Michael Chertoff, acting in concert with Congressman Duncan Hunter, was the driving force behind the ambitious plan to add extra walls to the first wall in the Tijuana region. To create these additional walls, whose construction continued after Chertoff was no longer in office, massive amounts of land had to be bulldozed from mesas near Tijuana, flattening the mesas in an effort to make the installation of concrete and steel walls easier (fig. 9). The soil that was removed was dumped into the gullies that lie between the mesas. This excess did not, however, stay where its producers had intended; seasonal rains washed the soil into the Tijuana Estuary and threatened to clog the vulnerable and fragile channels of the marshlands there. While some effort was made to plant grass on the bare slopes of the degraded mesas, this proved to be an insufficient antidote to the serious erosion problem that had been created by the construction project. This is just one example of the way an overall lack of consideration for the fragility of an ecosystem can, in an instant, threaten to destroy something that took a very long time to evolve (indeed,

Figure 9. Earth clearing for U.S. border wall, Spooners Mesa, Tijuana, Mexico. Photo by Mike McCoy.

thousands of years) and that required several decades of committed human labor and cost a large sum of money (over forty million dollars) to restore.

As Mike McCoy has recently observed, the result of the construction of the additional walls has meant "habitat fragmentation and cumulative impact on the entire resource area, resulting in a very ecologically destructive problem. The border mesas, riparian corridor, the estuary, and the ocean are all part of a larger ecosystem, so what happens to one happens to all, because they are interconnected and dependent upon each other" (personal communication, May 2, 2011). Everything is part of an immense ecological matrix comprising myriad edges in the form of intersecting boundaries. To impose walls on this matrix is to force borders on these boundaries—and this is to risk ecological catastrophe of major proportions.

PAUSING TO CONSIDER

Three points emerge from the foregoing analysis:

(1) The Tijuana Estuary, located as it is just north of the border walls at La Frontera, participates in a highly complex situation involving issues of

immigration and drug traffic, as well as environmental degradation. This estuary marks the southwestern limit of the United States, while Tijuana marks Mexico's northwestern limit. Despite their close contiguity and their shared extremity of location—as well as their intense interaction in the region—the two places differ dramatically. The city's green identity is severely compromised; not only does the downtown area include very few parks, but the bed of the Tijuana River as it passes through the city is entirely artificial. Moreover, although fully two-thirds of the overall watershed area in the region lies in Mexico, and certain canyons (e.g., Los Laureles Canyon) open directly into the estuary on the American side, no estuary or marshland is recognized, much less protected, on the Mexican side, where there are far fewer environmental laws and enforcement efforts. Far from being valued for its own sake, the surrounding landscape is pushed ever farther out, as the sprawling city grows by several hundred square hectares every week, engulfing previously freestanding communities. In this virtually out-of-control expansion, Tijuana has become an insatiable urban leviathan. Not only is the landscape at the outer edges of the city continually leveled for new building, but environmental degradation increases as unfettered trash and waste flow into the watershed from these new building sites and from the city itself.[12]

(2) Although the regions on the two sides of the border exhibit markedly different circumstances, they are linked by the common fate of the watershed and the estuary, both of which are now imperiled. The city of Tijuana agreed several years ago to clean up the massive debris that accumulates in Los Laureles Canyon out of a concern for what many felt was an impending environmental disaster; this project has, however, met with only limited success. In contrast, the United States, despite almost a half-century of serious commitment to improving the marshlands of the estuary (with many contributions from the private sector), has now put these restored areas at risk by building multiple walls along its southern border. Only recently have both countries begun to join forces in bilateral efforts to move from a purely exploitative approach to the natural world to a more broadly based coalition that aims at its protection and preservation.[13] Overall, retaining the region's irreplaceable natural resources will clearly require more vigorously pursued pollution controls.

(3) Were a commitment to such controls made, we would witness the transition from the predominance of borders to an augmented presence of boundaries—or more exactly, the two together in a state of dynamic coexistence. The success of the greenbelt zones (i.e., parks and open fields) in and around many contemporary cities show this to be no mere utopian dream. The entire watershed area around Tijuana should be supported in such a

way that its inherent natural boundaries become more fully compatible with artificially imposed borders, whether those of concrete river channelization, the grid plan of city streets, or the border wall itself. The porosity and smoothness of these boundaries must be allowed to cohabit creatively with the striation of these rigid modes of bordering.

A natural environment that surrounds and sustains a given place or region gives room for boundaries and borders alike, whereas gridded surfaces or vertical walls create borders that claim exclusive rights of domain and powers of determination. In the Tijuana Estuary—indeed, in Tijuana itself, as well as in San Diego—there is space for both kinds of edge, despite all their manifest differences and despite the discrepant rhythms of the natural and the urban.

ECOTONAL COMPLEXES

From these general considerations we turn to a more particular notion, that of the "ecotone." A term is needed to describe the specific way that boundaries come to presence in the natural world, subtending and structuring the flesh of that world. *Ecotone* is such a term,[14] and it is definable as "the boundary between two natural communities where elements of both as well as transitional species intermingle in heightened richness" (Krall 1994, cover). The result of such intermingling is a transitional zone that embodies what can be called an "edge effect." Thus an ecotone is not just a zone of contact between two discrete edges, as in the meeting of two separate surfaces; instead, it is characterized by a certain breadth or width. It is in effect a *band*. Thanks to the comparative amplitude and depth provided by this band, things happen in an ecotone that do not occur elsewhere. The unique environment that is found there can be attributed to the intimate interaction of several places with their unique contents (just *this* set of trees, *this* stream, etc.) or different regions with their characteristic flora and fauna, their soils and topographies. Given the multiple levels on which such interactions occur, ecological change is often conspicuous in ecotones: animals and plants meet and interbreed here, increasing genetic diversity while inducing altered behavioral patterns in both plants and animals.

Band, juxtaposition, change: these are three leading features of ecotones in natural settings. To these is added a fourth feature, *complexity of habitat*. Krall has given an especially apt description of this last feature: "In the natural world, edges where differences come together are the richest of habitats. Animals often choose these ecotones, where contrasting plant communities meet, to raise their young where the greatest variety of cover and food can be found. A doe will give birth to her fawn on the edge of a forest, where she can find shelter as well as food in the open area beyond the trees" (1994, 4).

Krall adds, "Transitional species, plants and animals such as those found in tidal zones, have become highly adapted for life 'on the edge.' Marshes where fresh and saltwater habitats meet are some of the most productive places on Earth in terms of fecundity and diversity of species" (1994, 4). It follows that the loss of marshlands such as those found in the Tijuana Estuary is tantamount to the loss of significant biodiversity. Their restoration is therefore not merely a nostalgic project of returning to an earlier state; it has everything to do with the future of proliferating life. Such proliferation requires supportive places and regions that allow for continual experimentation in adaptation and diversification.[15]

An ecotone is composed of intermediary spaces—what can be called "interplaces" (Casey 2009). In the case of the Tijuana Estuary, these interplaces are where we find "the transition between the terrestrial and marine, the estuarine and marine, the intertidal and upland zone, the maritime succulent and Coastal Sage Scrub Zone, and the riparian and Coastal Sage Scrub" (M. McCoy, personal communication, May 10, 2007). Ecotones are not limited to bringing together two sorts of land or water; they may implicate many kinds of landscape and seascape, each possessing quite different elements and edges. An estuary is a nexus of ever-changing interplaces, and it has a genius for bringing together many life-forms, each with its own characteristic set of edges that calls for separate description. Indeed, a unique assemblage of life exists in band-like ecotonal edges, an assemblage whose content and structure serve to define the local ecosystem itself. The result is a total edge effect that "carries the connotation of the complex interplay of life forces where plant communities, and the creatures they support, intermingle in mosaics or change abruptly" (Krall 1994, 4).

The full edge effect cannot be reduced to a mere collection of biotic and physical structures. The effect arises from the dynamic becoming— the complex interplay—of these structures. Tension is here at stake, as is implied in the *tonus* root of "ecotone." It is from their very tension with one another (i.e., differences of material constitution, species or type, habit or history) that the members of an ecotone interact—and draw one another to kinds and levels of actualization not otherwise possible. In an ecotone such as the edge of a forest or the edge of an estuary, differences are preserved, tensions remain, and imbalances occur. Indeed, *difference*, rather than sameness, is the leitmotif. Change, then, arises from a myriad of differences that elude exact measurement or totalization, since the structures that are mobilized contribute to the emergence of an entire place or region that is always exceeding itself—that is on its way to *becoming other* than one might have predicted or expected.[16]

Our discussion of ecotones has thus far considered them as belonging exclusively to natural environments, the domain where this concept was first proposed. But the same concept, suitably expanded, can be seen as illuminating other circumstances in which the environmentally given and the humanly constructed are both at stake. In keeping with this expanded usage, we shall now discuss a more complete panoply of ecotonal complexes (each with a dyadic structure to reflect the fact that at least two differential factors combine to form a given ecotone): nature/nature, culture/nature, and culture/culture.[17]

(1) *Nature/Nature.* Included here are classical ecotones such as are found in the commingling of saltwater and freshwater, as well as different kinds of local vegetation, in a given marshland. These interactions represent the literal meeting of material masses—say, tidal waters that flow into the marshland, coming right up to the stalks of *Spartina* grass at high tide and, by circulating around them, forming an aqueous matrix for them. In the ensuing ecotonal complex, the water provides essential nutrients to the grass, while the grass helps to purify the water. Here altogether natural differences combine to create edge effects in shared intermediary areas—areas that constitute "dwelling places that connect rather than separate" (Krall 1994, 4). We could say just as well that they constitute integral parts of the flesh of the natural life-world.

(2) *Culture/Nature.* In earlier parts of this chapter, we considered the impact of the metropolitan area of the city of Tijuana on the estuary across the border from it—mainly through the watershed that flows from the Mexican to the American side, carrying river and stream water from the interior along with chemicals from the maquiladoras; discarded plastic bags; metal containers; and human waste from Tijuana, Tecate, and other nearby villages. This is not to mention the pollution of the atmosphere throughout the region. All this constitutes a continual intrusion of human refuse of every description into the estuary system. Complicating matters still further, the double and triple security wall immediately east and south of the estuary puts the stamp of political and military culture on the local landscape even as it generates its own considerable environmental damage. Instead of the characteristic two-way interaction of the nature/nature ecotone (e.g., tidal waters with *Spartina* grass), in these instances we observe a one-sided intervention of the humanly produced into the natural world, with comparatively little reciprocity from the side of nature, except in purely reactive or self-protective actions.

(3) *Culture/Culture.* Mike McCoy remarks, "I also look at the border as a *social ecotone* where two cultures come together" (personal communication, May 10, 2007). McCoy here extends the original sense of *ecotone*, pertaining to the natural world, fully to the human sphere—to planned construction, language, custom, and history. When two or more cultural traditions meet at an edge (or several edges), they profoundly influence one another, sometimes manifestly and sometimes too subtly to trace easily. Rarely is there any exact equality of effect comparable to that of osmotic equilibrium, and any such equilibrium is conspicuously absent from the border situation at La Frontera. At the level of culture, difference predominates. In San Diego, Mexican food and souvenirs, Spanish-named streets, the sounds of Mexican pop and mariachis, and the image of the Virgin of Guadalupe are easy to find, whereas high-volume rock music, English signs, and Americanized food and drinks are in evidence on Tijuana's Avenida Revolución, a street filled with pleasure-seeking Americans. Beyond this level of two cultures clashing with each other, the disparity of economic and political power between the two countries in this region is striking, with the proliferation of American-owned industrial plants and the infrastructure of highways bringing products manufactured in maquiladoras to the United States being just two symptoms of this disequilibrium.

The border wall, in the very center of this intercultural ecotone, brings this same imbalance of cultures to a boil: it is in effect turned one way—tipped toward the south—by favoring crossing from the north. The one-sidedness of this wall is nowhere more obvious than in the fact that individual panels are numbered on the American side (to aid the Border Patrol in tracking migrants who attempt to scale the wall at particular places), while on the Mexican side some of the same panels sport lively words and images. It is difficult to imagine a contrast starker than the one provided by juxtaposing figures 10 and 11: on one side, neutral and indifferent numbers meant purely for the Border Patrol's pursuit of migrants; on the other side, colorful images that offer social critique or a vision of a better future (see chapter 8). One continuous and self-identical wall presents two very different sides that are not just in tension (as is often the case with a wholly natural ecotone); rather, the two sides manifest outright conflict. The wall splits an entire cultural complex right down its middle.

The border wall at La Frontera represents a striking reversal of a natural ecotone. We see not a band in which disparities and tensions play out in an extended interplace but rather a single concrete edge where two cultures run up against each other with a notable absence of common space in which to deal with differences. In its rigidity, this edge amounts to a zero degree of the breadth and range that is evident in ecotones belonging to

Figure 10. U.S. side of U.S. border wall at Tijuana/San Diego, 2010. Photo by Edward S. Casey.

Figure 11. Mexican side of U.S. border wall at Tijuana/San Diego, 2010. Photo by Lily Rosenthal.

natural settings. In its minimization of ecotonal equipoise, it excludes more effectively than it includes, rejects more concertedly rather than it shelters. Krall puts the situation thus: "The ecotone, which in the natural world provides a dynamic interchange, becomes exceedingly complex as a cultural metaphor and may represent a barrier that blocks some people from their rightful place in the scheme of things" (1994, 5). The wall along the U.S.-Mexico border is just such a barrier.[18]

One further aspect of ecotones calls for emphasis: "The richness and diversity in an ecotone is greater than that of the communities outside the edge" (M. McCoy, personal communication, May 10, 2007). Here is a forceful way of formulating the "edge effect." This effect is comparable to a multiplying or potentiating force one edge exerts over another (and, again, this is not confined to two edges but may involve a plurality of contiguous edges, such as those that make up the Tijuana Estuary reserve). When these edges interpenetrate, they exhibit a generative power that displays itself in a multiplication of life-forms or, alternately, of cultural formations—unless these formations are blocked by a counterforce, such as a separative wall that is expressly designed to curtail the free movements and open space that such cultural and natural multiplications require.

Ecotone as Interval, Gap, and Band

Ecotones are composed of divergences that constitute *intervals* between edges. They are constituted by active differences that collide and coexist in the gaps, however infinitesimal, between edges. "Intervals" (*diastēmata*) were a central concern of ancient cosmologists and philosophers, who accorded considerable generative powers to them; the intervals between elementary particles, for example, were regarded as more dynamically formative than the particles themselves (Casey 1997). Luce Irigaray has carried this thought further forward in our era by proposing that the gap between two sexuated human beings, that of "sexual difference," is profoundly constitutive of the interhuman ethical field. Thus conceived, an interval is not merely "some sort of extension between extremities" but a dynamic space that is capable of engendering places: "The interval would produce place," says Irigaray (1993, 48), who is here referring to the intimate space shared by human beings who are sexually attracted to each other.[19]

The issue of interval matters not just in ancient physics or in contemporary accounts of relations among sexuated human beings; it is crucial to the relations between distinct places—each with its own set of edges. For the full differentiating effect between these places to occur, their edges have to interact at a certain critical distance; if they were too close, their interactive powers would be inhibited, but if they were too remote from each other, they could not connect at all. In this place-specific version of what early modern physics called "action at a distance," we can say, with Irigaray, that "[t]he interval cannot be done away with. . . . Place is never closed. The boundaries touch against one another while still remaining open" (Irigaray 1993, 51). Irigaray adds nuance to this by pointing out that even when the edges of bodies touch (her paradigm is that of two lips touching each other), they still exist at an interval from each other: less a determinate physical space than an experiential opening, a crease within contiguity itself.

What I earlier characterized as the "band" embodied in the ecotone or transitional space between two different regions can equally well be regarded as an interval or gap between these same regions and more particularly between their edges—paradigmatically, between two or more *boundaries* insofar as edges are more dynamically interactive to the extent that they are porous. The porosity, not the physical distance, ensures that contiguity is not stifling (as it would be in the case of impermeable edges), that it allows room for motion or transport. Considered thus, an interval is an "intermediary *between the boundaries*" (Irigaray 1993, 48). It exhibits what Heidegger calls "the openness of the Open" (1971, 69), that is to say, the active spacing that is at play in quite diverse situations, in poetry and in politics, say, and in the interval between Tijuana the city and the estuary that lies just across the border wall from it. With the notable exception of the wall, both city and estuary are delimited by edges that act as permeable boundaries—for example, the edges of different species of marsh grass growing alongside different currents of water in the estuary or the edges of a given barrio or neighborhood in the city. Even though the edges in each case may be strictly continuous, the intervals between clusters of marsh grass or different parts of a neighborhood are genuine *places* in which humans and animals (and sometimes both together) are given space for cohabitation. Such places are at once bands, intervals, and boundary situations.

In contrast, the border wall offers no such dynamic intervals. It offers no room in which to move and thus cannot be considered as a band; it cannot be inhabited; it has no being of the between. It is not open, except at designated checkpoints (and only partially so there, in a highly regulated way). Its very essence is to be closed—and equally, to close down on surrounding open places, where living beings circulate freely. The wall stands still in the midst of motion, whether it be the motion of the sun or tides, of animals, or of humans. A solemn sentinel of "homeland security," it arrests all such motion, freezes it, and puts it into a site.

It also effects exclusion. Its aim is to *keep out*. If its main express purpose is to deny undocumented or undesirable human beings from entry into the United States, it also denies access to animals—and even more effectively so. As Scott Nicol puts it:

> Though humans have no trouble climbing walls, most animals are stopped in their tracks. Walls fragment their habitats, separating them from food, water, and mates needed to maintain a healthy population. Border walls built in New Mexico's Playas Valley block the movement of one of the last wild herds of bison, whose range straddles the U.S.-Mexico border. In Texas, the walls that slice through the Lower Rio Grande Valley National Wildlife Refuge have fragmented habitat that is critical for the survival of endangered ocelots, a beautiful, secretive cat. (Nichols 2011)

The exclusionary effects of the wall stand in dramatic contrast with the Tijuana Estuary, which embraces extensive biodiversity: birds, reptiles, humans, plants, water, air, fish, plankton. The wall also contrasts with the city of Tijuana, which takes in a very diverse array of humans of many ethnicities and races, several languages, many cats and dogs and insects, several styles of architecture—and many modes of music, including mariachi. If the wall is fiercely *repellent*, the city and the estuary are deeply *absorbent*: they incorporate all manner of things into the openness of the intervals and the breadth of the bands they offer. Each takes in, and holds, a remarkable range of denizens, allowing them to coexist—offering to each a "home-place," however differently configured this place may be.

Tijuana and its nearby estuary constitute what Irigaray describes as a veritable "double place" or "double envelope" (as cited in Casey 1997, 48). Each is a place of its own, with its own distinctive characteristics, but each is also a place by virtue of its many relations with the other place, by way of river and ocean, land and air, waste and trash, the animals that fly and those that burrow under the wall, the humans who cross the border easily (authorized workers, casual shoppers, members of the Border Patrol) and also those who pass over only with the utmost ingenuity and risk (migrants, as well as drug traffickers)—not to mention the transnational circulation of capital that holds both places in thrall.

While the human body may be "a place of passage" between spirit and matter (Bergson 1988, 151), the Tijuana region is a place of passage of another order: an interplace across and over (and sometimes under) which many bodies, human and animal, pass by day and by night, summer and winter, one year and the next. Here, in one delimited but expansive interval, one densely interwoven band, there is little stasis and much movement, all within the collective flesh of one co-inherent place-world.

However different they are in historical development and in geographical extent, city and estuary make up a dense skein of internal relations. These relations are composed of differences that coexist within the same region, however uneasily. Thanks to the ecotone they coconstitute, and to the world's body to which they both contribute, Tijuana and the estuary to its north present us with a dense zone of transition that is at the same time a place of immense actual and potential transformation.

Border walls such as those at Tijuana convert the open intervals of ecotonal complexes into lethal sites capable of killing those humans or animals audacious or desperate enough to try to cross them at the wrong moment.[20] Even apart from such attempted crossings, these walls do damage to almost every creature dwelling or moving close to them, whether by wounding or starving them or by causing them to live in confusion and fear. All manner of living things, including plants and trees, are caught up in the wall's life-endangering effects. Utterly artificial themselves, impervious walls undermine the lives of those who are unfortunate enough to inhabit or just pass through the land adjacent to them.

It does not matter whether nearby ecotonal complexes are urban or rural—whether they are located in Tijuana the city or in the estuary bearing the same name—given that both are under the influence of the wall's pervasive presence at all times and without exception. Very few living beings can flourish in such circumstances, not even the drug traffickers who make immense profits but are subject at all times to deadly infighting, or even the well-paid Border Patrol officers, who testify to tedium in their work. Those who cannot testify, the fauna and flora of the bioregion, are perhaps the most sorely afflicted. With rare exceptions, they suffer in silence even as heedless human beings drag deafening earth-moving machines over the earth when constructing new stretches of the wall and then drive special patrol cars over the leveled-down earth. Until this pandemonium ends, life will be vexed for man and beast alike.

The double and triple border walls at Tijuana are the primary source of the continual jeopardy to which those who live in their proximity are exposed. Any such walls, above all those that are patrolled closely, take life to the limit: not just the legal limit of international agreements and proper documentation but the acutely felt limit of barely viable living conditions.

We are far from being able to say that "on the edge or crossing over, we are held tenderly and tenuously in transition" (Krall 1994, 3). It may well be the case that human beings are, as Kristeva describes, "crossroads beings" (1987, 254). However, the figure of Hermes, god of the crossroads, reminds us that there is crossing well and crossing ill: crossing safely into welcoming hands versus crossing dangerously into harm's way. All too often, a border wall that keeps living creatures of every kind apart from each other makes the critical difference. It undermines continuity of experience; it tears asunder the shared flesh of all who live in its vicinity, pulling them apart limb by limb.

It follows that ecotones can be drawn in two disparate directions: they may furnish "sanctuary, solitude, and peace, growth and transformation," but they can also be the occasion of "isolation and inner or outer conflict" (Krall 1994, 6). When the dynamic intervals of ecotonal spaces are divided by walls of the sort that exist at La Frontera, the future of these spaces is at high risk.

The Tijuana region today presents a strange pairing, not a hinge joining twin cities, as in the case of Ambos Nogales, but a perplexing commixture of city and estuary separated by diremptive walls that, far from offering security or sanctuary, heighten conflict and rend the living flesh of the local world. From the forced construction of these walls, we can draw important lessons about how life on earth can be closed out and choked off—or else pursued in more life-affirming and sustainable ways.

CHAPTER 4

Wall and River in the Lower Rio Grande Valley

The river is a strong brown god—sullen, untamed and intractable.

T. S. Eliot, "The Dry Salvages" (1971)

This place has been shaped by the river, and . . . the shape of this place tells the river where to go.

Susan Griffin, *Woman and Nature: The Roaring inside Her* (1978)

GETTING WALLED IN

"We are occupied," remarks Eloisa Taméz as we sit in the living room of her modest home in El Calaboz, Texas.[1] Several people had previously urged us to seek out Eloisa as a person at the heart of the storm that has arisen in the southeastern corner of Texas along the Rio Grande River. This is a region apart, having once declared itself an independent republic, from 1836 to 1846, ending with the Mexican-American War of 1846 to 1848; still earlier, the Lower Rio Grande Valley had been a province of Spain.

The two nation-states are situated on either side of the Rio Grande, which acts as their common border for more than 1,200 miles (representing two-thirds of the entire U.S.-Mexico border). Whether flowing in rainy seasons or drying up at other times, the river provides the channel through which the borderline between the United States and Mexico is drawn in the geopolitical imagination. Later, we shall confront the question of *just where* this borderline is located in the river. For now, it is a matter of underlining the axial position of the river in the cultural and historical life of the people of this region; it silently supports this life, serving as the constant horizon of everyday activities there. Even when distant from the river, people inhabiting the region have a sure sense of where the river is to be found. It orients them, furnishing an ongoing framework for thought and action. For this reason, El Río Grande del Norte (its full official name) provides the leitmotif for the region that bears its name.

Far from being merely separative in its effects, the river sustains the highly hybrid "mestizaje" culture of the Lower Rio Grande Valley, including its own quite distinctive music. For centuries, American and Mexican families mingled with one another here in ways too numerous and too subtle to tabulate. They lived on both sides of the river, which was easily traversable during most of the year, whether by small ferryboats when the water level was at its height or on foot during the dry season.

Into this tranquil but complex world came the border wall. By the terms of the Secure Fence Act, passed by Congress in 2006, a wall was to be built in the corridor, starting from Brownsville at the eastern end of the Lower Rio Grande Valley and ending with Laredo as the westernmost point. As of May 2009 (when we were first in the region), the wall was still under construction but by then had been completed in many stretches of this corridor, which is more than two hundred miles long. The constructed wall includes a segment straight across Eloisa's backyard, effectively cutting off half her land. Her home in this place has special significance to Eloisa. The property has been in her family since 1767 and is thus intimately connected to the family's historical memory; it is also where she chose to return to after her husband died. Indeed, it was the land itself that offered her a place to seek solace. It was here, in the land of her early youth, that she had hoped to begin her life anew—a life that would take shelter in a new house that was to be built in close proximity to her childhood home.

She recounts that her dreams were rudely interrupted when she received a call in August 2007 from Border Patrol Captain Cavazos, who announced: "We need to discuss something with you. . . . Your property is in the path of the proposed wall. You will need to sign a waiver for a survey of your property—to determine if your land is appropriate for the construction of the wall. If you don't agree, your land will be subject to seizure by eminent domain" (E. Taméz, personal communication, May 30, 2009).

Eloisa, taken aback but managing to collect herself, suggested that the captain come to her office at the university the following Monday so that they could discuss the matter. He did not show up, nor did an engineer from the U.S. Army Corps of Engineers who later called her concerning the same waiver. By November (three months after his initial phone call), Captain Cavazos himself finally appeared in her office, holding a letter for her. She discovered that signing it granted permission to the corps to study her land for one full year. As if this were not already intrusive enough, it also authorized the surveyors to enter and exit Eloisa's property at their leisure. When she refused to sign, another letter was sent to her, proposing that the corps be allowed six months instead of a year to survey her land—with the right to occupy her property during any or all of that time. She also rejected this new letter, and as a direct consequence, the Department of Homeland Security filed a lawsuit against her in January 2008—a lawsuit that requested that her property be condemned and put at the disposal of the U.S. Army Corps of Engineers. Eloisa, however, decided to fight back, and with several friends from the area she filed suit in early February against the head of the Department of Homeland Security (DHS), Michael Chertoff. Her suit, joined by others, pointed out that the omnibus bill on which Homeland Security was basing its claims explicitly stated that the state must consult with the property owners whose land would be directly affected by the construction of the wall—a consultation that had never taken place.

The very day this suit was filed (February 7, 2008), Michael Chertoff gave a speech at Harvard University claiming that those seeking to block the wall's construction were radicals and property owners who did not want to "lose their [personal] view of the Rio Grande" (Chertoff 2008). He also claimed that the locals were peeved because the wall would prevent them from watering their cows at the Rio Grande. Clearly, Eloisa and her fellow litigants did not fit any of these descriptions: they owned no cows, had no view of the river, and were by no means political radicals.

For the property owners who were directly affected by the construction of the wall in this part of Texas, "consultation" was an empty word. A town hall meeting that had taken place in Brownsville on December 12, 2007, for the presumed purpose of openly discussing the situation, was in fact organized by the construction companies that were active in the wall's construction. This meeting amounted to nothing more than a show of posters claiming to prove that the wall had to be built to handle issues of immigration and drugs. "It was a farce," exclaimed Eloisa. Border Patrol agents, dressed in plain clothes, attended the discussion and checked out individual citizens' reactions. The only one of its kind, the meeting was strategically scheduled during the very evening of the main celebration for the Virgin of Guadalupe—with the predictable result that very few people were in attendance.[2]

At Eloisa's insistence, U.S. District Judge Andrew Hanen agreed to let the DHS do a preliminary survey of Eloisa's property. Eloisa's main concern was the effect of the sheer weight of the wall on the fragile soil of her property. This survey was never done, despite her urgent request, and all responsibility for possible damage to her property was waived without any serious inspection. By this time, Eloisa realized that the wall would probably be built in her backyard, and she petitioned the same judge to ask that the wall be built on an earlier fence line (as had happened at the University of Texas and Texas Southmost College in Brownsville). Ignoring this request,

Judge Hanen, on April 16, 2009, instead approved the condemnation of (in Eloisa's words) "a significant swath" of her land—without compensation, financial or otherwise.

As a concession, Ms. Taméz asked that a pedestrian's gate be included in the wall on her property so that she could gain access to the other half of her three acres of land (over which she retained ownership). When a corps official showed up soon after she had made this quite reasonable request, she asked him about such a gate, whereupon he texted a message to his supervisor. Within minutes, however, he said that it would not be possible. Eloisa strongly suspected that he was only pretending to send the message containing her question. She pointed out to me that other landowners had been granted this very same concession, but these were wealthy persons who owned much larger tracts of land and who had political clout in the county. She had to conclude that these people, thanks to their financial and political influence, had persuaded the Army Corps of Engineers either to relocate the wall on other people's property rather than on their own or, if this was not allowed, to build gates in the wall so that they could have access to the walled-off part of their lands.

The construction of the wall in Cameron County had been underway since the summer of 2008. By April 2009, it had been built on both sides of Eloisa's slim strip of land, whose open space constituted an awkward caesura in the wall's continuous flow. When Judge Hanen ordered her property condemned in mid-April, she filed for a restraining order on the grounds that the DHS had neither consulted with her adequately nor offered any compensation for the damage that the wall would cause to her property. But by the time Judge Hanen was in a position to consider her request, it was already too late. Construction quickly began in Eloisa's backyard, within the very week following her land's condemnation on April 16. Heavy equipment was brought in, and within twenty-four hours the wall across her backyard was completed, permanently closing her off from half of her own land.

The wall itself cannot be missed as one speaks with Eloisa in her house. It is dark and massive, casting very long shadows into her backyard. It looms just behind her house, at a distance of less than fifty yards. Its size dominates any view from her house in the direction of the river; indeed, it stands out even when seen from Highway 281, which runs in front of her property. Less than half a mile away, the wall is even closer to the backside of other houses that are still more modest than Eloisa's: the smaller the property, the more intrusive the wall's presence. The fact that private property remains in the possession of the owner does not mitigate the effects of the severe bisection. The wall is hulking: it is built of tall iron spikes (approximately sixteen feet high) that rise directly out of a sizable concrete base placed deep in the ground. The sharp points on top of the spikes, reminiscent of medieval weapons of war, ensure that climbing over it is no picnic. Only cats and miniature dogs could make it through the spikes, which are placed less than six inches apart, effecting closure for many animals, as well as all adult humans.

Nevertheless, one could scale such a structure with a rope ladder and jump to the ground on the other side with comparative ease: "It really isn't that difficult," remarks the border activist and local resident Scott Nicol, "though it does get rust on your hands" (personal communication, June 7, 2011). But Eloisa assures me that *no one had ever tried to enter her property before the wall was constructed.* Her area of the county was never a channel for immigration or drug traffic, much less terrorism; she views the wall as being entirely futile, nothing but a barbaric scar on her land and that of her neighbors. However assiduously the Department of Homeland Security may have advocated for this wall, she is certain that it makes no significant contribution to the security of the United States either in her region or in any other part of Texas. She says that it is evident to all those who have eyes to see that the wall has been built in vain. For those who actually reside in the Lower Rio Grande Valley, it is both a burden and an eyesore, an incubus on the back of the land and those living there.

VICISSITUDES OF THE WALL AT LA FRONTERA

The newly erected wall acts to reverse a century and a half of cultural continuity and ease of movement between Mexico and the United States. Cross-border sociality, largely based on the family, was especially prominent in the Lower Rio Grande Valley—the area between Brownsville and Laredo, in which the Rio Grande (called Río Bravo del Norte on the Mexican side) figures as the central connective ribbon. Thanks to the many bridges over the river, families and friends got together frequently; businesses between the two countries operated with a minimum of regulation and oversight. In this earlier era, La Frontera was an open boundary: porous in both directions, welcoming to residents of the region without undue attention to questions of citizenship when crossing the borderline. Although proper documentation began to become a concerted issue as early as the 1950s, the building of the wall from the middle 1990s onward brought home the gravitas of being asked to prove one's national identity. The stolid presence of the wall epitomized the inhospitable spirit of separation and exclusion that arose with the institution of NAFTA, in concert with more rigorous criteria for the entry of noncitizens from south of the border; it was not coincidental that the first portions of the wall (euphemistically called "the fence") were built at that time. After 9/11, the construction of a more complete and more formidable wall became an obsession in the wake of heightened public and political concern with the presumed threat of terrorism, spurred on by fears of massive immigration. The most concrete expression of these various economical and political concerns is a wall that enacts the very meaning of "border" as an arbitrary and exclusionary edge, an impervious limit.

It is notable that in Brownsville, at the very university where Eloisa Taméz teaches, there was a remarkable compromise realized in the wall's design and placement. Instead of the gaunt structure that bestrides Eloisa's backyard, the wall at the university's southern edge is of modest height and is built of a pleasing beige brick. When we first saw it, we didn't realize that it was the border wall at all; indeed, we thought it was a purely decorative structure that graced the edge of the campus. Far from being forbidding, it invited appreciation of its aesthetic properties. Who would take this for the official *border wall*? Only if one follows it for a mile or two in either direction does one discover the resumption of the familiar presence of the border wall in its usual daunting height and rigorous structure.[3]

In the city of Brownsville itself, less than one mile west of campus, one comes on a strikingly different scene. At Hope Park in downtown Brownsville—so named at a moment of optimism in 1976, on the occasion of the two-hundredth anniversary of the American Revolution—there is the bleak prospect of a somber wall composed of iron spikes whose sharp edges are aggressively arrayed at the top. Peering through the spikes is like looking through prison bars. One sees Mexico just across the river, grimly perched on low cliffs. Two bridges across the Rio Grande connect Brownsville with Matamoros on the other side. When we gazed through the tall spines of the wall one Monday morning, vehicle and foot traffic on both bridges was at a trickle, which seemed to mirror the limited flow of the Rio Grande below. The contrast of a formidable vertical wall and a flat river at low ebb could not have been more graphic—or more telling.

The same situation was characterized by its own absurdity. In the midst of the very same wall that imposes itself between the river and Hope Park, there is a sizable opening, gateless and unguarded. This opening was clearly meant to give access to Border Patrol vehicles that cruise alongside the river on a special road, a river byway that also serves as a military highway. Any migrant or drug smuggler can easily step through this glaring gap if members of the Border Patrol on duty are distracted from their surveillance, as then appeared to be the case; we looked around and saw no officers. Again, walls may well be built to be breached, and here the breach was offered up for all to see, undermining its vaunted invulnerability. It was as if the wall had sprung a leak sufficient to convert a border into a boundary.

Militarizing the Border

Unsolicited, Nick Braune opened our talk with him by remarking bluntly that "we have become militarized" (personal communication, May 30, 2009).[4] By the time we spoke to him in May 2009, the "occupation" that Eloisa Taméz had described in such painful detail had indeed taken a specifically military turn. This is hardly surprising. Thanks to their forbidding presence, border walls collude with practices of control and surveillance of many kinds, to which military personnel, equipment, and weapons, as well as intensive strategies of surveillance, all contribute substantially. If borders are created to enforce order, the ordering forces are very likely to be military or paramilitary in character.

The ways in which such militarization is now happening at La Frontera are legion. Among the more obvious is the ever-present Border Patrol, which one encounters not only at official checkpoints but also all along the border. Given the stationing of Border Patrol agents at virtually every turn of the river and many points in between, one is not surprised to learn that the number of these agents has been increased fivefold in the past decade—doubled between 2004 and 2011 alone—at the urging of the Department of Homeland Security; the current total number stands at more than twenty thousand (Isacson and Meyer 2012). Contemporary discussions of comprehensive immigration reform within the U.S. Congress are calling for still further augmentation of these forces.

But this rapid growth in the number of surveilling forces is only one symptom of a more massive militarization. Guards perform a variety of functions. They inspect cars and trucks passing through the checkpoints. At the same time, Border Patrol police are found throughout this part of Texas. Their other duties include running "inner checkpoints" that are found on all major highways as far as ninety miles from the border itself; these are designed to apprehend migrants and drug smugglers who have slipped through the safety net of the border itself. This is not to mention constables and sheriffs, also much in evidence in the region. Less obvious, but still quite a potent presence, are the federal ICE (Immigration Customs Enforcement) agents who are found throughout the entire border region. Members of this enforcement group are especially active in bus and train stations; they are authorized to arrest those traveling without proper papers, arrests that rarely involve warrants. ICE agents often collude with local police in raids on households and businesses undertaken to capture "illegal aliens." Beyond this, they are empowered to go into local jails to check on the immigration status of those held there on even the most minor infraction.

The Border Patrol and ICE agents, acting in concert with local police and sheriffs, are joined by self-appointed Minutemen, border vigilantes who effectively deputize themselves to identify and report any migrants they spot. When we were inspecting the easternmost end of the wall outside Brownsville—a surreal spectacle, for a lack of federal funds has caused the wall to suddenly stop there—we were asked by a man in a private car what we were doing there. This man was wearing a fluorescent security vest similar to those commonly used by private guards at shopping malls, but beyond this he offered no further identification. We inferred that he was patrolling the wall on his own initiative.

In short, the Department of Homeland Security, acting in concert with local and state police forces, as well as with federal agents and self-appointed vigilantes, has brought about what is in effect a military state in this part of the world. One result of this militarization is that those who are employed for purposes of detection and apprehension now constitute the largest part of the working population in the entire Lower Rio Grande Valley region. Nick Braune cites this striking fact as the main reason for low enrollments in his humanities courses at Texas Southmost College in McAllen. He is disappointed that the current commencement brochure shows 12 students graduating in history and 4 in philosophy, while there are 177 in criminal justice. The reason seems all too evident: when employment opportunities are running so high in the area of immigration control, one can understand why young people might be tempted to enlist in programs that train police and border officers.[5]

The demand for law enforcement is not surprising in a situation where corruption is so rife. Not only do many people benefit from the corruption, they have come to depend on it. Jay Johnson-Castro Sr. tells how U.S. inspectors of trucks that pass over the Laredo bridges may be handed a roll of bills worth as much as $50,000 to wave through the truck driver and his cargo. If an inspector refuses to do this, his life may well be in jeopardy in the days afterward. Johnson-Castro estimates that only 1 percent of the numerous trucks that pass through these checkpoints on a daily basis are actually searched, though many of them are almost certainly carrying concealed drugs to the American market. Given this circumstance of unchecked corruption, there is indeed a need for more trained officers to combat the problem—if these officers can themselves withstand the temptation to participate in the cycle of corruption.

Greed, always a central motive in capitalist cultures, is reinforced at every turn and touches on many parts of the population. Not only inspectors and customs agents but also members of the Border Patrol and local police officers are tempted to participate in a culture in which "money speaks"—all the more so in the difficult financial times that set in during the fall of 2008 and continue to this day. One might argue that this very circumstance implies the need for increased law enforcement at the border, but this line of thought does not withstand scrutiny, for the extra personnel will in turn become prime targets for bribery. One must not forget that there is an entire world that exists in the dark shadow cast by the wall, a world in which one is given the choice of receiving either "a silver or a lead bullet," as the local saying goes: either accept bribe money or face death from a bullet.

The bribery arising from drug traffic and the evasions of the law that loom in circumstances of undocumented immigration are bad enough; equally odious, however, are the numerous "detention centers" located at or near the border. These centers (discussed in chapter 6), although sanctioned by federal and state governments, are often managed by private corporations on a for-profit basis—and the profits are extensive. Besides the considerable money made by the companies that run such centers, a significant financial reward is reaped by the county in which a center is located. When asked why these centers exist, the immigration lawyer Jodi Goodwin replied with one word: "money." Avarice joins forces with fear and racism, both of which are actively exploited by the owners of these facilities while being tacitly affirmed by all who support the construction of the wall.

This array of dubious motives was nowhere in better evidence than in the T. Don Hutto Residential Center at Taylor, Texas, not far from Austin. This detention center was named for T. Don Hutto, a founder of Corrections Corporation of America, one of the largest for-profit prison businesses in the United States. In the case of Hutto, a "processing center" was created as a designated place for the temporary detention of mothers and children. These vulnerable individuals were kept in eight-by-twelve-foot unheated concrete cells, often locked up there for twenty-three hours a day—even the children. The food was frequently contaminated, and the health care conditions were abysmal. Despite—or perhaps because of—these primitive penal conditions, the center generated profits that some have estimated to be nearly three million dollars a month (N. Braune, personal communication, May 30, 2009). Most detainees were not informed of their right to legal counsel.[6] Jay Johnson-Castro Sr. led a major march to Hutto from Austin on June 20, 2009; he was joined by Nick Braune and his family, along with many others. Their purpose was to make this outrageous situation known to the people of the region and to the American public at large.

Thanks to this protest and several others, the center at Hutto was no longer allowed to house families after September 2009; its population was restricted to five hundred adult women, many of whom were seeking political asylum. The cruel conditions at Hutto—where sexual assaults on women detainees were common practice—persist in other detention centers in the area.

From all this—from the political confusion and the cowardice to the corruption and the economic exploitation—Jay Johnson-Castro Sr. was forced to conclude that many, indeed most, of those living at or near the border in the Lower Rio Grande Valley "live under tyranny." If we accept Mussolini's dictum that "fascism is corporatism," they inhabit a fascist state. In effect, ordinary residents of the area have been "deconstitutional-ized," in Jay's term. They have "lost their constitutional rights," as Eloisa Taméz prefers to put it, the basic rights of being a citizen: life, liberty, and the pursuit of happiness. And for those many who are not citizens, such rights are nowhere in sight.

Even if someday the wall will come down, this much-desired event will not solve all the problems that have arisen, and will continue to arise, at the U.S.-Mexico border. Other deep-lying difficulties will have to be addressed as well, most notably those stemming from the drug traffic and rampant corruption, not to mention an entrenched racism and nationalism, and the profiteering of private American corporations that have invested heavily in the wall and associated institutions.[7]

Bridging the River

Life along the Río Grande del Norte was very different in earlier times. As we know, the original border was established in 1848, but the acute suffering of recent times was unknown during the first century of the border's existence. As if to foreshadow contemporary difficulties, trouble erupted in 1954, with the abrupt deportation of up to one million Mexican workers in "Operation Wetback." Many of these workers had entered the United States as "guest workers" who, under the bracero program, did not require visas for the duration of their stay in the United States. Once these workers were no longer needed for their manual labor, they were summarily expelled.[8]

Nevertheless, until very recently many places in the Rio Grande Valley were relatively unaffected by such tribulations or even by the intense occupation and militarization that have occurred since 2001. These oases of comparative calm included the small town of Candelaria, located far to the west of the Laredo/McAllen/Brownsville region. Referring to Candelaria,

Nick Braune exclaimed that "the border didn't exist there," as if he himself could hardly believe that this had once been the case, given the vexed character of La Frontera in the rest of southeastern Texas. For many decades, a simple footbridge spanned the river at Candelaria. Schoolchildren, shoppers, and families would use this bridge to visit the small town of San Antonio del Río Bravo on the Mexican side. The bridge allowed people to pass over the river freely in both directions and at all times of the day and night. There were no border guards or checkpoints, much less surveillance cameras or klieg lights overhead. As a boundary phenomenon, the bridge played a decisive role in shaping this Texas town's unique history. This history has its own subtle nuances, and was certainly not without pain and conflict, yet it was remarkably free from the direct imprint of the forces that were set into play in the mid-1990s and then intensified after 2001.

In Braune's moving narrative, the tranquil world of Candelaria was shattered forever one day in 2008 when bulldozers destroyed the footbridge that had united peoples from the two sides of the river over which it arched. Ordered by the Border Patrol acting as agents of the DHS, this destruction happened without consulting those most affected. The justification for this drastic action was stated by a Border Patrol officer who claimed, without citing any evidence, that the bridge had become "a route for terrorists, drug traffickers, and illegals" (conversation, May 2009). Unannounced and unbidden, the bulldozers emerged with something like the sudden force of the hurricanes that can descend on the southern Rio Grande area. All at once, in the course of a single day, a world was lost: a literal *interworld*, to use Merleau-Ponty's term, a world shared at the level of lived flesh, of concrete transactions, and personal relationships. Robust as the experience of this shared world had been in its heyday, its fragility was evident in the speed with which it was removed.

Despite the similarity to Eloisa Taméz's circumstance—the same lack of consultation, with the decisive event happening in the space of a single day—no wall was involved in the case of Candelaria. It doesn't require a wall to establish and maintain a contested border. Good neighbors can be lost by something other than a wall, even if a wall can certainly augment (and may even first set up) tension between neighboring peoples. In the absence of a wall, a bridgeless river can very well serve as a force that separates whole peoples from each other.

As Braune put it, trenchantly, "The wall is not the issue." Not the whole issue, anyway. We suspect he meant something different by this striking statement: he was referring to the real possibility that virtual surveillance may someday become so efficient—thanks to continual camera oversight from towers, land sensors, drones, and other instruments of advanced technology—that a physical wall may become superfluous. Yet a virtual wall of this description is *still a wall*. Keeping human beings apart in accordance with the wishes of a dominant nation-state does not require a wall of bricks and mortar, sheets of metal, or iron spikes. "Consciousness of the wall," Braune observed, "is all it takes," even if the wall in question is only projected or virtual. A border wall has a force that can be felt in the very absence of its material embodiment. Such a wall exists not only in its physically built or militarily maintained presence but also in people's minds and bodies, as the forced arrest of free movement between two countries or, on another scale, two communities. These countries and communities are forcibly divided in an action they never chose and certainly do not want to continue. The walls that stand at Nogales or at the San Diego–Tijuana border materially instantiate such forced separation, but the destruction of the footbridge at Candelaria effected an equivalent separation upon those living on different sides of the Rio Grande.

In the case of Candelaria, the bifurcation of an existing interworld was visited on local residents from without. It was a consequence of forces beyond their full comprehension and powers beyond their control. These forces and powers emerged from a history they could not claim to be their own but that from then on became an insistent and undeniable presence in their daily lives. This literally otherworldly history was visited on them in such a way that it could no longer be held at arm's length, for the pedestrian bridge on which they had long counted and that had formed the most concrete basis of a living community, shared with relatives and friends just across the river, had been abruptly removed without any prospect of its restoration.

THE BORDER WALL AS A REAL AND SYMBOLIC PRESENCE

Occupation, militarization, or outright destruction and deprivation: these do not paint a pretty picture—certainly not one that fits the image of "America the Beautiful." Yet they are the grim costs of a policy of exclusion and separation that brooks no facile compromises, no easy solutions, no false syntheses. At the same time, the border, so integral a part of this disjunctive circumstance, does not fit easily into the fierce logic of either/or, with its exclusive alternatives. It is not simply present or completely absent; rather, it can assume either form. This fact is made clear in two of the leading examples we have so far considered: the obtrusive wall in Eloisa's backyard and the destroyed footbridge in Candelaria. On the one hand, we witness an unwanted and unwarranted presence: an obtrusive wall in one's backyard; on the other, we see a glaring (and quite literal) gap between two towns formerly united in friendship by a simple footbridge. Whether materially present as a massive wall or felt as the absence of a bygone link between communities, the border intrudes into human lives with real and lasting effects.

The vexed history of the U.S.-Mexico border is reflected in the differential fate of a wall that was built to substantiate its existence. The wall that was supposed to extend continuously west from Brownsville, and to do so in rigorously uniform succession, is in truth an inconsistent and discrepant entity. There are significant variations in its structure and appearance, beginning with its style of construction. The spiked style has variable heights, and all of it rests on a base that is sometimes set deeply into the earth and at others almost fully exposed. An altogether different style of wall appears in the case of the "levy wall" that was built at McAllen in the same region. This dirt mound belongs to an encompassing flood-control system and is mostly underwater when the river rises. Furthermore, the positioning of the wall vis-à-vis the official border differs considerably from place to place. Sometimes the wall clings to the north bank of the river, but it can also be found miles to the north of the same bank, creating a transitional zone between the wall and the borderline, which runs in the river. Between wall and border, this space is a literal no-man's-land of forbidden turf, a space over which one moves only at one's peril given its exposure to the eagle eyes of the Border Patrol.

At still other places, the wall doesn't exist at all, whether because it remains to be built or because it paradoxically includes interruptions. As we were driving west from Eloisa Taméz's house, we were dumbfounded to see at least three gaps in the wall. In each case, a dirt road led directly from Highway 281 in Texas up to the wall and right through a sizable hole. As we drove toward one such gap, we saw no sign of warning; for all intents and purposes, we were being asked to ignore the wall and flout it by driving straight through it. Had we done so, we would have landed immediately on top of a levy just south of the wall. This area had been leveled in order to create a roadway—one no doubt intended exclusively for Border Patrol vehicles.[9] In another case, the road through the wall simply continued on the other side without a break, and one could drive due south into Mexico. We soon realized that such openings, including the one at Brownsville mentioned earlier, were built to allow the Border Patrol to cross to the other side directly, without having to pass through distantly located checkpoints.[10] But even if this is so, couldn't the migrants and drug dealers also pass through these same openings? Given the lack of apparent surveillance—we saw no Border Patrol personnel or surveillance cameras nearby—one would think these openings would become quickly known and favored by those attempting to enter the United States. We were not the only ones to be puzzled by these conspicuous breaks in the wall, which could be spotted from a considerable distance. As we were inspecting the first such break, a car drove up, and several visitors from Japan emerged to examine the phenomenon and to photograph it with intense interest.

When confronted with a situation in which gaps in the border wall are openly tolerated, one cannot help but wonder whether the wall here becomes as much a symbolic as a practical entity. A strict commitment to the wall as a physical structure would surely have led to the construction of one continuous entity, no matter what practical difficulties that might have entailed or what objections local citizens might have raised. We know that builders of other security walls or wall-like barriers have prided themselves on permitting no breaches in their constructions—notably, the Berlin Wall; the DMZ between North and South Korea; and more recently, the West Bank barrier, between Israel and Palestine. In these various circumstances, openings in the basic structure of those walls are unthinkable; they present themselves as remorselessly gapless. Such undertakings are obsessed with a wall's full, literal presence, while in the case of La Frontera, absence is allowed at many locations along the border.

Even in the various instances just mentioned, walls are not just undeniably real—chunks of matter set on the ground—but also powerfully symbolic in status, standing for the strict security required by sovereign nation-states. We are speaking here not just of their status as purely posited cultural entities (as emphasized in chapter 1) but also of the insistent symbolism of being a wall protecting a nation at its border—that is, physically exemplifying the integrity and intactness of a nation that proclaims itself to be impregnable to "foreigners" of many descriptions. In relation to such a symbolic dimension, the exact size, form, and degree of impenetrability of a given wall become secondary concerns. Indeed, gaps in the wall and other inconsistencies become tolerable as long as the wall's symbolic message of "No Admittance" is conveyed effectively to would-be trespassers and to citizens who support anti-immigrant policies. In this way, the wall's symbolic status trumps the either/or logic of simple presence versus sheer absence; put differently, this status can be expressed in either modality. The border's presence is felt as keenly in a missing bridge as in a completed wall, for the force of sovereignty is based on the sanction of the symbolic and not on physical construction alone.

From here it is but a short step to the view held by many natives of the Rio Grande region: "it's a joke—a five-billion-dollar joke."[11] If the wall's legitimation is ultimately symbolic, the wall itself can be taken as an object of humor or satire as easily as it can be viewed as a matter of grave literal fact.

In the case of the U.S.-Mexico wall, even authorities at the highest levels, including the president and U.S. Congress, probably lack clear political intentionality. Certainly the mixed signals continually picked up from both levels suggest this. In this vein, Scott Nicol maintains that the wall between Brownsville and Laredo was "nothing but a bargaining chip," a ploy in the congressional debates over comprehensive immigration reform that occurred during the summer and fall of 2006.[12] No agreement emerged in the extensive debates over reform, and in a desperate move to come up with something concrete, Congress passed the Secure Fence Act two weeks before that year's midterm elections. The wall here became a metonym, a symbolic stand-in, for the full-scale political reform that was so pressingly needed at that historical moment but around which no consensus could be achieved; a material wall, even if partially built, is at least something tangible to which one can literally point. Little thought was given in these debates as to whether such a structure would be *effective* in deterring immigration or drug traffic. Even a brief consideration of such effectiveness reveals the flaw that stares everyone in the face: if they don't go through one of the gaps in the existing wall, those determined to migrate or smuggle drugs will simply go *around* the end of a given stretch of wall or else (where no direct surveillance takes place) will climb *over* the existing structure by means of ladders just high enough for the purpose. A common joke in this part of the world is this: "What is the solution to the problem of a twelve-foot-high wall? A thirteen-foot ladder."[13] No wonder, then, that any discussion of the wall itself is so easily transformed into a form of political football that is kicked ever further downfield, without ever coming close to entering the end zone.[14]

ENVIRONMENTAL CONSEQUENCES

This brings us to the untoward environmental effects of the border wall's construction in the Lower Rio Grande Valley. We see these effects most dramatically in three wilderness tracts near Brownsville: the Sabal Palm Sanctuary, Las Bocajes de la Palma (belonging to the Lower Rio Grande Valley National Wildlife Refuge), and an unnamed tract managed by the Nature Conservancy. The areas are supervised by three distinct bodies, but all three are meant to provide congenial habitats to wildlife. The U.S. Fish and Wildlife Commission's ultimate goal is to amalgamate these areas into one continuous preserve, to be called the Lower Rio Grande Natural

Wildlife Refuge. Although merging them makes environmental as well as economic and ecotouristic sense, large parts of these tracts have now been walled off, discouraging visitation by humans and animals alike. The U.S. Fish and Wildlife Commission's goal has thus become virtually impossible to achieve, since the Department of Homeland Security has treated the three areas quite differently.

Local environmental activists are convinced that the booklet recently compiled by the DHS to discuss environmental impacts of the wall, here and elsewhere, is nothing but a padded text to be waved in front of members of Congress and local citizens, as if to say, "Look at all we are doing." Yet little is being done to avoid the environmental damage that the wall will cause, notably the sequestration of the three wildlife areas in the Lower Rio Grande Valley. Even worse, whenever environmental well-being conflicts with the construction of the wall—as happens in the Tijuana Estuary (see chapter 3)—the wall invariably wins out.

The wall wins, but creative compromise is possible. For example, the Sabal Palm Sanctuary was threatened by the wall's projected construction across its entire northern side, which would have closed the sanctuary to visitors, who must enter from this side. Struggling under the shadow of the anticipated wall and suffering from lack of revenue, Sabal Palm was forced to close in May 2009. It did not reopen until January 2011, when a generous offer of financial support was made by a local philanthropic group, the Gorgas Foundation, without whose help the sanctuary would probably have remained shuttered. By that time, a compromise had been achieved in the construction process that would provide for an opening just large enough to allow visitors' cars and vans to enter and exit the sanctuary. This opening was to be outfitted with a heavy gate that would be closed overnight, with the intention of cutting off migrant and drug traffic. This amounts to a middle path between complete inaccessibility and unsupervised openness—a compromise made in consideration of saving the sabal palm forest, which is one of the very last preserves in the United States for this rare species of tree and contains a bird sanctuary with an extraordinary diversity of species.

Whereas the Sabal Palm Sanctuary was kept open by this last-minute action, other wildlife areas in the Lower Rio Grande Valley remain endangered, and their future is deeply clouded. They provide a cautionary tale showing how the border wall at La Frontera brings with it a very broad destructive wake—a wake not only of human suffering and deprivation but of outright damage to the natural environment, which is the ultimate setting of all human activity. This environment surrounds the wall on every side, encompassing and penetrating the humanly constructed at every turn.

The wall runs through the region like an insidious knife, threatening whatever natural life it encounters.

WHY THE WALL?

Why the wall? We constantly posed this question to people during our most recent visit to southeast Texas. Why was the wall planned in the first place, and why is it now being built, at very great expense to the federal coffers and at an even greater cost to humans and their environment? Those to whom we spoke in the region converged considerably in their replies. Moving beyond the official arguments for the wall's existence (stemming immigration, drug traffic, and terrorism), they pointed to less savory factors that are rarely discussed in the media yet are no less pertinent for their being covertly operative. These factors include unvarnished xenophobia and outright racism; the exploitation of impoverished Mexicans with the aim of maintaining them as a permanent underclass; the claim of general criminal proclivities on the part of these same people; the moneyed interests of corporations and private citizens; and highly protective feelings toward English as a first language (motivations to be discussed in chapters 6 and 7). Given this mass of cherished if inchoate beliefs and thoughts, few of which would survive critical scrutiny on the part of those who hold them, it becomes less surprising that something like a wall might be built. The not-so-hidden message comes down to this: "Let's keep 'em out!" Such exclusivist and separatist thinking, which proceeds in binary terms such as us versus them, legal versus illegal, and white versus brown, makes it tempting to regard a wall or its equivalent as a definitive way of dealing with whatever is perceived as contaminating citizens of the United States. After all, won't a high wall keep out the undesirables?

The irony of this situation should not escape us. The lack of substantial justification in xenophobic and self-serving aims stands against the massive materiality and palpability of a wall. This contrast has its own logic: if the presumed reasons are in fact baseless, or based on little more than prejudice and unenlightened self-interest, they require something physically imposing and visually impressive to bear them up—to embody them concretely, as if by a process of reverse sublimation that goes from belief to matter rather than the opposite. At play here is the fact that the wall is a physical *thing*; it has "determinate presence," which is Heidegger's (1962, 47) term for the perpetual temptation to seek the assured in the face of the flux and uncertainty of human experience. It is a matter of the "freezing of being," as Merleau-Ponty (2012, 55) puts it. As such, it serves to crystallize and sanction nationalistic and racist beliefs rather than to confront and change them.

A wall is as inanimate as it is mute; it doesn't speak back. Given this, it does not take long to agree to the building of a wall without regard to its immediate or eventual consequences for human beings and the environment, and then to claim that this is "the will of the [American] people." When this line of reasoning is buttressed with concerns about rising unemployment in the United States and the perceived danger of drug trafficking and other crimes, the wall presents itself as virtually irresistible to those who are obsessed with protection and security. In its stolid actuality and mute presence, it absorbs and withstands doubts and reservations— or such is the hope of those who support its construction and continued maintenance.

And yet we know by now that "the wall" is a highly ambiguous entity, at once literal and symbolic, actual and virtual, physical and political, material and psychological—a collection of contrary terms that do not invite neat distinctions and separations. Instead of offering determinate presence, the being of the wall is radically indeterminate.

Why then was the wall built when the wall at La Frontera is riddled with such ambiguity and indeterminacy—indeed, with outright contrariness? Why does it exist if it does not constructively solve any urgent problem and instead evades any lasting solutions? Why was it built if it entails such expense and inflicts such suffering? Why the wall? And where do we go from here?

Jay Johnson-Castro Sr., our intense and immensely well-informed host in Laredo, says, "I don't like fences: we will see the day when they will come down" (personal communication, May 26, 2009). He recounts the moment when he first heard that Congress had passed the Secure Fence Act: "I couldn't believe it. I just could not comprehend building a wall to divide our community. It makes no sense. It is unreal. How can the U.S. build another Iron Curtain?" He was so outraged that he decided, on the spot, to protest by walking from Laredo to Brownsville, continuing over the bridge to Matamoros to show solidarity with the Mexican side: "I had to do something." Starting out alone on a hot and grueling walk of 206 miles (the first day left him exhausted, with painful blisters on his feet), he was soon joined by others along the way, and before he knew it, his lonely action had become a media event. This led to a series of protest walks in Texas and elsewhere, as well as an event dubbed the "Border Caravan," in which a group of cars drove from San Diego to Brownsville/Matamoros during a single week in early February 2007. More recently, Jay has sponsored collective kayaking on the Rio Grande, the boats linking up with one another all across the river, signaling, "The river is ours." In

October 2009 he staged a "Día del Río," which involved more than five hundred kayakers. In other events of protest, Jay, along with area churches, encouraged human chains that stretched over the river on certain bridges, the people holding hands to indicate their solidarity across countries and across cultures—bodily demonstrating, as he put it, that "this was a community before it became a border." In undertaking such acts of protest and resistance, he said, "We are taking the sting out of their strategy." He made this last remark with a mixture of satisfaction and sardonic irony.

The irony stems from his acknowledgment that there is a long way still to go before the wall disappears. He is the first to insist that, although "the wall must come down," there are formidable obstacles to this happening in the near future. Beyond the lack of any national-level concerted political resolve to dismantle the wall (bespeaking a collective *akrasia*, to employ Aristotle's term for "weakness of will"), and in addition to the racism and xenophobia manifest in the circumstance (the United States "wants to wall off the brown people," as Jay put it bluntly), there is the fact of the extensive graft and corruption that now besets virtually every aspect of life on both sides of the border. As Jay says, "The border is set up to be corrupt."

The border may well invite corruption at every turn, financial as well as moral (Collingwood speaks of "the corruption of consciousness" [1938, 331]); but the river that bears the border offers hope at another level. How is this so?

THE RIVER RUNS THROUGH IT

Throughout Part 1, the emphasis has been on the wall as an implacable physical fact. But we have also been tracking implacabilities in the natural world: bodies of water, whether in the form of oceans (the Pacific Ocean), marshlands (the Tijuana Estuary), inland streams (the Nogales Wash), or (as now) a river (the Rio Grande del Norte). We shall conclude this chapter with a series of reflections on the role of the river that is such a formative presence in southeastern Texas, where the border wall begins its long journey westward.

The Río Grande del Norte takes on a special significance given its position as the southernmost limit of a landscape densely arrayed with the poignancies we have been tracing. It subtends much of the contemporary conflict and corruption, repression and imprisonment, and fear and suffering that pervade the Lower Rio Grande Valley region. Not only does this lengthy river run along the border between the United States and Mexico, but it *is* the border from the westernmost tip of Texas to the Gulf of Mexico. As a natural phenomenon, the river is a boundary with porous edges, but by its geographic situation and its central role in the history of the region, it figures as a border.

"Rio Grande": the Spanish name evokes a history wherein this body of water belonged first to Spain and then to Mexico long before the United States claimed it; its full Spanish name, El Río Grande *del Norte*, implies that it runs north of the land inhabited by those who christened it. As a creature of climate and topography, it is indifferent to the destiny of nations. After 1848, however, it gained a new identity, a new status. It became a basis of decisive demarcation between two countries, albeit only as defined by one of these countries, the United States. The international border established by the Treaty of Guadalupe Hidalgo runs right down the back of the river in a continuous line that marks the middle of its deepest channel, an invisible line that changes its position as the seasons bring different widths to the river and change the shape of its channels. The borderline imposed by the treaty is perched like an imaginary plumb line in the river, there when the river is coursing with new waters in the spring, and still there when it runs dry in many stretches in late summer. What was once a force of nature alone—a sheer watercourse—has become a force of separation between entire nations. Whatever was once the case, and may yet be the case in the future, the current historical truth is that the Rio Grande serves more to hold peoples apart than to bring them together.

In contesting this fact, Jay Johnson-Castro Sr. must also acknowledge it: "The river unites us rather than divides us" (personal communication, May 26, 2009). Instead of describing the contemporary moment, he is here pointing to a past in which the river was easily and often traversed in both directions (a situation once common throughout the Lower Rio Grande Valley), as well as to a future in which the separation now effected by the border wall will have been overcome.

A river is far from a human phenomenon. In its impersonal flow, it does not attend to human affairs; it just keeps rolling along, at its own speed and at its own bidding. As long as it is a river with its own flow and its own bottom and sides, it is its own master, determining its own destiny. Even where its overall contour has been altered by the U.S. Army Corps of Engineers, as at El Paso, where the original course of the Rio Grande was considerably altered in favor of a virtually straight course, set in concrete, it retains its essence as this singular river. However much it is reconfigured, it remains the Río Grande del Norte. It is as if the river itself had accepted its new form and course while still moving on with its own force, a force that becomes manifest when the river overflows its banks in times of flooding. In the words of T. S. Eliot, in his poem "The Dry Salvages" (1971, 31):

I do not know much about gods; but I think that the river
Is a strong brown god—sullen, untamed and intractable,
Patient to some degree, at first recognized as a frontier;
Useful, untrustworthy, as a conveyor of commerce;
Then only a problem confronting the builder of bridges.

We might put it this way: a river is *one*, not something to be divided, however much we may wish to control and measure and span it, or to use it for political gain in the desperate power games played between nations, cultures, and classes. Just as it runs under and through all that human beings attempt to build under or above it or impose upon it—from beds to banks, and from boats to bridges—so it survives all their efforts to manipulate it for their own tendentious purposes. James Joyce's *Finnegans Wake* opens with the word *riverrun*, as if Joyce were attempting to capture in this flowing neologism the way in which a river moves at its own rate and goes to its own fate.

In contrast, a border wall does nothing but divide, forcing and keeping peoples (and animals) apart. Its essence is separative. Not only does such a wall divide human beings from one another, but it is divided against itself: as we have argued, it is self-undermining. Unlike a river, which continues to affirm its aqueous essence throughout its whole course, a constructed wall bears contradictions that threaten to undercut it at many points. These contradictions can be summed up in our claim, made in chapter 1, that the wall's status as a border is continually ceding place to its becoming a boundary. Despite itself, its being as a border (tightly containing, strictly excluding) gives way to its original and resurgent boundary being—which is to say, to something permeable, open, and ever-changing.

Another contradiction lies between the wall's physical reality and its symbolic status. To construct the wall at La Frontera, weighty equipment and highly resistant materials (concrete, iron, steel) had to be assembled, all exacting a heavy toll in cost and labor: about $16–$21 million a mile, depending on the location, without figuring in the cost of land and labor to maintain it. It is estimated to have cost $22.4 billion so far, with an annual expense of $6.5 billion for maintenance and repair (Preston 2011b). Yet, as we have shown, the wall's significance remains largely symbolic; its primary force lies in its message, not in its materials. This explains why it may someday be replaced by a virtual wall and why, when its point and purpose no longer obtain, it will someday collapse.[15] As a compromised outcome of conflicting political interests, a border wall can offer no effective equipoise between these interests. The wall as a physical object can effect no lasting reconciliation between the conflicting forces that have brought it into being and that are often exacerbated by its literal presence. Beyond its physical deterioration, any abatement of the wall's entrenched divisive power will come from changing economic and political conditions, or else from devastating climate change.

Unlike a wall, a river is not divided against itself, nor is it self-undermining. For the most part, it is "sullen, untamed and intractable." At the same time, a river can be very wily. Beneath its placid surface, complexities abound. I refer not just to the invisible undercurrents that cut across its depths but also to its varying directionalities and inconstant contents. It is no wonder that measuring these depths is difficult. Not until the nineteenth-century development of surveying instruments adapted to the purpose could the depths of rivers and oceans be determined. Even so, this measurement is far from perfect when it comes to a major river such as the Río Grande del Norte. Its depth alters radically as the river alternates between flooding and drying down to its bed, extremes common to this body. In the former, the conditions are too turbulent to sound the depths; in the latter, there is no depth to be measured. In between, many circumstances render such measurement highly tenuous. For example, the two channels bordering an island in the river often have different depths; when multiple islands cluster together in the river, the measurement is further compromised, since the channels become interbraided. All this complicates the rule that the borderline is located in the middle of the deepest channel of the river.

Still other difficulties foiled the best efforts of the first U.S.-Mexico border survey, undertaken between 1848 and 1857. Time and again, these efforts had to be abandoned, whether because of sand-, wind-, or thunderstorms; lack of supplies; Indian attacks; political interference; or threatened mutiny on the part of overworked and underpaid workers. As José Salazar Ylarregui (the name appears with various spellings), the Mexican commissioner of the United States–Mexico Boundary Survey, put it, in high frustration, "You cannot imagine what labors we have suffered and are still suffering" (quoted in Werne 2007, 135). Ill with fever, Ylarregui had to suspend the survey in September 1852 because of a "lack of funds, engineers, and an adequate escort [for protection in Apache and Commanche territory]" (Werne 2007, 127).[16]

As for the Americans, they called a halt to their efforts soon after, on November 5, 1852. What is striking is that the survey bogged down as a result of the attempt to determine the deepest channel of the Rio Grande as it made its way through Texas—that is, the basis of the border itself (Werne 2007, 121–122). M. T. W. Chandler and the remaining Americans abruptly turned away from the river and headed over dry land to Santa Rosa and Fort

Duncan. They had been tested by the river's wiles and were found wanting. The river's challenges included the fact that during the six months separating the U.S. and Mexican survey efforts, the Rio Grande changed its channel in one area. A note appended to the commissioners' review of the resulting maps stated, "The two Maps agree, except in the bed of the River, which circumstance is the consequence of the two Surveys being made at different periods, six months apart, during which time the River changed its bed [thus its channel], as it is constantly doing" (quoted in Rebert 2001, 177).[17]

In fact, the exact depths of many of the river's channels were never determined in the nine years of binational surveying that provided the official basis of the U.S.-Mexico border; they literally escaped measurement. Since then, these depths have changed many times thanks to the constantly altering course of the Rio Grande itself.[18]

We must conclude that "you cannot step twice" into this river (Heraclitus 1959, 21 [fragment 21])—such are its vagaries and vicissitudes. Indeed, if you step into it even once, you will find its bed and channels changing shape, with no set depth or shape.

In positioning the wall, its designers had to respect this continual metamorphosis. One way they did this was by placing the wall several miles north of the meandering river so as to avoid the damage that comes from periodic flooding. In so doing, however, they created a limbo between the river and the wall—a space that has the effect of walling off many Americans from their property, even though they are located many miles from the river itself, as in Eloisa Taméz's case, rather than keeping migrant Mexicans off American soil. In the end, the river's inconstancy triumphs over human ingenuity, the river thus taking its final revenge over the wall, deconstructing it from below, as it were.

Despite its wiliness and incessant mutations, a river such as the Río Grande del Norte remains at one with itself: it flows forth out of its own forceful essence, moving resolutely in one direction, irreversibly eastward, toward the Gulf of Mexico. In it, "everything flows" (Heraclitus 1959, 29).[19] It flows with one manifest purpose: to sweep along both itself and its contents, all at once (viewed in simultaneous crosscuts) but also all in succession (considered over time).

A river is indeed "a strong brown god," but any divine dimension discerned in it is entirely immanent to it: the god is within it. At the symbolic level, a river is the very embodiment of immanence, since it *takes in* and *takes on* all that comes to inhabit it, flowing on in its "riverrun." In a further twist, a river can bend downward—down into the earth, as with underground rivers, like the Styx in the ancient Greek imagination—or else down into the self: "The river is within us, the sea is all about us" (Eliot 1971, line 15). Going down within is especially characteristic of a river with a long and dense history, such as the Río Grande del Norte, which gets incorporated into the shared memories and entire imaginations of whole peoples. The river becomes one with the collective psyche of the humans who have lived along and from it. Even if it has come to divide populations in the course of human history, its natural essence as a river is to unite all that streams in and through it—however submerged, however unknown.

The Río Grande del Norte runs through a single riverine region, holding it together, dissolving differences as it flows over more than 1,250 miles. As a river, it remains one, even if the same river, reinforced by the wall recently built at its northern flank, divides the region in two. This suggests that what looks all too bleak in the treacherous terms of contemporary human history—unresolvable, lethal, spinning into the abyss—is seen in a different light when viewed against the backdrop of the river that is the origin and continuing cynosure of the afflicted territory: a river that remains its ever-flowing foil and its elemental source. The single body of the river bears up, from below as it were, the many suffering bodies and souls of those who live on either side of it and whose intersecting destinies it reflects and supports.

In view of this basic elemental being, the very idea of the Río Grande del Norte serving as the basis for an international border appears in all its absurdity. Any such role is literally superimposed upon it, something we can see most graphically in the borderline that is imagined to traverse it longitudinally as determined by the midpoint of the channel that happens to be the deepest at any given moment. The arbitrariness of any such line is apparent for all who have eyes to see or minds to think. For one thing, it is literally invisible and impalpable. For another, it is a creature of the fortunes of economic and political history. With another turn of the wheel of the fortunes of empires, the locus and import of this imaginary line will transmute.

The likelihood, however, is that the border at La Frontera will persist for quite a while, thanks to its formal ideality as a human construct, as a creation of a treaty whose terms are unlikely to alter. A border and its linear representation in a borderline, despite their contingent origins in a conflictual past, possess momentum of a peculiarly powerful sort. Once established, they become capable of determining the fates of millions of human beings, as has happened many times elsewhere on the earth. In regard to their tenacity, they are rivals of natural forces such as rivers, the latter persisting from their naturality rather than from a posited ideality materialized in such things as walls and armed guards who patrol them.

The linear and the elemental are held in the embrace of a single river like the Río Grande del Norte, as occurs in other comparable circumstances in world history, those surrounding the Rhine, the Danube, the Volga, the Mekong, the Yellow River. This is a strange partnership indeed. Even if the partners end by making a certain peace with each other, this peace is decidedly imperfect, since it happens, all too often, at an unacceptable price of human suffering on the part of those whose lives are affected by their forced marriage—affected at every level that matters, from the concourse of daily life to long-term futures.

When a borderline, at once imposed and imaginary, is reinforced by a fortified wall of separation, as happens at La Frontera and elsewhere, we have a redoubling of the exclusion at stake in virtually every political border, especially in an international border such as that between the Mexico and the United States. The very idea of being a "border"—at once irreal and symbolic—here gains the rigor of the real: the formality of the line, intact on its own terms, is overtaken and overborne by the materiality of the wall. This materiality was brutally evident in the wall that was peremptorily built in Eloisa Taméz's backyard. This wall divides her property as surely as the same wall, extending for miles to the east and many more to the west, divides the United States from Mexico. What is designated as "la línea divisoria" in the original maps of the Boundary Survey of 1848–1857 has become *un muro divisorio* (a divisive wall) that at once reflects and shapes the relationship between two nation-states and their respective peoples. In so doing, it has also become a *muro de contención*, a retaining wall that is a cause of continuing strife.[20]

In the Lower Rio Grande Valley, near this wall, runs the river that gives the region its name. Even as it is diverted by the U.S. Army Corps of Engineers and overshadowed by the wall, this river is ongoing. It keeps coming. It flows on, and will do so long after the formidable wall on its northern flank has fallen into disuse and disappeared. However turbulent it may be under its surface in times of heavy rain, and diminutive as it becomes in the dry season, the Rio Grande undergirds the whole region, the entire watershed. As a naturally given boundary, it is a nonrepressive presence, a porous source of life and movement. It is a force of nature, speaking with its own voice amid the confused din of human voices that clamor from beyond its bed and banks in the citadels of corporate and state power.

In the river, the wall reaches its limit. A conflicted border encounters an outright boundary. Therein it meets more than its match.

Walled Up and Walled Out

The only thing the wall won't stop is people," says Scott Nicol, adding that it is at most a "speed bump" for migrants and drug smugglers. For other species, however, it is a massive obstacle: a "bisection of vast eco-systems that has changed the face of the land" (personal communication, June 12, 2009). Even as it fails to halt human migrations, it disrupts those of animals, stopping ocelots and pronghorns, jaguars and javelinas, snakes and rodents; the wall cuts their movements short and undermines their habitats. It has been estimated that it will take centuries to restore these habitats and the landscapes that surround them.

Whether a given border crossing succeeds or does not in terms of sheer numbers is a straightforward matter; the success rate can be directly tabulated (even if the eventual human consequences defy calculation). Effects on the circumambient natural world, however, are much more difficult to track, both in the lives of individual animals that are thwarted by the wall and in lingering effects on entire generations of animals—not to mention the harm to streams and marshes, and to plants and other flora in the vicinity of the wall.

These differential effects of the wall reflect the intrinsic difference between something that is constructed and placed on the landscape by human design and organic processes among living things—processes that are natural, plural, and belonging integrally to the land rather than imposed upon it. The wall is a fiercely condensed material entity—a sheer Thing located at a definite Site—while living beings in the natural environment are distributed across entire landscapes. Where the wall as a Thing is isolated from its surroundings, standing up in defiant singularity, the surrounding bioregion is inherently interstitial, being composed of myriad interactions of all its denizens within such concrete matrices as soil, seasons, air, and weather. It is open to any significant influence, however major (e.g., desertification) or modest (e.g., a single dry spell, a sudden shower) it may be. A wall, in contrast, is closed in upon itself and thus closed off from the surrounding world. It is more an anti-Thing than a Thing in the Heideggerian sense of something that brings together sky, earth, gods, and humans. These cosmic dimensions are riven by a wall (Heidegger 1971).

Despite its manufactured materiality, its isolation and its self-enclosure, a wall is subject to massive projection by human beings: to idealization by those who believe in its necessity and to vilification by its critics. The very simplicity of its repetitive structure (composed of panel after panel, spike after spike), its blankness and muteness, invites multiple readings of its meaning, its reason for being, and its legitimacy. Sometimes, the projections take the form of graffiti written directly on the southern side of the wall, as if the wall were one vast writing surface on which to express one's rage. Short of assuming such dramatic form, the projections take the form of beliefs and claims that are entertained by humans whose lives intersect with the wall on a daily basis: beliefs such as "This wall is a very good thing, since it will stem illegal immigrants"; "It is important to guard against terrorists"; or "It will stop drugs from being smuggled into the United States."

The open landscape invites projections as well, but rarely of any comparably opinionated sort: for the most part, it is there to contemplate or savor, to appreciate in its biodiversity or its beauty. The sheer array of life-forms discourages simplistic reductions that reflect matters of personal belief. The wall, however, is there not merely to behold (except perhaps on its first perception) but prompts the beholder to *take a stand*. The two-sidedness of the wall's very structure encourages the kind of either/or thinking that suits the generation of intensely held convictions of right versus wrong, a theme taken up earlier in chapter 4. This exclusivist way of thinking departs radically from that occasioned by the natural world, about which we are rarely tempted to say that it is simply "good" or "bad"; such definitive, dualistic thinking is out of place in that context.

Beyond noting these basic contrasts between the wall at La Frontera and the environing world around it, we may discern six paired differences:

First, the wall is *for humans only*. Being built by them from scratch, it reflects their history, ideologies, politics, cultures, forms of racism, design preferences, and so on. It is "human, all too human" (Nietzsche 2012), yet its larger setting is characterized mainly by the *other-than-human*: desert, mountains, rivers, cacti, multiple species of wild animals. The setting exists *for these other species*; if humans enter it, they come into a place that is decidedly not theirs and on whose own terms they must manage to live—or perish if they fail to do so.

Second, the wall is a *nonliving* entity. Not only is it made from inorganic, industrially produced materials, but these materials come from somewhere else, where they may have been put to very different purposes (the panels of the first version of the wall came from landing strips for military aircraft). In contrast, the environs of the wall are composed of *living things*, whether animal or plant, or else forms of matter (soil, sand, stones) that are native to the region.

Third, while the wall has been in existence for *a brief time* only—its oldest parts dating from 1994—the natural world around it has evolved over millions of years (it is estimated that the Tijuana Estuary took 1.5 million years to reach its current form). The wall has changed its overt form every several years since its construction began, depending on the most current technology, while changes in the desert and mountains in which it is set are *long in coming* and difficult to discern for all but geologists, climatologists, and long-term residents.

Fourth, despite the brevity of its existence, the wall has been enormously *expensive* to create. In contrast, the landscape on either side has no determinate real-estate or other monetary value attached to it; as Thoreau remarked, "The landscape is not owned" (1991, 84). It is there to be savored or traversed, not to be sold or exchanged.

Fifth, the wall is an altogether *artificial* thing; it is wrought by humans for a particular purpose and from materials that have been manufactured by these same purposeful beings. It is *constructed* in every sense of this term. A landscape, however, is not built, not even by God; it has evolved on its own, by way of processes belonging to it alone. It is altogether *natural*, something given to or found by humans and other species, not made or crafted by them.

Sixth and finally, the wall encourages *obsession*. As a single continuous thing that is densely overdetermined in its cultural and political significance, it calls attention to itself as an object of intense controversy and debate. Anyone engaged in such discussion seeks the single best argument with which to defend one's beliefs or opinions regarding the wall and what it stands for. At the same time, a landscape calls for a receptive and open attention that expresses itself as *absorption*, an attitude fostered by a lateral thinking that is diffusely polycentered rather than monofocal.

The most definitive difference between a border wall and its natural surroundings is found in the fact that the wall aims at *exclusion*, at keeping certain things out of the area found within the perimeter of the wall—in the case of La Frontera, presumptively "illegal" immigrants, drug importers, and potential terrorists. This is done in the interest of protecting those human beings who live within its confines, shielding them from these various "undesirables" and the effects of their projected actions. A natural landscape, in striking contrast, proceeds by *inclusion*, by supporting all beings who are situated there as its denizens and tolerating many who pass through. It embraces all things that grow or move there, or live there because their species or type has adapted to that natural habitat. Whereas the citizenship in question when one passes through a checkpoint is shown by papers confirming one's country of birth, occupants of the natural landscape possess their own natural birthright for which no legal documentation is required.

By its structure and history, a border wall is perforated by as few openings as possible, and these few portals are overseen by state-appointed agents whose primary task is to assess evidence for authenticity of documentation on the part of those who seek to gain admittance. In stark contrast, the surrounding landscape is open through and through—being a matter of "wide open spaces." Here greatly diverse living and nonliving things commingle without proof of right of residence. The only qualification for living in such a setting is being able and willing to *live there*, on its terms and under its aegis.

Despite these various contrasts and differences, an international border wall such as that at La Frontera must *ultimately coexist* with a circumambient natural world. A wall of any kind has to be set *somewhere*. It could be in an urban scene, as in the case of the Berlin Wall, but it can also be in a natural setting, as with the Great Wall of China (for most of its considerable length). Powerfully divisive as they are, humanly constructed walls never make up the entirety of a given situation; they exist to differentiate and demarcate at least two portions of a larger space, dividing that space into two regions with sufficient room for their respective populations to survive, however minimally and at whatever cost.

The wall at La Frontera runs mostly through open land, though it also passes through certain key cities. In this respect, this wall is more comparable to China's Great Wall than to the Berlin Wall. Unique to the circumstance at La Frontera are not just its exact forms of construction (a range of styles stretching over a period of twenty years) but also its stated purposes of controlling immigration, blocking state terrorists, and denying access to drug smugglers—all this within the distinctive landscape settings of northern Mexico and certain southern parts of the United States. It is as if the complexity of its various aims, all too human in origin, somehow matched the multifariousness of the natural environment in its variegated geomorphic configurations, multiple microclimates and bioniches, and animal and plant species.

La Frontera is a very dangerous part of the world. Human beings who wish to cross the border to enter the United States may pay with their lives, while those who fail to take this risk often suffer from severe poverty caused by dire unemployment. But jeopardy is not foreign to life in the desert, whether that life be those who manage to get over or around the wall and into open land or members of the many other species found there: danger lurks, day and night, for every denizen of the deserts, plains, and mountains. Just as Mexicans are adversely affected by the current economic situation and the dangers brought on by drug-trafficking violence, no member of any natural species is immune to the harsh extremities that obtain in the vast, arid bioregion that encompasses them all.

By the same token, each factor, wall and natural world, reaches out into the other and is capable of wreaking havoc in that other. The leveling of the Spooners and Border Mesas east of Tijuana to make way for the second and third walls in the San Diego area has had potentially disastrous effects on the Tijuana Estuary, as Mike McCoy attests: the leveling has "destabilized the structure of this eco-system [in an action that] . . . causes habitat fragmentation. [The] cumulative impact on the entire [ecosystem] is very destructive" (personal communication, May 2, 2011). We have noted the detrimental consequences for animal species in other stretches of the wall, notably in the Lower Rio Grande Valley National Wildlife Refuge.

At the same time, the character of the local landscape affects the flow of legal and illegal traffic across and around the wall in very particular ways. In this two-way interaction, the wall and its surrounding world not only coexist but copenetrate each other and influence their respective destinies—so much so that in the end, they are inseparable, no matter how distinguishable they may be for analytical purposes. This is true to such an extent that a change in the character or form of one brings with it massive, if sometimes subtle, effects on the other. What McCoy says of the situation at the Tijuana Estuary applies equally to the incursion of the wall into any given natural environment: "The border mesas, riparian corridor, the estuary and the ocean are all part of a larger ecosystem[;] . . . what happens to one happens to all because they are interconnected and dependent upon each other" (personal communication, May 2, 2011). Despite its pretense of self-sufficiency and its assertive stolidity, the wall is a major player in the ecology of the region through which it passes—while this region in turn affects the fate of the wall itself.

Man-made wall and other-than-human world: what happens to one happens to the other, and vice versa. Deeply divergent in all the ways we have outlined, this wall and this world undergo intermingled fates in the many places they share along the U.S.-Mexico border.

Now, in Part 2, we will assemble with a different guide, Mary Watkins, at Friendship Park, where the wall extends into the Pacific Ocean.

Part 2

LOOKING BOTH WAYS
AT THE BORDER

Friendship Park: First Encounter

I, Mary Watkins, invite you to begin our journey together in Part 2 at Friendship Park, where I first encountered the U.S. wall at the U.S.-Mexico border. In the summer of 2002, I took off a week from work to be "a friendly adult presence" on a teen work camp that went to Tijuana, Mexico;[1] two of my daughters participated in the work camp. We had recently moved from Boston to Santa Barbara, a small city whose population is about 38 percent people of Mexican ancestry. I knew little about southwestern U.S. and Mexican history and had not studied immigration in any detail. I was having a hard time deciphering the California town to which my job as a psychology professor had taken me and welcomed the opportunity to learn about some of the issues facing Mexican communities at the border.

We were to spend one long day near Tijuana helping a young Mexican couple build a house from four cast-off garage doors, a frequent method of cheap construction in the towns that have sprung up around the maquiladoras, the vast manufacturing plants created following the passage of NAFTA, the North American Free Trade Agreement. The rest of the week was to be spent participating in a gesture of solidarity, joining in a community art project in Maclovio Rojas, a community of (at that time) ten thousand that had been founded in 1988 by a group of visionary women from Oaxaca. These women had imagined a better life for their families and organized an autonomous community to promote education, health care, and local self-governance. Unfortunately, their plan for such a community began to conflict with the master plan for the "free-trade" zone that developed around them. To prepare for the passage of NAFTA, the Mexican government amended Article 27 of the Mexican Constitution of 1917, which gave people rights to communal land ownership. This article made it impossible to sell communal lands (*ejidos*), thus protecting them. Maclovio Rojas's claim to the land, however, was jeopardized by this amendment and the surrounding corporations' desire for more land as firms sought to expand their manufacturing plants in the free-trade zone. Because of their resistance, Maclovio Rojas's leaders have periodically had to go into hiding, seeking to avoid periods of house arrest or even imprisonment. Several human-rights groups, including the American Friends Service Committee, which sponsored our trip, have volunteered as international witnesses in an effort to curb the human-rights violations that have occurred as powerful forces seek to intimidate the community's residents in order to dislodge them from their land. We were to be a small part of this long effort; specifically, we were to help to create a memorial for migrants who had died crossing the U.S.-Mexico border.

Before NAFTA, there was no record of such deaths because they were so rare. Since NAFTA, more than six thousand people have died trying to cross from Mexico to the United States. In order to help us understand this sharp rise in deaths, we were taken on a field trip to Friendship Park to meet with Christian Ramirez, the American Friends Service Committee's national coordinator for immigrant rights. It was a beautiful and bright San Diego day as we got out of our cars at Friendship Park, also known as Border Field State Park. Despite the serious topics of our trip, we were in a light mood as we got out of the van, for we could see and hear the Pacific Ocean.

It was here, at Friendship Park, that I first encountered the U.S. wall at the U.S.-Mexico border. My reaction was visceral and unexpected. As my eyes slowly began to take in its extent, I began to feel physically ill. To the east the wall bisected sharp hills and stretched as far as I could see. In front of me, it divided an ocean beach, cutting off one people from another, Mexicans and Americans. To the west, at the water's edge, a place associated with freedom and the unfettered meeting of land and water, the wall continued directly into the Pacific Ocean, as though to part even the great waters. The hubris required to attempt to part nations and an ocean seemed sickeningly stark. Ralph Waldo Emerson once exclaimed, "Suffice it for the joy of the universe that we have not arrived at a wall, but at interminable oceans" (1981, 283). This joy, on which we rely, collapsed. I had no sophisticated understanding of border politics. I did have a gut sense, one arising with startling intensity, that building a wall between two friendly nations was wrong.

It would be a while before I heard the term "una herida abierta," an open wound, applied to the wall at the border. Anzaldúa (2007, 3) describes the border as the place "where the Third World grates against the first and bleeds." Later still, I would find the wall described as "bleeding" and even as "crying." Having spent time with it, I can now see and hear this in my imagination.

Figure 12. The U.S. wall, westernmost point, San Diego/Tijuana. Photo by Lily Rosenthal.

That first afternoon, my sudden sense of visceral disgust and distress began to lift as we talked in broken Spanish with Mexicans on the Tijuana side of the wall. Everyone laughed as young children with small bodies—Mexican and American—put an arm or a leg between the narrow slats of the wall, amused at being in two places with one body, in Mexico and the United States. I even put my own hand through the slats, as though to resist the wall's attempt to put us all in our places, confining us by nationality, and, as I later understood, by economic class.

In 1971, Pat Nixon, the president's wife, christened a 418-acre area between the border and the Tijuana Estuary, south of San Diego, naming it Friendship Park, Parque de Amistad. She said she hoped that Mexican and American children could play there together one day. In fact, they had played soccer at this place together before the first fence was built, but she did not mention that in her talk. She too passed her hand through a barbed-wire barrier to the other side to shake a few hands as she dedicated the park to binational friendship and goodwill. Reportedly, she asked the security guard to cut a hole in the barbed wire so she could embrace a few Mexican children, saying, "I don't like fences at all, and I hope this one is not here for very long" (BorderLinks 2012, n.p.). Friendship Park was a site where families separated by the border could meet for a picnic and share their news and hopes of being reunited, despite the presence of the fence.

By 2010 you wouldn't see any child defying adult borders by putting a hand through the fence at Friendship Park. The first wall was fortified by an additional barrier fence, built about ninety feet from the first one, and authorized by the Secure Fence Act in 2006. Access to the main park area was allowed only on the weekends between 10:00 a.m. and 2:00 p.m., and only twenty-five to thirty people were permitted to enter a cage-like space near the monument marker for a maximum of thirty minutes—and they had to seek permission even for that. Often that permission was denied. The road was closed Monday to Friday and flooded out five months of the year. Except for the supervised visits arranged through the Department of Homeland Security, no one was allowed past the new fence, thus separating people from the original wall, as well as from the first border marker, placed in 1849. The binational friendship garden that was built before the second wall was installed has now been torn up on the U.S. side so as not to impede Border Patrol activity. There was concern that, in addition to the food, occasional birthday presents, and weekly communion wafers made of tortillas that were passed from one side to the other, drugs and illegal documents might also be handed back and forth. In 2012 the Friends of Friendship Park succeeded in prompting a redesign that once again allows visitors to approach the "fence," now reinforced by a thick, dense mesh that precludes clear vision to the other side but does allow for conversation. The deafening roar of surveillance helicopters, however, often makes it difficult to hear conversation or even the sound of the ocean surf.

It would be beautiful if this area could ever be a true park of friendship. True friends acknowledge grievous wrongs, apologize, and make amends. They make special efforts not to exploit each other, holding each other's best interests at heart and acting to facilitate each other's self-fulfillment.

Now, years later, I understand that declaring a park of friendship at the very site of a marker inscribing a border won through war and treachery is not enough to make it so. We appear to have tightened our defenses against what went unacknowledged and thus unspoken in Pat Nixon's visiting remarks. At Friendship Park, psychic, cultural, historical, and physical defenses converge so powerfully that a literal wall has issued forth, announcing a zone where surveillance and "operational control" have crowded out impulses toward hospitality and friendship.

The northward path of Mexican migrants, usually forced but sometimes chosen, brings them back to lands that, prior to 1848, were part of their country. As though caught in a reciprocal osmotic process, I have been pulled southward over the last decade, as if a compensatory process in my own psyche and bodily presence had been activated. My pilgrimage has taken me southward in order to more fully arrive home in Santa Barbara, to have a better understanding of my neighbors and myself. It has drawn me "off center" and has offered me a deeper way of being at home.

I naively thought that the desperate situation I encountered in 2002 could be ameliorated through federal immigration reform and that local and state efforts could be launched in the meantime, helping those migrants whom the wall has left stranded in our communities. Instead, I have found myself witnessing and learning about a tragic and shameful chapter-in-the-making of American history. While my interest began with the literal wall that has been built during this period, it gradually widened to encompass the global and local implications of this wall building. We live in an age when forced migrations occur across the globe and threaten to multiply as the number of environmental refugees soars, and the most destructive effects of globalized capitalism are felt by those furthest from seats of power and influence: the poor.

I have now traveled many times to Mexico, to the border region of both countries, to the site of the Berlin Wall, and to the Derry wall and the "peace walls" in Northern Ireland. I have turned back toward the "walls" in my own community of Santa Barbara. It became clear to me early on that our government could not build such a wall at the border if we were not already living within metaphorical walls in our towns and cities, walls that separate citizens from noncitizens. The wall at the border snakes itself into our communities, dividing schools and classrooms, hospitals, and neighborhoods. Those dining in the front of our restaurants are cut off from those working in the rear; those riding in cars rarely meet those on buses and bikes.

Perhaps these more local and invisible walls have their final outcome at the border in now the most militarized and technologically sophisticated wall in history. I have listened carefully to my neighbors, who labor hard for little and who live in my town without documents. They bear witness to this dark and inhospitable period of history. And I have listened to those who fear they will lose their language, culture, and jobs because of the influx of migrants—indeed, what they see as "the invasion" of Mexicans.

Gradually the American history I had learned as the daughter of Memphis-born white parents growing up in New York—the history of the relations between black and white people in the United States—began to echo in the history I was learning of Anglo relations to people of Mexican ancestry. The aberrant gene of American racism remains hearty as it moves from one incoming group of immigrants to another, gathering those with black and brown skin into a vast racial underclass, supported by legislation in some instances and by the lack of legislation in others.

Why is this so? How does this happen? What is at stake for us as human beings, as citizens and noncitizens? How do we resist inhospitality and instead create communities that value all of our members? I write these chapters first to fellow white citizens, for I am closest to understanding the psychological and spiritual price of this state of affairs for those whom Mexicans call "Anglos." It is considerable. But I have found that the issues of hospitality and inhospitality need to be omnipresent concerns for all of us. Every society, and each individual within that society, must both reckon with the arrival of "the stranger" and ultimately face the shame that accrues when one locks one's door against those on whom one has come to depend.

To arrive back at the wall with any depth of understanding, we too must become migrants, tacking back and forth between Mexico and the United States, between the Anglo and the Mexican sides of our towns and cities, and between the struggles of migrants who are locked out and the fearful Americans who are now locked in.

It was only through such a migratory and circular nomadic path that I could begin to understand the small city where I live. While these understandings came last, I would like to begin with them in chapter 5, for they lay bare the historical dynamics that are often unknown or repressed in the American citizen psyche. If we look at them closely, we can begin to see the resonance between black and white relations and Mexican and Anglo relations. In chapter 6, I explore the creation of the racial caste system in the United States that has consigned Mexicans to their ostensible "place," alongside Native Americans and African Americans. How do we continue to create and sustain racial caste in the United States? Whom and what does it serve? How does it function with Mexican migrants, and what are its effects on them? In chapter 7, I look at the psychological and soul costs for Anglos of our present immigration system. My focus lies particularly with the psyche, the soul, of citizens, the price of social and historical amnesia, of othering and scapegoating, and of closing one's door in the face of others' needs. How might we recognize and face our legacy of shame, and see this acknowledgment as a crucial step to restoring our souls? Finally, in chapters 8 and 9, I try to feed a prophetic imagination, picturing how we might live our borders differently. What happens when we refuse to accept an imposed limit, such as the U.S. border wall, and instead not only contest it but also create an altogether different mode of being that resists and transfigures it? I begin by describing the functions of the art on the Mexican side of the U.S. wall at the border, and continue with examples of already embodied prophetic imagination in many American towns and cities.

CHAPTER 5

The Creation of an Internal Colony

Santa Barbara, a City Divided against Itself

WALLING OFF OTHERS

If we were to take wing at Friendship Park and fly eastward above the U.S.-Mexico border, the triple wall would come into view. This part of the wall shares its design with the Berlin Wall, creating paved lanes between walls that the Border Patrol can oversee and police. Migrants may succeed in scaling the first wall, but they are slowed down by subsequent barriers and thus easier to apprehend. The once rugged and rural terrain has been turned into a highly militarized zone, with surveillance and control as the primary aims.

As we rise and fly northward, past the stretch of forbidding walls, we are awed by the beauty of one of the few remaining estuaries along the Pacific coast, the Tijuana Estuary. Here there is a meeting of an altogether different sort, where the worlds of freshwater and ocean water freely meet and mingle, and the creatures and vegetation that thrive in this hybrid environment grace a gentle landscape. In the natural world, this meeting place between two ecologies, ocean and river, spawns a third that gives rise to new species and plants and to a remarkable fertility and capacity for regeneration. How ironic and sad that our effort to halt the borderlands' human culture that has developed at La Frontera mortally threatens this estuarine preserve as well (see chapter 3).

Borders forcibly imposed in one domain have their echoes and effects in others. The natural flows that happen at edges—between people, animals, earth, and water—give rise to great creativity. Assault on them reverberates across species. This is the case at the border.

When we look straight down at the wall between San Diego County and Tijuana, we cannot help but be struck by the disjunction between the heavy urban sprawl of Tijuana and the relatively bucolic aspect of southern San Diego County. Looking south, we see Tijuana, at a population over 1.5 million, with densely packed buildings. Further east we see a vast complex

Figure 13. Looking at the "triple wall" from Tijuana, Mexico. Photo by Lily Rosenthal.

of maquiladoras, industrial plants whose owners have taken advantage of the free-trade zone. Unfortunately, these plants largely assemble parts that are brought from elsewhere and create products primarily destined for export. Neither the manufacturing of constituent parts nor the finished items themselves offer any significant support to economic life in Mexico. Rather, through the low-paid labor of primarily young women, corporate factory owners are able to make sizable profits. As Mexicans and Central Americans move northward to cross the border, the wall and U.S. securitization of the border make passage extremely difficult and costly, often marooning migrants south of the border in this free-trade zone. They need jobs and take what is available: almost always low-wage nonunion jobs with poor working and safety conditions. If we were to swoop down at a change of shift, we would see thousands of Mexicans pouring in and out of these windowless factories.

Looking next to these industrial zones, we see what Mexicans call "pigeon housing," echoing, at the intimate level of the family, the border wall's containment of the population. Such housing crowds whole families of maquiladora workers, side by side, into one-room living spaces. You will not see any playgrounds or central community gathering areas (*zócalos*) in pigeon housing areas. The residences are not formally called slave dwellings, but their form and function suggest just this. Close by these quarters, you can look down and see acre upon acre of tractor-trailer units, all of them ready to take the finished products to market, primarily in the United States. The poor quality of housing construction contrasts sharply with the sophisticated infrastructure for transportation: toll roads, ports, and railways that have been built for the movement not of people but of consumer goods.

Each U.S. city along the border has its twin, its Mexican counterpart. Ambos Nogales was explored in chapter 2. In every case, the latter is more swollen with population, more densely settled, less green because it has less water available, and profoundly poorer. While the paired cities are twins, sharing a bioregion and a borderlands culture, they are far from identical.

This tale of two cities echoes metaphorically within my own city of Santa Barbara, California, a little more than two hundred miles from the U.S.-Mexico border. Here, however, the proportions are reversed: the smaller "city" is the one of Mexican descent. What remains the same is that the relative poverty and the precariousness of daily life, the sheer difficulties of making ends meet, lie predominantly on the Mexican side of town. This is also the case in other cities throughout the southwestern United States, such as Tucson, Phoenix, San Antonio, and Los Angeles.

Just as the U.S. wall at La Frontera attempts to divide a nation of great relative wealth from a much poorer one, a metaphorical set of walls in my city of Santa Barbara divides those with legendary financial resources from those with few. These "walls" abruptly and decisively curtail the potential human estuary where these communities could intermingle, giving rise to new forms of conviviality and civic imagination.

Santa Barbara, not Los Angeles, was the center of power in Spanish, and then Mexican, Alta California, so it is a good place to begin our understanding of the history between communities of Anglo-American and Mexican descent. It is a comparatively small city, where two populations—Mexican and Anglo—came into contact 150 years ago. Rather than develop an estuary teeming with new life-forms—borderlands at their best—one life-form overpowers another, eventually surrounding it, containing it, and reducing it. This is a possibility at any edge where two sets of life-forms meet, but it is not preferable or inevitable. How did this happen? Santa Barbara's small size, as well as its repetitive process of extruding difference, makes its dynamics easier to discern than those in a megalopolis such as Los Angeles, eighty miles to the south. It thus can serve as an exemplar of the dynamics of internal colonization, one response to the meeting between cultures. Using it as a starting point will prepare the ground for chapter 9, which explores decolonizing alternatives that could give rise to a vitality and hybridity rivaling that of estuaries.

WALLING OFF THE PAST

Americans have been criticized for living almost solely in the present and the near future, rarely looking at either the present's deep roots in the past or the long-term consequences their present choices will have in the future. This historical amnesia can be understood in part as a defense against the largely unacknowledged and unclaimed darkness and destructiveness of Americans' own history. Without looking carefully at our history, we misconstrue the present, particularly the situation facing members of those groups that continue to carry the burdens of past insults and assaults. We are sorely in need of what Aurora Levins Morales (1999) calls "medicine history," as opposed to official or imperial history that supports efforts of domination. Medicine history retrieves extruded history from the margins, bringing to the table what has been unacknowledged and silenced. These restorative acts give us an opportunity not only to reconcile with the past but also to lay the foundation for undertaking processes of reconciliation with those of our neighbors who have been profoundly affected by these histories. In the absence of such a restorative history, we are unable to understand intimate details in our daily life that otherwise remain opaque.

Lacking knowledge of my new town's history, I found many things about it puzzling. If you go downtown early in the morning, the road is full of Mexicans on bikes. In certain parks and neighborhoods, there are many young Mexican men carrying backpacks. When you drive down Quinientos Street, the labor lines are long, and all those looking for work are Mexican. Why is this so?

Why aren't the Mexican teenagers I know taking driver's education? Why aren't they filling out their FAFSA financial aid forms so they can get federal loans to help them go to college?[1] Why are so few Latino students going on to four-year colleges? Why are young Mexican Americans who get accepted to Berkeley or Harvard unable to attend? Why is a very smart Mexican friend of my daughter still working in the back of a restaurant, as she has for ten years, since she was fifteen? When a member of a family dies in Mexico, why does the family drive to Tijuana and then fly to their home city instead of flying directly from Santa Barbara? Why are there so many Mexicans standing in concealed lines on the first of the month, paying landlords/slumlords with cash? Why are Mexican families afraid to have their teenage children go out at night? Why are the neighborhoods and the schools so segregated? Why are all the Mexicans to be found at the back of most establishments (restaurants, supermarkets, clothing stores) and not at the front? Why are they working, always working? Why are 25 percent of Hispanics in our county living in poverty? Why do the gardeners at my workplace not want to speak Spanish with me? Why do small traffic accidents or violations seem to terrify my Mexican friends? Why doesn't Marguerite call the police when her husband is beating her in front of her children? Why do young people involved in gangs choose State Street, the main shopping corridor, as their dividing line? It is possible to live as an Anglo in Santa Barbara without thinking about these questions. To grapple with them, it is necessary to understand the history of our town. The same is true for your city or town. I offer Santa Barbara as an example.

MAKING THE FIRST THE LAST

When you lay out the history of Santa Barbara, you begin to notice tragic patterns familiar from other parts of the world, *colonial patterns*: divestiture of earlier groups' claims to the land; cultural invasion; the outlawing of language; disfranchisement; the consolidation of political power by wresting power from indigenous groups; the erasure of local history and a substitution of the colonists' history; racism that derogates those who were here first, as though to justify the grab of land and economic and political power from an "inferior" people; and violence and threats of violence to force the dislocation of those with prior claims—claims based on a long history of inhabitation.

As we know from colonial processes elsewhere, the first become the last. Within impressively short periods of time, newcomers using excessive force can displace a native population, driving it onto ever-smaller parcels of land and reducing it to a labor pool for the control and profit of the occupying power.

This is also the story of Santa Barbara, and it is inseparable from pernicious forms of capitalism that feed on colonial arrangements. The Anglo-Latino relations we now see in this town largely resulted from events that began in 1847, just 167 years ago, and were mostly accomplished within the first forty years. The events left a history of a stark income divide between Latinos and Anglos, and patterns of social distance accrued through a history of racism and the exploitation of others for the accumulation of capital. The present situation has other tributaries as well, but it is the colonial one we hope to clarify here. The relegation of the native population to something like an internal colony would be breathtaking had it not been normalized through historical revisionism and the proscription of narratives that describe its actual practices.

Displacement and Confinement of the First by the Last

In 1782 King Carlos III of Spain ordered the establishment of the Presidio in Santa Barbara "to provide the benefits of government" for the inhabitants of the Santa Barbara Channel region of California. The inhabitants were Chumash people, the most populous indigenous groups in what we now call California. That was the pretext. The subtext was to secure Alta California from Russian and British encroachment and to protect the trade route between the Philippines and Mexico. Alta California, which Spain claimed as a province, included what is now California, Nevada, Arizona, Utah, western Colorado, and southwestern Wyoming. Santa Barbara was well positioned to defend the central Pacific coast. The Presidio was built by soldiers as well as by Chumash people.

The Santa Barbara Mission was established four years later, up the hill to the north. The function of the Presidio (where the soldiers lived) was to deter invasions, protect settlers from Indian attacks, and provide governance. The manifest function of the mission was to convert Indians into Christians and loyal Spanish subjects.

When the Spanish and indigenous Mexicans from Sonora first arrived after a one-thousand-mile northward journey, some 15,000 to 17,000 Chumash lived in the area extending from Malibu to San Luis Obispo; 8,000 Chumash lived in the region that was soon to be named Santa Barbara. By the early 1800s, the three Chumash communities near Santa Barbara had ceased to function. By the time of the 1834 Secularization Proclamation, 2,500 Chumash remained; by the time of annexation, in 1848, a mere 1,150; by 1880, only a few dozen. Within one hundred years, a thriving population had been tragically decimated, removing the Chumash as a possible challenge to Spanish and then Mexican domination of the region.

By 1803, twenty-one years after the founding of the Presidio, the Chumash in the Santa Barbara region had been absorbed into the mission. Thirty-one years later, when the missions were secularized, the Chumash worked as laborers, servants, and vaqueros. In effect, the Chumash were "civilized" to death; 4,000 lie buried in a mass grave under what is now the mission garden and cemetery. Their claim to the land others came to call "home" was vitiated because they themselves and their culture were almost completely destroyed.

At issue here is a history of relations between Anglos and those of Mexican descent that echoes the themes of displacement and containment, both elements common to colonialism. We begin with those twenty-seven or so indigenous people who came to the Presidio from Mexico and who were later joined in Santa Barbara by many more Mexicans. Now, a century and a half later, the city is 38 percent Latino, largely of Mexican descent. The story we are going to tell concerns how the first to arrive became "the last" as wealth was divested from one group and accumulated by another. We want the reader to become aware of the pattern of "disappearing" others that is foundational to American cities' histories.

In 1782 fifty-five men, along with some wives and children, arrived at this location to build the Presidio under the Spanish flag. Half of these men were Spanish. They and their flag provide the basis of Santa Barbara's celebration of its Spanish origins. The other half, now largely forgotten, consisted of people listed as "mestizo" (born to a Spanish man and an Indian woman), "coyote" (born to a mestizo and an Indian), or "Indian" (i.e., indigenous). The Spanish conquerors of Mexico created an extremely elaborate caste system based on skin color. Faced with an impressive array of developed cultures—Aztec, Maya, Chimu, Aymara, Inca, and Chibcha— the Spanish set about performing "the homogenizing task on which colonialism depended in order to abruptly disinherit a multitude of people from their specific cultures—their languages, customs, and achievements" (Quijano 2000, 551–552). The soldiers who came to Santa Barbara in 1782 were enlisted to extend the Spanish empire up the coast. The pueblo, or town, was established across the street from the Presidio. It housed Mexican settlers who helped supply food and secure the area for the benefit of the Spanish crown.[2]

In 1821, Mexico gained its independence from Spain, and all Alta California came under Mexican rule. Santa Barbara's claim to a Spanish history is thus limited to thirty-nine years and to a handful of men and families. Most of the residents during this period, including rancheros, were Native Americans and mestizos from Mexico.

While there were distinct social classes before the United States annexed Santa Barbara, there was also a marked "cohesiveness, solidarity, and common tradition" that was enhanced by baptism and the accompanying *compadrazgo* system of godparents (Camarillo 1996, 12). In the first half of the nineteenth century, many came north from Sonora, Mexico, to work in the California mines; before long, they were displaced by a law discriminating against nonwhites. Many then settled in the Santa Barbara area.

In 1848, after a short war used as a pretext for a massive land grab (see chapter 1), the United States bought from Mexico much of what is now California, New Mexico, Colorado, Arizona, and Texas. Many Mexicans were basically trapped in territory that now belonged to the United States, which explains why some Mexicans say, "We did not cross the border; the border crossed us."

Prominent figures including Emerson, Thoreau, Grant, and Lincoln denounced the 1846–1848 war, but the annexation of formerly Mexican land continued apace. The aggressors' speculative greed for more land was fueled by the rhetoric of Manifest Destiny (and by the earlier Monroe Doctrine). This ideology acted like a magic wand, making the worst human aggressions appear a blessed part of some divine unfolding. The war was justified on the pretext of protecting Texans, but only a half-dozen of the Alamo's defenders had been in Texas for more than six years (Acuña 2000). The American soldiers were badly controlled by their commanders, and many committed atrocities with abandon. Among the acts of brutality were many fueled by outright prejudice against Catholics, including violence against nuns and priests. They were moved, it seems, not only by a sense of unbridled entitlement but also by a conjoined sense of superiority that forged the conquest. Scalping Mexicans, raping women, and murdering civilians of all ages and both genders occurred routinely, with the slaughter often constituting mass murder. Even Mexican allies of the United States "became disillusioned by the harsh reality of American rule," saying Mexicans were being treated "worse than brutes" (Rodriguez 2007, 105). While the infamous Texas Rangers were a particularly brutal and racist force that terrorized those of Mexican descent in Texas, the latter group fared little better in California, where they were commonly robbed, beaten, and even lynched in the mining camps by 1849 (Rodriguez 2007). In Texas and California alike, many Anglos made no differentiation between Mexicans with U.S. citizenship and those without it, treating all Mexicans as migrants, even if their families had antedated Anglo presence. This was also true in Santa Barbara.

American history in the Southwest gained gringos a highly dubious reputation: first, for the "stealing" of a half-million square miles of Mexican land (the federal government paid $15 million for the present-day states of California, New Mexico, and Nevada and parts of Colorado, Arizona, Utah, and Oklahoma); and second, for the state-sponsored plan to empty Texas of Mexicans, which spawned a campaign of terrorization intended to force Mexicans southward. Anglos took land, rivers, gold, silver, zinc, copper, uranium, and ports on the Pacific.

Nicholas Trist was sent to Mexico in 1847 as a peace commissioner. Before Trist began peace negotiations, however, President James K. Polk ordered the commissioner back home, having decided he wanted more land from Mexico. He wanted to send a tougher negotiator than Trist. Trist, with the support of General Winfield Scott, decided to continue. "The negotiations were difficult for Trist. He was aware of Mexicans' humiliation and felt a strong sense of embarrassment. Trist himself knew that the war had been a pretext to seize Mexican land" (Acuña 2000, 51).

Trist wrote to a friend of the family upon his return: "If those Mexicans . . . had been able to look into my heart at that moment, they would have found that the sincere shame that I felt as a North American was stronger than theirs as Mexicans. Although I was unable to say it at the time, it was something that any North American should be ashamed of" (quoted in Acuña 2000, 52). In 1859, Juan Cortina, protesting the oppression of Mexicans in and around Brownsville, Texas, called Anglos "tyrants" and "flocks of vampires in the guise of men" (in Acuña 2000, 67). This history of usurpation, violent displacement, and terror is still being suppressed in the United States, most recently in Arizona, where books detailing this history have been banned from the public schools.

Denigration of the First by the Last

While Santa Barbara was the "stronghold of Mexican socioeconomic and political influence in nineteenth-century southern California" (Camarillo 1996, 3), this stronghold was gradually dismantled. From 1847 to 1848, the United States Army occupied Santa Barbara. While no combat took place, there was "a pattern of racial conflict that became ingrained in Santa Barbara society" (ibid., 13). The main occupation force "created intense racial antagonisms" (ibid., 14). The Mexicans resented the soldiers' disrespectful behavior, their destruction of Mexican private property, and their punishment of the whole community for a crime that was presumed to be committed by a single Mexican, though never even proved as such. Some of these soldiers became private citizens and were believed to have contributed to racial enmity (Camarillo 1996).

In 1850, Anglos constituted 20 percent of the population. They did not care about the meticulous divisions the Spanish had made between those of Spanish descent, of Indian descent, and their commixture, the mestizos. The Spanish found themselves victims of an American version of their own racial misogyny. The Anglo newcomers were unable to imagine those who had settled before them—Spanish or Mexican—as part of the future of their newly claimed town. Indeed, before any actual encounters between potential neighbors could have occurred, Anglos already believed that they were bringing progress and that whatever they presumed to be Mexican would be in the way of it. Such was the hierarchical model of civilizations that gave kudos to Anglos even as it stripped other cultures of their unique strengths and modes of sophistication.

One of the new settlers, Charles Huse, editor of the *Santa Barbara Gazette*, referred to Mexicans in his diary: "[The] dregs of society are collected in this town. . . . The greatest part of the population is lazy, does not work, does not pay its debts, does not keep its word, is full of envy, of ill will, of cunning, craft and fraud, falsehood and ignorance" (quoted in Camarillo 1996, 15). The gazette published Anglo attacks against Mexican society while it promoted the Americanization and anglicization of Santa Barbara. In 1855 the editors wrote that the Mexican residents were "habitually and universally opposed to all progress whatsoever, and they look with decided disfavor on every innovation." They considered Mexicans to be an "impediment to the development of the city as a desirable home for Anglos" (16). The editors joined the Know-Nothing Party and partook in its nativism. Aided by Frémont veterans, they called for vigilante violence against "Californios," Spanish speakers residing in California before 1848, all of whom were branded as public menaces (Chalquist 2008). This use of the newspaper to discredit the native population is familiar to us from other colonialist efforts to remove a preexisting group of people in order to seize control of the political, economic, and social life of a locale. Once a population is sufficiently maligned, unseemly and even cruel removal strategies are made to appear more justifiable.

During the 1850s, racial antipathies ran high. Neither Anglos nor Californios sitting on juries would punish defendants of their own ethnicity. The gazette emphasized any crimes committed by Mexicans. The editors were infuriated that there was little enforcement of the Vagrancy Act, known as the Greaser Law, an anti-Mexican law enacted in 1855 in California. The law defined vagrants as "all persons who are commonly known as 'Greasers' or the issue of Spanish and Indian blood . . . and who go armed and are not peaceable and quiet persons" (quoted in Bender 2003, xiii).

Mob lynching was not unknown. In 1859, in nearby Carpinteria, Francisco Baidillo was accused of stealing a horse. Not only was he hanged, but his son was lynched as well. The perpetrators were not convicted, while the Mexicans who had beat the main perpetrator were (Camarillo 1996, 21). "Troops from Fort Tejon briefly occupied the city to prevent more killing; an officer noted that intolerance of the Californios was 'exceeding' and 'almost a monomania'" (Chalquist 2008, 303). Contemporary Anglos are largely unaware of how mob lynching was used in the United States to control and forcibly displace not only African American communities in the South but also Mexican communities in the Southwest. From 1848 to 1928, white mobs lynched at least 597 Mexicans in the United States, and from 1848 to 1860, at least 163 Mexicans were lynched in California (Carrigan 2003).

Seizure of Economic and Political Power

From 1863 to 1873, the balance of economic power between Anglos and Mexicans shifted as the cattle-ranching industry that had been the source of Mexican rancheros' prosperity was undermined. American courts contested Californios' claims to their land. Fighting the dispossession of their lands was costly in legal expenses. Extended litigation often resulted in Anglo lawyers entrusted with these cases owning the land as payment for their legal fees. New land taxes forced many rancheros to sell their land cheaply. As the mining camps in the north disbanded, the need for beef diminished. In addition to a succession of floods and droughts that also weakened the cattle industry, Anglos began to import their beef from Texas, depriving their Mexican neighbors of income (Camarillo 1996). As a result, many rancheros had to mortgage their lands to Anglos. Anglos began to squat on many of the extensive tracts of land. When rancheros no longer had the economic means to pursue ranching, some simply left their ranches, yielding their land to Anglo squatters. Through these means Anglo agricultural interests replaced cattle and sheep ranches, undermining Mexican rancheros' livelihood. As a result, poverty and hunger set in for many, particularly during the floods and droughts of 1863–1865. Many were reduced to subsistence farming on rented land. As a result of these varied tactics, rancheros and landowners were converted into agricultural fieldworkers and railway construction workers. Mexicans were relegated to the lowest rungs of labor, where there was little possibility of moving into more skilled categories—a situation that still obtains today.

Anglo capital investment from northern California and the rest of the United States began to reach Santa Barbara after the Civil War, taking advantage of the weakened economic circumstances of the Californios (Camarillo 1996). Anglos also became merchants and made an inroad into the economics of the area. Anglos with capital accumulated from their businesses bought up Californio-owned lands. The ranches were split up and subdivided, luring other Anglos west to own a plot of land. Land speculation thrived. As Anglos entrenched themselves in the skilled labor market, they gained further assets to accumulate land and property, pushing more Californios into the lower economic rungs.

In 1873, the boom created by Anglos' westward migration to Santa Barbara ended. The downturn in the economy most affected those Mexicans who had sold their lands at a low point and then later tried to buy land at much higher prices. Now they were broke.

In 1878 the *Santa Barbara Daily Press* blamed Mexicans for hurting the economy by refusing to accept marginal work (Chalquist 2008). Anglos felt that Chicanos, given their destitution, should be willing to accept any job at a low wage. The victims of economic disfranchisement were now viewed as lazy and irresponsible. Those of Mexican descent wanted to remain in their traditional jobs. While some did seasonal work elsewhere herding cattle, by 1880, 74.8 percent were unemployed. Their resistance had been strategically undermined. When the majority of Chinese workers were driven out of Santa Barbara in the 1870s, the Anglos turned to those of Mexican descent to fill these low-paid menial jobs. At first they resisted, but before long they realized they had no other options.

Joseph Johnson, the owner and editor of the *Santa Barbara Daily Press*, started the newspaper in order to promote three aims: the growth of tourism, the marketing of Santa Barbara as a place for white people to regain or further build their health, and the transformation of remaining ranches into agricultural tracts.[3] While immigrants from Sonora enlarged the Mexican community, the Anglo population was rising at a greater pace, fueling the takeover of both economic and political power.

Seizure of political power became the next battlefront for the newly arrived Anglos. As this fight ensued, racial conflict deepened in Santa Barbara. The editor Charles Huse lamented, "The Americans have very little influence in the elections, but in a few years they will have all the power and they won't consult the Californians [the Californios] about anything" (quoted in Camarillo 1996, 23).

Mexican politicos recognized the importance of keeping the political power that the Anglos were trying to seize. In an attempt to retain political power, Mexicans most often voted in a bloc. While Anglos split their vote between Republican and Democratic candidates, Mexicans voted Democratic. In order to defeat the Mexicans, an Anglo coalition across parties was created. In 1873, the election went Anglo, except for the county sheriff. Within twenty-five years of their arrival, Anglos had gained the reins of political power, and they still hold them today.

In 1874, the Anglos changed the voting and ward system so that the Californios could win only one seat on the city council. Thanks to the gerrymandering, there was never again a mayor of Mexican descent, and contenders for other positions were consistently defeated by the Anglos. This made it increasingly hard to rally the Mexican vote, for political involvement began to appear fruitless. In 1880, Mexicans were purged from county Democratic proceedings. They were locked out of political affairs, becoming, says Camarillo, foreigners in their own city. "Without political, judicial, or law enforcement representatives the Chicano people were defenseless against Anglo racism" (Camarillo 1996, 76). Chicanos were not placed on juries, and they received harsh sentences if convicted of a crime. Anglos who assaulted Mexicans were not prosecuted. Seventy percent of the arrests and convictions reported in the *Santa Barbara Daily Press* involved people with Spanish surnames.

In the late Mexican and early American period, from 1840 to the 1880s, the Presidio and the area around it went from being "the heart of a Mexican pueblo to an antiquated neighborhood" (Schultz et al. 1993, 1). Mexican adobes were demolished to make way for wood structures. In the last two decades of the nineteenth century, Anglos thought that Mexicans were disappearing, but they were not leaving town. They were disappearing from sight as the area of their pueblo shrank. Camarillo describes Mexicans as a segregated minority confronted by a hostile outside world. Anglos rarely traveled the alleyways of the Pueblo Viejo. There was little commingling of the two communities. The "wall" between Anglos and those of Mexican descent was largely in place. Racial and ethnic differences were now conflated with a stark—and intentionally created—economic and class divide, a situation that still obtains.

The incorporation of Mexicans and Chicanos into the capitalist labor market had a profound effect on traditional family work roles and family structure. By the 1880s, their desperate economic situation forced women and children to become laborers for the first time, the former as domestic help and both as agricultural laborers. The children would miss much of the school year because of their involvement in agricultural labor. In the summer, families would go north to Goleta and sleep in the fields as they harvested walnuts. The mothers would forage to feed their children. The growers made sizable profits, for their labor costs were only 1 percent of their operating budgets.

Racism and Economic Marginalization

Albert Memmi (1991), in his classic study of the psychological dynamics of colonization, describes racism as a daily ingredient of colonial relations. Redefining "the other" as inferior legitimates all manner of abuses as understandable and necessary or even "helpful" and charitable to those harmed. This process of racist definition of the other is clear in Santa Barbara. The mestizos in Santa Barbara were no longer referred to as Californios or Californians, a term that described their families as part of the original settlers; now they were called "Mexicans." The Anglos saw even those with citizenship as interlopers. Some, in order to escape a racist net, attempted to emphasize or claim Spanish origins at a time when things Spanish struck a romantic chord with Anglos. The homogenizing logic that the Spaniards had first imposed on many different cultural groups in Mexico ended up being used against anyone of Spanish descent. Anglos gathered Spanish, Mexican, and indigenous into the same racist net.

Mexicans and Mexican Americans suffered from Anglo stereotypes of them as "'an idle, indolent, sleepy set'; an 'illiterate . . . wasteful people,' who were also 'shiftless and indigent, little caring for work, and not given to progress' . . . unsanitary 'riffraff'" (quoted in Camarillo 1996, 77). The Anglos now viewed all Mexicans as foreigners, even though many of their families had been in Santa Barbara long before the arrival of Anglos. The Mexicans now saw themselves as residing within an Anglo society.

In the 1890s, the Ku Klux Klan established a small chapter in Santa Barbara. In the 1920s, it reemerged with great enthusiasm. Over four hundred Klansmen were initiated in Santa Barbara and Ventura in 1923. In Santa Barbara, the chapter boasted that its members were "of the highest standing, being composed of preachers, doctors, lawyers, bankers, merchants, in fact, men of every walk of life" (quoted in Camarillo 1996, 193). It also included policemen, business executives, and public officials. It took pride in members being 100 percent native born and Protestant. It wanted to eliminate "Jews, Negroes, and Catholics" from Santa Barbara (quoted in Camarillo 1996, 194). While there were few Jews and African Americans in Santa Barbara, most Chicanos were Catholic, and the Klan clearly sought to terrorize that population. The Anglo community was sufficiently open to the Klan that its members felt no need to hide their faces during their rallies down State Street, Santa Barbara's main boulevard.

From 1890 through the 1920s, migrants came to Santa Barbara from the Mexican states of Guanajuato, Zacatecas, and Michoacán. They settled mainly on the east side of Santa Barbara, in a racially segregated neighborhood, living near their workplaces, which included the railroad yard, lumberyard, and fruit-packing establishments. Some worked on the train line to San Francisco; many others worked in the agricultural sector. More Mexican immigrants came northward, fleeing the worsening economic conditions in Mexico and the destruction caused by the revolution of 1910. Many Mexican immigrants did not know that, having been radically restricted over the last half of the nineteenth century, their opportunities in Santa Barbara were far from wide. Little by little, extended family members migrated from Mexico to join their family members.

Mexican Americans born in this country often did not mix with the new Mexican immigrants, fearing that Anglos would see them as "dirty Mexicans." The newcomers felt put off and discriminated against by the old-timers, who were resentful that the new influx of Mexicans had made finding and keeping jobs even more difficult. Hostility arose between the Eastside barrio and the Pueblo Viejo, the latter populated largely by the original families of mestizos who settled Santa Barbara. Horizontal aggressions developed between members of different waves of immigration, a basis of gang violence today in youths who have no sense of how a long history of racism and disfranchisement has affected their own behavior to others of Mexican descent.

In the 1900s, Anglos distinguished between groups of "Mexicans" according to skin color, excluding darker "Mexicans" from the community swimming pool, Los Baños. Darker "Mexicans" were also segregated from Anglos in movie theaters. Local Baptists tried to convert the "Mexicans" to Protestantism, while simultaneously segregating their church services (Camarillo 1996).

Ninety percent of Santa Barbara's Chicanos lived in the Pueblo Viejo by 1890. The Anglo city that grew up around it was experienced as a foreign city (Camarillo 1996). By the 1890s, those of Mexican descent had dwindled to 20 percent of the overall Santa Barbara population. City resources were not shared equitably with the barrio. The barrio school was decrepit. There were no fire hydrants. The adobes were run down. Poverty was widespread, requiring the county to provide some assistance until charities were set up to address it, at least in part. A diphtheria outbreak struck the Mexican barrio.

Leonard Pitt (1970) succinctly described the process and the end result:

> Yankee settlers then swept in by the tens of thousands, and in a matter of months and years overturned the old institutional framework, expropriated the land, imposed a new body of law, a new language, a new economy, and a new culture, and in the process exploited the labor of the local population whenever necessary. To certain members of the old ruling class these settlers awarded a token and symbolic prestige, at least temporarily; yet with that status went very little genuine authority. In the long run Americans simply pushed aside the earlier ruling elite as being irrelevant. (296)

By 1900, Chicanos were locked into occupational structures "that not only restricted their opportunities for advancement but perpetuated their poverty as well. Although they formed the largest single sector of the manual labor market that was indispensable in building the region's economic prosperity, they did not themselves benefit financially" (Camarillo 1996, 100).

The walnut growers in Goleta, as well as other businessmen, used seasonal child labor because it was cheaper. This practice, which began in the 1880s, meant that children missed school during certain periods, leading authorities to shut one school. In 1911, the California Labor Commission cited the walnut growers for violations of child-labor laws. The compromise decision permitted any family that could plead hardship to send their children to work the groves. Many families needed to plead such hardship. Not only had they been assigned to the lowest labor rung, but they were paid half what Anglos were paid for doing comparable work. Wage differentials and contract-labor arrangements made it impossible for Mexican workers to ascend the ladder of economic viability. When assigned to the same job as white counterparts, they were given the more difficult tasks and then not promoted. Confined to the most menial of tasks and the lowest wages, Mexican families found it largely impossible to improve their living conditions.[4]

Mexicans were precluded from entering into certain professions, such as carpentry. Even if a man left the city and trained elsewhere, joining the relevant union, this did not ensure him a job and union membership on his return to Santa Barbara. Length of residence or number of years on a job made no difference; Chicano workers were not advanced in the workplace. They were consigned to a lowly socioeconomic position. The economic system that required a permanent low-paid laboring class perpetuated the patterns of Chicano employment far into the twentieth century (Camarillo 1996).

World War I introduced a labor shortage across the United States, one that lingered. New immigrant families came to Santa Barbara from Durango, Chihuahua, and Sonora. Mutual aid societies, or *mutualistas*, were created to support families and to provide sociality and help during difficult times. The need for Mexican workers increased in construction and agriculture, but the jobs open to them were unskilled or semiskilled, locking them into the bottom of the labor market. During the 1920s, the standard of living fell still further for those of Mexican descent, with infant mortality rising to five times that of white infants. Most Mexican families could not own their own houses, and many could not afford rents of ten to fifteen dollars a month, the average for housing on the East Side. This forced multiple families into single dwellings, sometimes with ten families sharing a toilet. Living conditions were unsanitary and overcrowded. Small children scavenged in refuse and garbage to find food and playthings. Even in the early part of the century, there was a labor line forming off Haley Street where the unemployed waited for daily work.

From Social Exclusion to Extrusion and Deportation

Once the wall of social, political, and economic exclusion was complete, the steps toward social extrusion were also largely complete. Indeed, in the last decade, we have again witnessed how quickly American society can turn on Mexicans, on whom they have relied for many essential services, as well as amenities. As long as social, economic, and political walls surround groups of our neighbors, the latter are at risk of removal, be it through deportation, detention, or imprisonment.

As poverty increased, Anglos began trying to rid the community of Mexicans and Mexican Americans. Poverty-based deportations began in 1926 and intensified during the Depression. The first included a mother and her four children. The rationale was that indigent Mexicans created a burden on the welfare lists, an argument that has been made down to the present day. The charge was untrue, according to Camarillo (1996). The percentage of Chicanos on the welfare list only slightly exceeded their percentage of the population. The elderly placed the greatest burden on the coffers.

Interpreters at the East Side Social Center aided immigration agents in their deportation efforts. They encouraged people to leave for Mexico, often painting a pretty but false picture of what would await them in Mexico and even lying to them by saying that southbound immigrants would be offered land and supplies in Baja California. Many of those who voluntarily left for Mexico later tried to return. Between 1926 and 1934, between one thousand and two thousand people—that is, 200 to 250 families—were deported. Mexican workers had worked for many years in the railway yard in Santa Barbara. Now they were to find themselves back in that yard being deported in a humiliating fashion. Mary Ortega, an interpreter at the East Side Social Center, recalled the scene: "[The immigration officials] put all the people that went in boxcars instead of inside the trains. . . . They sent a lot of people from around here too. A big exodus. . . . They were in here legally but the moral part of it, like separation and putting them in boxcars, . . . I'll never forget as long as I live" (quoted in Camarillo 1996, 163). Many of those deported, particularly those who had been born here and were citizens, returned in the 1930s and 1940s. Tens of thousands of Mexicans and their U.S.-born children were deported from Southern California in the wake of the Depression, and over one million from the United States. These deportations weakened the Eastside Mexican community, separating people from their friends and families. It temporarily halted the growth of the Chicano community in Santa Barbara during a critical phase of its history. It certainly contributed to the community's sense of itself as little respected and as ultimately expendable and discardable.

During World War II the United States facilitated the immigration of 4.5 million Mexicans to meet wartime labor shortages. Once servicemen returned to the domestic labor market, attempts were made to deport the Mexicans. Operation Wetback was a repatriation effort that modeled itself on the Mexican repatriation during the Depression. Throughout postwar America, agents searched neighborhoods for these immigrants, ultimately deporting over 1.1 million Mexicans, who were often taken into the interior of Mexico in an effort to hinder their return.

When Chicanos' labor was needed, the status of their documents was ignored. When their labor was no longer needed, they were deemed a social threat (Camarillo 1996). Denying legal status allows employers to use workers as they desire, without moral constraints. Until the 1960s, you could see signs throughout the Southwest that said "No dogs or Mexicans."

This is a shameful history. Unfortunately, it is not over.

Miseducation and the Transgenerational Perpetuation of Walls

In 1933, Carter Woodson wrote *The Mis-Education of the Negro*, describing how American schools prepared Negroes to assume inferior positions in society. He could have been describing the situation for children of Mexican descent in the town of Carpinteria, the town next to Santa Barbara. The following account is drawn from research done by John McCafferty, author of *Aliso School: "For the Mexican Children."*[5]

Looking back on the opening in 1919 of Mexican-only classes at the Aliso School, an Anglo newspaper, the *Carpinteria Herald*, described it as "the first step on behalf of the Mexican population. . . . This gave those Mexican children who would find it difficult to keep apace with the American children an opportunity to receive more individual instruction" (quoted in McCafferty 2008, 19). These were ungraded classes, for, it was claimed, Mexican children were unable to make age-appropriate progress. By 1922, the Aliso School was completely segregated, with all Mexican students in two classrooms. Most of the children were in grades one to five. Not until 1931 did any Mexican child make it to high school in Carpinteria. The elementary school functioned as a funnel into work in the lemon groves. Poor education based on racist notions of the children's limitations created a cheap labor pool even as it yielded "proof" of the group's supposed inferiority.

In 1925, the Carpinteria school board directed the principal to arrange the schedule of the children so they could harvest walnuts in the afternoons during walnut-packing season. There was no such directive for the Anglo students at Main School. Anglos saw the Mexican neighborhoods as labor camps and the children as destined to move from part-time to full-time employment in the agricultural sector.

From 1920 to 1947, the Mexican children who did not speak English were educated apart from the Anglo children. At school they were required to speak only English, a language many did not know. If they were caught speaking Spanish, they were spanked or struck with rulers. Chicano students in Goleta, a nearby community, enjoyed an integrated school setting; when compared to this otherwise similar group, Aliso's pupils showed less English-language proficiency. They lived in a Spanish-speaking world where the only native speakers of English were their teachers, whereas Goleta's children had Anglo children in their classrooms. The segregation was neither de facto (by location) or de jure (by law). It was one of the last racially segregated schools in California.

In the late 1920s, the Aliso School became progressively overcrowded. The class time of the younger students was cut to make room for the older students. In 1931, Assemblyman George R. Bliss, of Carpinteria, introduced a bill to the California legislature that would have legalized the segregation of Mexican and Mexican American students in all California primary and secondary public schools. Bliss, a school-board member, wanted the state to use the same logic that had been followed in establishing Carpinteria's segregated schools—namely, to think of Mexican and Mexican American children as Indians, whether born in the United States or not. Schools already had the power to segregate Indian children.

Mexican children were in fact called "Indians." One father, Joe Montoya, moved from Santa Barbara to Carpinteria and wanted his children to remain in integrated schooling. His children were assigned to Aliso. He protested to the state's attorney general, but the latter supported the prevailing arrangement. While the town awaited the verdict, the *Carpinteria Herald* reported: "[T]he action of Montoya has caused Carpinterians to pause and ponder over the multitudinous things that have been done for our Indian population[,] and it is likely there will be a reduction in the misplaced benevolence." The Anglo press responded to Montoya's legitimate objection with the threat of reprisals against the Mexican population.

When Mexican American servicemen returned from fighting in World War II, their consciousness of civil rights was heightened. Finally, in 1947, the district was pressed to integrate, as the winds of change were blowing in California for increased civil rights for Mexicans. The board decided this privately and never publicly discussed its rationale; it simply complied with a letter sent by the district attorney.[6] In a case tried in Orange County in 1947, a judge ruled that Mexican American students who were considered Caucasian could not be segregated. Until 1954, California law allowed the segregation of Indians, African Americans, and Asians.

CONTEMPORARY EXPLOITATION AND CONTROL

In Santa Barbara today, the Anglos' presence, as well as their social, political, and economic control, has been so normalized that most people—Anglo, Chicano, and Mexican—do not know about a time when no Anglos lived there; indeed, they probably never imagine such a period. There is no boast of an Anglo victory, because the conquests of an earlier era are not even remembered. Comfortable in this amnesia, Anglos rarely grasp the pain of exclusion and prejudice that Mexicans and Mexican Americans experience daily.

Today the classrooms of many of the public schools are de facto segregated. Most are predominantly Latino. Many white families have fled to private schools or to more exclusive "gate" or charter programs within the public schools. Neighborhoods are largely segregated. Many churches are still almost wholly Anglo or wholly Mexican/Mexican American. While almost every business in Santa Barbara depends on Mexican labor, Anglo employers and Chicano and Mexican employees maintain a social distance. Anglo and Latino families rarely socialize. Wages are still not comparable and fair.

Federal and state policies place additional burdens on families without proper immigration documents. In California an immigrant without documents cannot get a driver's license. To compound these injuries, the county increasingly derives funding from impounding the cars of immigrants who have been stopped at checkpoints purportedly established to find drunk drivers; the cars are seized not because the drivers are intoxicated but because they cannot produce a valid license. Until recently, these cars were impounded for thirty days, costing over $1,000 to retrieve. Many impounded cars are abandoned, for their owners fear being apprehended by Department of Homeland Security agents. The cars are then sold, the profits going to the county. Adults are left without cars to get to work or to take their children to school. It is important to understand how maintaining a population in a state of illegality creates profits for individuals, municipalities, and the federal government. It has been argued that the practice just described is an unconstitutional measure, an "unreasonable seizure" of private property.

Once at work, those without documents cannot safely argue for fair wages and work conditions. Without owning land, without a path to citizenship, without equal wages, without ways to climb the job ladder, without access to adequate scholarships for college, and without adequate health care—without any of these things, a population is restricted in its possibilities for advancement. While this works out well for employers who want the cheapest labor and for consumers who desire cheap goods and services, it also provides all the ingredients for maintaining a permanent underclass. Access to the labor of an underclass allows income gaps to deepen, as well as a seemingly unbridgeable abyss to form between those who have been able to accumulate capital and those who are living hand to mouth.

The immigrant community in Santa Barbara calls the Secure Communities program ("S-Comm") of the Department of Homeland Security "The

Insecure Communities Program." An editorial in the *New York Times* (May 11, 2011) remarks,

> [This is an] ill-conceived program . . . which sends arrested people's fingerprints through federal immigration databases, turning all local officers and jails into arms of the Department of Homeland Security. Many lawmakers and police agencies say it erodes public safety by making immigrants, especially victims of domestic violence, afraid to report crimes. They worry about giving rogue officers a convenient tool for racial profiling. And they feel betrayed because what the administration once billed as a transparent, voluntary program aimed only at dangerous convicted criminals turns out to be none of those things.

Under this initiative, approximately four hundred thousand immigrants were deported each year in 2010, 2011, and 2012. In 2011, there were ten to fifteen deportations a week from Santa Barbara County.[7] Santa Barbara was the sixth community in California to opt into this program. There was no public process of deciding this, no discussion of the merits of the measure.

When you are stopped in Santa Barbara for a relatively minor traffic infraction, such as having a broken headlight or changing lanes without signaling, your identification and your fingerprints are checked against not only Department of Motor Vehicle databases but also federal immigration ones. If you lack the legal status to be in the United States yet are innocent of the charge for which you are arrested, the Department of Homeland Security has seventy-two hours to take you into custody. Once this happens, you are placed in a detention center, and paperwork is readied for your deportation. More than half of those deported last year have no criminal records, or committed only minor crimes. Many of the deportees have children at home, some of whom are U.S. citizens. These children often depend on the deportee's income for their physical survival, not to mention his or her presence for their emotional well-being. So many parents have been deported in California that orphanages have been created in Lancaster and Sacramento to house minors left behind after raids swept up their parents. In Santa Barbara, 58 percent of S-Comm deportations have been of noncriminals.[8]

Family members left behind live each day with heightened anxiety. They worry that they should move because now the Border Patrol has their address. Yet leaving would make it difficult for family members to find them, particularly sons and daughters who were deported as minors. This program of close surveillance has compromised community policing. People are afraid to call police when they are needed, as in cases of domestic violence. Indeed, they are often counseled not to do so, since both parties may well be arrested. They are aware that if they are arrested and taken into custody, their fingerprints will be run through Immigration and Customs Enforcement (ICE). Even if they are not convicted of the offense for which they were arrested, they may be deported.

Daniel Kanstroom, author of *Deportation Nation: Outsiders in American History*, describes deportation as a "powerful instrument of discretionary social control, . . . a mechanism of scapegoating, ostracism, family and community separation, and, of course, banishment" (2007, 5). The fear of arrest, detention, and deportation serves to force many in the Latino community into ever-greater invisibility. A mother recently broke down when she recounted an argument with her sixteen-year-old son, who wanted to go downtown for the evening. The mother did not want him to risk being stopped by the police and then possibly deported to Mexico, where he had not been since he was two years old. She knew of families who could no longer locate a teenage child who had been taken into custody. Sometimes these minors are transferred to detention facilities in other states and have no reliable way for their families to find them. Essentially left to their own devices, they have no one to advocate on their behalf, and they face the very real threat of deportation to some place in Mexico where they do not know anyone; indeed, since many have been raised in the United States, they may not even speak Spanish very well. At the same time, families caught in such circumstances are afraid to pursue their children, fearing their own detention and thus separation from other children remaining at home.

Recent "gang injunctions" add to the anxiety besetting Santa Barbara's immigrant community. Young persons named in such an injunction cannot be outside in their neighborhoods in the company of other gang members (including close relatives) or in any park, on the waterfront, or on State Street. Chavo Romero, of the Oxnard-based advocacy group Todo Poder al Pueblo, says that the message is clear: "Disappear, leave town, or go away to jail or deportation."[9]

INTERNAL COLONIES: COLONIAL PRACTICES CLOSE TO HOME

If you study colonialism in various locations—Ireland, the Congo, South Africa—you will no doubt notice pernicious patterns. It can be shocking that a few people with excessive relative power can go to another people's home territory and, within a short number of years, hold almost all economic and political control. That the newcomers can outlaw the original people's languages, religions, and customs is nothing short of breathtaking.

That they can remove people from their land, force them to pay taxes and rent, appropriate their labor, and bring them to submission through terror and violence is aberrant and abhorrent. That people who have been self-sufficient can quickly and collectively be reduced to poverty, subservience, and dependency is bad enough. That their reduction to an inferior mode of life is then used as evidence to justify the harshness of the exploitation and racism imposed on them is almost unspeakable. This process of colonization makes the newcomers the citizens and those who were present at the beginning the interlopers. Indeed, it often forces those initially present to leave, to migrate elsewhere. As the native population dwindles and those from abroad multiply, history is rewritten, and soon most of those now present give little thought to the period of injustice and violence that paved the way for the kinds of excess privileges they now enjoy.

Colonizers have been forced out of the lands they seized; it has happened, for example, in Kenya and India. Elsewhere, however, the settlers crowded out the surviving earlier groups, settling into a fixed cultural and historical amnesia. Many Anglos would like to think that this colonial treatment happened far away, that it is now over, that our families had nothing to do with it, and that our own lives are made relatively easy and pleasant by dint of our own hard work and responsibility. I wish it were so, but it is not.

Three groups have, above all others, been subjected to extensive colonial practices in the United States: African Americans, Native Americans, and Mexicans. In differentiating immigration from colonization, the sociologist Bob Blauner defines three factors. The first is an effort to make "colonized groups become part of a new society through force or violence; they are conquered, enslaved, or pressured into movement" (Blauner 2001, 46). This distinguishes them from immigrant groups, whose members enter voluntarily, even though the conditions in their homeland may have made migration a necessity. The second is the imposition of "various forms of unfree labor that greatly restrict the physical and social mobility of the group and its participation in the political arena. The third is a cultural policy of the colonizer that constrains, transforms, or destroys original values, orientations, and ways of life" (ibid.). Anglo Santa Barbarans do not think of their city as an "internal colony," but that term is an altogether appropriate description. The original Mexican and Spanish populations were almost literally encircled by a rising Anglo population. The latter group seized land as well as political, economic, and social power. It outlawed the Spanish language in schools and restricted or eliminated pastimes that were part of Mexican culture. It failed to fairly allocate city resources. Terror and fear—produced through lynchings, vigilantes, and KKK activity—were used to control the population. Racial and ethnic stereotyping were used to justify the demeaning treatment of Chicanos and Mexican immigrants. While their labor was exploited, their full personhood was denied. Unfortunately, Mexican newcomers were assimilated not into the larger Santa Barbara society but into the internal colony, with all its deprivations and restrictions on economic mobility and political power. Today, others from still further south join them: migrants from Guatemala, El Salvador, Brazil, and elsewhere.

The concept of internal colonialism helps us to understand why African Americans, Native Americans, and Mexicans have not met the success many immigrant groups have achieved in the United States. Native Americans resisted the slave agrarian labor into which the Spanish mission system sought to press them. Their resistance to colonization was so great that they were subjected to massive displacement from their home regions, and their numbers were vastly reduced though genocidal policies. African Americans and many Mexicans were relegated to agricultural labor, with the ladder to other, more upwardly mobile work positioned out of their reach. After the Civil War, many African Americans became sharecroppers and tenant farmers, but they were often pressed back into servitude through racist vagrancy laws and other unjust paths to imprisonment that siphoned them into convict agrarian labor pools—"slavery by another name" (Blackmon 2009). Mexicans and Mexican Americans have experienced a myriad of legal, economic, and social forces that have pushed them to the periphery of the working world and maintained them there, restricting them largely to unskilled labor. In addition, policies that withhold citizenship have placed twelve million Mexicans in an exceptional legal status, bereft of basic rights, including the right to representation (which is not part of current deportation proceedings).

IMAGINING THE FUTURE

Many Santa Barbara residents want to imagine their city differently. They want to see it as a city where the wisdom and decency of living wages are adopted throughout. Where each Latino child is helped to realize his or her promise. Where friendships are as common between Anglos and Latinos as they are among the members of each group. Where federal and state laws that cause fear and insecurity are protested and resisted. Where police practices that increase insecurity and economic precariousness are given up and genuine community policing is restored. They want their town to support its young adults in gaining the education for which they are ready to strive, whether they are citizens or youth brought as children to this country.

To achieve these ends, it would help for residents to be aware of their city's history and to grapple with its shame, particularly, in this case, the shame of Anglos at the amassing of fortunes from the labor of so many without more decisively and generously redistributing that wealth. Shame can be a creative emotion when it leads to restorative and reparative actions, as we shall see in chapters 7 and 8. When philanthropic activities proceed from a historical awareness of past injustices, they can act as reparations for a history that cannot be erased but that needs to be remembered and addressed with apology, justice, and compassion.

A skeptical Anglo might be thinking, "Well, my family wasn't from here. I had no part in this." But, allowing for variation, almost all the American towns and cities in which most of us grew up were cities of two or more tales. They were homes to those with adequate or excessive resources and to those struggling against the odds of poverty and miseducation. In most cases—even if not in all—this division was traced along racial and ethnic lines. When a city is unaware of its own history of marginalizing ethnic groups and displacing them—as has happened in Santa Barbara with the Chumash, Chinese, Japanese, African Americans, and Chicanos—it is more likely to mindlessly repeat these same patterns, blind to the way this reinscribes psychic and communal wounds. To learn and reflect on our history is the first step to reparation. Through intentional dialogue between Anglos and those of Mexican descent, we can come to understand more clearly how we continue to live the destructive divisions that consign us to being a city divided against itself by pernicious "walls." Chapter 9 summarizes some of the steps other cities have taken to address similar histories and to create more inclusive communities less fraught with economic and political injustice.

CHAPTER 6

Juan Crow

The American Ethnoracial Caste System and the Criminalization of Mexican Migrants

> There are people who say, the laws say that a person who crosses [the border] is a criminal. It's more criminal to let your children starve to death. If I have to lose my life, at least I wanted to try rather than let my children die of hunger.
>
> Clara, quoted in Brabeck, Lykes, and Hershberg,
> "Framing Immigration to and Deportation from the United States"

We are caught in a centrifuging process. In neoliberal globalization—neocolonialism—those who accumulate capital are spun apart from those whose labor is necessary for this amassing. This is happening at an ever-faster speed and intensity. It manufactures an almost unbridgeable gulf between the experiences of the privileged and those of the undercaste they rely on. As trade barriers between countries are dismantled, local economies are disrupted, forcing many to migrate. This has turned whole regions, as well as segregated areas within and around cities, into pockets of poverty and zones of sacrifice (Hedges 2012). Both race and ethnicity have been inexorably linked to the unjust division of labor and thus to a caste-like existence in the lowest socioeconomic class. Speaking of African Americans, Kenneth Clark (1965, 11) described "dark ghettos" as "social, political, educational, and—above all—economic colonies. Their inhabitants are subject people, victims of the greed, cruelty, insensitivity, guilt and fear of their masters." Such is the plight of economically and politically dispossessed Mexicans in the United States, many of whom speak of their lives as *esclavizante*, enslaving (Wong 2006, 43).

Cities throughout the United States have created internal colonies of Mexicans and Mexican Americans. Whole regions can also be likened to internal colonies where the American racial and ethnic caste system manufactures the racialized underclass that has characterized U.S. society since its beginnings. This pernicious "creation" is accomplished through constriction of occupations, predatory financial practices, unjust laws, miseducation, disfranchisement, the withholding of human rights, the engendering of discourse that begins in pernicious "othering" and ends in criminalization of a racialized group, imprisonment, and psychic colonization. The effects of these practices on children are particularly pernicious and destructive, not only for the children themselves, but for our common future as a society. The dominant narrative of American hospitality toward immigrants and the freedom of opportunity for them to rise into the middle class is mostly false for Mexicans and Mexican Americans in the United States. Unless we understand how this situation is created and maintained, we cannot successfully construct a society of integrity, where narrative and reality are aligned for the sake of shared opportunities and increased recognition of human rights. These are the themes of this chapter as they pertain to those of Mexican descent, particularly migrants without documents.

Colonia/Colony: Colonized Settlements, Colonized Regions

> Here [in El Paso] the poor are considered as dangerous as those with a contagious disease.
>
> Olga Beatriz Torres, "Memories of My Journey, 1918"

In Mexico, the Spanish word *colonia* refers to all kinds of neighborhoods and settlements, both those that are resource-rich and those that are resource-poor. In the United States, the term has taken on a more constricted meaning. In the U.S. law code (specifically, Title 42, chapter 8A, subchapter III, para. 1479), a colonia is defined as any identifiable community within 150 miles of the U.S.-Mexico border, in Arizona, California, New Mexico, or Texas, that was established as a colonia before November 28, 1990, and "is determined to be a colonia on the basis of objective criteria, including lack of potable water supply, lack of adequate sewage systems, and lack of decent, safe, and sanitary housing." It excludes metropolitan areas that have a population exceeding one million. A term that denotes a neighborhood is reduced to one that describes extremely poor, primarily Spanish-speaking settlements lacking adequate infrastructure to sustain healthy human living.

At the eastern extreme of the U.S.-Mexico border, in the counties around Brownsville, Texas, that lie in the Rio Grande Valley, the Spanish word *colonia* can be understood in two senses. This whole border region is described as a colonia, a colony, by Antonio Zavaleta, an anthropologist and director of the Texas Center for Border and Transnational Studies (personal communication, April 11, 2011). The same region is also composed of many colonias, poor neighborhoods or settlements, scattered on the outskirts of Brownsville and all along the border. Texas has approximately 2,300 colonias in the border region, home to approximately half a million residents. The actual number of residents is uncertain, however, for many were too frightened to join the 2010 census, fearful of deportation for immigration violations. Indeed, many are too frightened to leave their homes. These communities—primarily made up of Mexicans and Mexican Americans—are heavily surveilled by the Border Patrol. Their residents are burdened by the daily anxieties and insecurities such a situation breeds.

Jay Johnson-Castro (personal communication, 2011) calls the Rio Grande Valley "the bastard child of the state," its "dumping ground" for nuclear and toxic waste, and a site dotted by proliferating internment camps for desperate immigrants and refugees, such as the Willacy Detention Center in Raymondville, also called the United States' "largest concentration camp." Eliot Shapleigh (quoted in Johnson-Castro 2008) calculated that if the forty-three-county area that makes up the border region in Texas were made a separate state and then compared to interior Texas and to the other states, it would rank first in poverty and unemployment. It would be larger than thirty-five other states and have the highest percentage of people who speak Spanish in their homes. It would be the third-largest state with a foreign-born population, the sixth-fastest growing, and the last in average income.

Beginning in the 1950s, with agricultural land being exhausted by continuous crops of cotton, farm owners became eager for another way to profit from their land. Developers began to create unincorporated subdivisions using agriculturally worthless land or land that lay in floodplains. They surveyed and divided it into small plots and put in dirt roads. They provided no or little infrastructure, taking advantage of sparse zoning laws and lax enforcement. There were nebulous promises of infrastructure to come. They offered these plots to poor migrants and other poor people for a low down payment and a low monthly payment, but the buyers were not given title until the last payment was made. Due to these "contracts for deeds," many lots have been sold many times over, serving to increase already huge economic disparities between the landed and the landless. This system was familiar to Mexicans from an analogous hacienda system in Mexico.

Hidalgo County, where Brownsville is located, has the highest number of colonias in the United States. In 2011, 64 percent of the colonias' residents were Hispanic, and 85 percent of those under eighteen were citizens. These colonias exist outside the formal city and county structures and often lack basic infrastructure for running water, roads, electricity, sewer drainage, wastewater treatment, solid-waste disposal, clean water, and reliable transportation to places where jobs might be found. High unemployment and school dropout rates plague the region. Because 80 percent of the residents have no health insurance, prenatal care is poor, many chronic and even life-threatening diseases go untreated except in emergencies, and continuity of health care is almost nonexistent. "Health care" too often consists of nothing more than visits to a doctor volunteering one day a year in the back of a church or a community center. Emergency rooms treat immediate complications of serious diseases, such as diabetes, cancer, and heart disease, but do not address the underlying diseases, which fester without adequate medical intervention.

Emily Ramshaw reports on health issues in the colonias.

Water- and mosquito-borne illnesses are rampant, the result of poor drainage, pooling sewage and water contaminated by leaking septic tanks. Burning garbage, cockroaches, vermin and mold lead to high rates of asthma, rashes and lice infestations.

And the poor diet so intrinsically linked to poverty contributes to dental problems, diabetes and other chronic conditions, which residents of the colonias rarely have the health insurance, money or access to regular health care to treat, . . . rates of tuberculosis that are two times the state average and four times the national rate, and the lingering presence of Hansen's disease, or leprosy, almost unheard of in most of the country.

There are cases of Dengue fever and Lyme disease carried by mosquitoes and ticks, the result of flooding and non-air-conditioned homes where windows and doors stand open. There is the nagging asthma and bronchitis stemming from the agricultural dust that wafts from nearby sorghum, corn and cotton fields, and the trash burned in the colonias, which often have no waste collection. Public health departments report rates of cholera, hepatitis A, salmonellosis and dysentery in the colonias that far exceed the state average. (Ramshaw 2011, n.p.)

According to the U.S.-Mexico Border Environmental Health Initiative, the border region as a whole is plagued by poor air and water quality, residual agricultural pesticides, increases in soil salinities, and heavy metal contaminants.

These real problems have been used to construct Anglos' ideas about colonias as filthy and disease-ridden places where, it is alleged, the septic systems are often placed so close to hand-dug wells that people end up drinking their own sewage (Hill 2003). Indeed, Sarah Hill (2003) maintains that the highly publicized threat of disease crossing from colonias to more prosperous areas of the region has served to carve a sharp dividing line between an "us" and a "them," as well as inscribing and domesticating the word *colonia* in the Anglo imagination.

To the Anglo, the word *colonia* is no longer attached to the earlier meaning of "colony" as a place where local self-governance and the local economy have been forcibly disrupted by a foreign power that now uses the land and people for its own aggrandizement and profit. In fact, however, the lived reality of colonias cannot be understood apart from our grasp of the dynamics of neocolonialism and global capitalism. These colonias are examples of the euphemistic term "uneven development," where development for some is inextricably linked to underdevelopment and deprivation for others. The derogatory attributions made by Anglos about colonia residents float detached from any acknowledgment of the unethical business practices that planned and created the colonias and that have reaped (and continue to take) substantial profit from them. They also fail to acknowledge the wider racial caste system that generates the conditions found to be problematic.

The structure and purposes of a colony are not decided by those who reside in it. Indeed, these residents are not part of the local region's planning and visioning process. The purpose of a colony is to serve those with more power. Zavaleta (2011) says that the function of the Rio Grande Valley is to act as a buffer between Mexico and the rest of the United States. The buffer absorbs the influx of Mexican migrants and retains the majority of them. Internal checkpoints help to ensure that many Mexicans will remain in the Brownsville area and not enter the "real" United States. At the border with Mexico, the United States has created internal checkpoints throughout a ninety-mile radius. The repressive measures include policing airports, railroads, and bus stations, as well as making frequent traffic stops on major highways, where one must show documents if one happens to look like an officer's image of an "illegal alien."

These efforts to curtail the northward movement of Mexicans result in Brownsville's being supersaturated with poor Mexicans, "protecting" an anglicized America that sees Mexicans as threats to the economy and to white culture. It separates an extremely poor region from one less so, though the latter is still quite poor.

From the history of colonization, we can see that where there was a constant availability of workers, little or no care was given to their well-being. Zavaleta underscores the fact that there has not even been an expectation of, let alone a dedication to, developing industry and jobs for the people of Brownsville. Ironically, Brownsville is laced by a transportation infrastructure, a benefit of NAFTA that helps to bring manufactured goods from Mexico to the U.S. market; these highways and train systems cut through

Brownsville, however, bound for other destinations. They are there for products and the corporate profits they help to accrue, not for people. The unincorporated settlements, the colonias, often exist so far from adequate transportation that residents cannot get to jobs. Indeed, many residents report being marooned.

Some say ironically that the "industry" in Brownsville is poverty and even that Brownsville's "investment" has been in poverty. A high proportion of those with jobs work in the service sector, where continuing poverty enables them to remain. There is no ready coalition of people in power seeking to help the poor move out of poverty. A paucity of efforts to attract capital and businesses keeps people poor, which appears to be a tacit goal generally achieved. Because they remain poor, most Mexicans will never make it out of this county and get to other parts of the United States. They are treated by the United States as a throwaway population, useful only as a dense collection of brown bodies that prevents other brown bodies from getting through the membrane to the rest of the United States. We shall come to understand that poor people can mean big business for others. Nowhere is this more evident than in the rise of the detention and deportation industry, a subject we will soon broach.

The principal employer in this region is the Border Patrol. Their patrolling and policing activities are evident wherever you go. A few years ago, we were walking on a remote riverbank of the Rio Grande near Laredo, Texas. A very young white Border Patrol officer appeared seemingly out of nowhere and walked toward us. "How is your day going?" we asked him in a friendly manner. He answered in a serious and grim tone: "Well, we found a body in the river this morning." We said how sorry we were, imagining the trauma of the young man recovering the decaying body of an accidentally drowned migrant. "Oh, no," he reassuringly replied, reading the concern on our faces, "We [just] arrested someone." Here a young American speaks what he has been taught: a human being of Mexican descent is *a body*, dead or alive.

To many Anglos, Brownsville does not feel as though it is in the United States, yet neither does it have the liveliness of Mexican cities. Something different, outside the margins, has been created here: ghettoes of people who increasingly need to remain as invisible as possible because they lack documents. If the goal is to have a buffer of poor Mexicans that protects the rest of the Unites States from others' arrival, it is being realized right here.

The beltway of colonias surrounding border cities along the Rio Grande has its analogue in the outlying districts of European cities of former colonizing nations. Once the colonizing force has imposed its culture on others, those others and their descendants feel some affinity to the culture of their colonizer, even if ambivalently so. Algerians—so harshly repressed by French forces—now inhabit the far suburbs of French cities and struggle to have their own effects on French culture and debate. Intensive securitization marks these kinds of settlements on both sides of the Atlantic.

Blanca Villalpando (personal communication, 2011), working in the office of the Texas state legislature, describes the borderlands of Texas as the place where Mexican American culture has its American roots. From this area, some Chicanos manage to press through the protective membrane and spread to other parts of the United States, many sending money back to feed their relatives in the south. Those who do make it out of the Rio Grande Valley are often the most educated, with a resulting tragic "brain drain" that is steadily occurring in this region, leaving the rest to fend for themselves as well as they can.

National Guard soldiers, police, and the Border Patrol attempt to seal this breach. The effect is that Latino residents—largely of Mexican descent—cope with surveillance that directly intrudes into their daily lives. The United States has created out of this border region a funnel with gaps, Villalpando says, lacunae that aid human traffickers and drug runners. These days, drug-cartel violence on the southern side of the Rio Grande acts as yet another kind of wall, hemming in the Mexican population in that direction, too. Families are reluctant to return to Mexico not only because it still offers the harsh poverty they initially sought to escape but also because ugly drug-related violence now frequently threatens life there, even in broad daylight.

Despite hopes for improvement in their life situation, many indigenous Mexican migrants find they have moved from a country with one caste system to a nation with another. The multiplication of oppressions amplifies the acculturational stress that all immigrants suffer in any new country. The wall at the border is not the only U.S. limit they will encounter on their journey northward. It is merely the first.

What Are Racial and Ethnoracial Caste Systems?

A caste system contains a population within a number of "walls." This system functions, among other things, to relegate particular segments of the population to a low rank, blocking them from any higher status. It thus obstructs some groups from serving their own interests so that those in higher-ranking groups can satisfy their desires. Sometimes a caste functions to provide a particular kind of labor that others desire. At other times, profits may be derived from efforts to contain the population, such as securitization, patrol and policing, and detention or imprisonment. Occupations within a caste are ordinarily fixed and regulated, and they fall within a narrow band of possibility in a way that serves some function for those higher up. Even unemployment and underemployment can fit in a caste system; although inevitably onerous to those caught in it, unemployment can further upper-caste interests. While all involved may in time psychically internalize the racist premises of a caste system, coming to experience it as natural and normal, such systems are imposed and held in place largely from above through the exercise of violence and other forms of power. The derogatory images projected on those of lower-caste status are used to justify their position. Indeed, the consequent deprivations are often understood not as systematically imposed distortions but as effects wrought by qualities of the lower-caste members themselves. Many become psychologically trapped in this illogic, coming to believe they are inferior and that they deserve the crueler fate meted out to them on a daily basis. Others may clearly grasp how they are demeaned by racist stereotypes and actions, but this knowledge by itself yields no effective escape. A caste system may be based on notions of ethnicity, as well as on those about race.

Anibal Quijano's (2000) ideas on the coloniality of power help us to see that the Eurocentric imagination of Anglos homogenizes those from Mexico into a single group, paying little to no respect to their many cultural differences, including the sixty-two indigenous languages found there. Mexicans are too often simplistically imagined as living in a traditional and primitive past, one that contrasts with civilized and modern European and American cultures. Within Mexican culture, this same division echoes in the imagination of the upper classes with respect to the largely indigenous lower classes.

In *The New Jim Crow: Mass Incarceration in the Age of Colorblindness*, Michelle Alexander defines the phrase "racial caste" as denoting "a stigmatized racial group locked into an inferior position by law and custom" (2010, 12). Slavery, post–Civil War Jim Crow laws in the South, and contemporary mass incarceration of African Americans are examples of practices that create and sustain a racial caste entrapping African Americans. Members of a racial caste are not as free as others to move up in their society. There are always exceptions, of course, and these exceptions will be promoted in the public imaginary to obscure the plight of the majority, but they are just that: exceptions. Alexander argues that racial caste members find it nearly impossible to move upward not just because they suffer from poor education, poverty, and restricted opportunity but also because they are "barred by law from doing so" (13). To create and sustain a racial caste, a society must deploy "a tightly networked system of laws, policies, customs, and institutions that operate collectively to ensure the subordinate status of a group defined largely by race" (13). Alexander sees the criminal justice system as "a gateway into a much larger system of racial stigmatization and permanent marginalization" (12). Steel bars, virtual bars, and invisible walls cooperate to lock many African Americans into second-class citizenship just as effectively as Jim Crow laws did earlier. Alexander argues that, since the mass incarceration system has been largely immunized from legal challenge, dismantling it will require a social movement to build a critical consciousness of the existing problems and to forge effective social action.

Those of Mexican descent, particularly those without documents, similarly find themselves part of a stigmatized "group locked into an inferior position by law and custom"—in this case, a position defined by varying intersections of race, class, ethnicity, and nationality. The feminist philosopher Linda Alcoff (2011) argues for the term *ethnorace* as a means to escape a simplistic white/black binary in the United States that fails to address the intersectionality of race and ethnicity critical both to identity and to the racism inflicted on Latino groups. In an effort to see a "more variegated map of racism," freer of a white/black binary, she differentiates kinds of racism along four axes (color, physical appearance, culture, and nativism). She proposes the use of the term *ethnorace* to help avoid choosing "between binary concepts imagined as independent" and argues that with regard to racism targeting Latinos, accent, language, documentation status, and body type are often as important as color is.

For this reason, we will speak of the "ethnoracial caste system" to which Mexicans and Chicanos find themselves subjected. Spanish colonizers racialized multiple Mexican indigenous groups but later fell prey to the same phenomenon when Anglos failed to reliably differentiate between Mexicans of Spanish descent and those of indigenous descent. Many Mexican Americans find themselves still struggling against and within the dynamics set into motion by this caste system. Ramón Grosfoguel (1999) uses the term "cultural racism" in describing Anglo derogation of Mexicans. Much like their counterparts engaging in other such "isms," the cultural racists' ignorance of cultural variation among the many groups indigenous to Mexico is profound.

State and local legislative initiatives are now operating to displace Mexicans without immigration documents from housing, workplaces, colleges, health care providers, and even, via fearmongering, from some public schools. This pattern of discrimination and exclusion has been dubbed "the new Juan Crow," continuing earlier anti-Mexican discrimination and suggesting a parallel with the "new Jim Crow" that has instituted the mass incarceration of African Americans (Alexander 2010). The federal government's disinclination or inability to pass immigration reform that acknowledges the United States' need for immigrant laborers locks them into ongoing disfranchisement. Such reform would need to acknowledge that Mexicans, as well as many other immigrant groups, bring skill sets complementary to those of American workers, thereby both increasing the labor force and boosting production in ways that are mutually beneficial for themselves, U.S. workers, and the U.S. economy generally. Instead, fear-mongering, particularly by right-wing media and politicians, encourages workers of low economic status to think of Mexicans as interlopers who are stealing their job prospects.

Since the time of slavery, American racial hierarchies have relied on sustained attempts to engender racist thinking in less economically advantaged white people. By stimulating racism, xenophobia, and the fear of even deeper deprivation of economic status, those behind such efforts have used poor whites to provide a popular base of support for anti-immigrant policies and legislation. Alexander (2010) points out that the white elite sought to create a wedge between poor whites and African Americans so that these groups would not join together to undermine them. Fostering white supremacy allowed the poor whites' antagonisms to be focused downward, toward African Americans (and presently Mexicans). While subjecting African Americans to projected feelings of inferiority offered no material recompense, it gave many poor whites a psychological payoff, allowing them to view themselves as "superior" despite the demeaning rigors of their lives otherwise.

BEHIND THE CURTAIN: CONSTRUCTING CASTE WALLS

Like prisoners and former prisoners, undocumented migrants not only encounter overt legal exclusion but also "enter a hidden underworld of legalized discrimination and permanent social exclusion" (Alexander 2010, 13). Rarely can they effectively contest the oppressive and unjust situations in which they find themselves. Just as those affected by the system of mass incarceration encounter a system of control that "has been largely immunized from legal challenge" (15), migrants likewise find themselves facing deportation procedures that give them little or no access to due process and representation (Kanstroom 2007).

Occupational Constriction and Structural Unemployment

In a racial caste system, a caste member is restricted to unskilled or low-skilled jobs that offer no or little possibility for upward mobility. As we discussed in the last chapter, the Mexicans already living in what was to become California in 1848 were systematically dispossessed of their land and status and reduced to occupations such as agricultural and railroad work. By restricting the jobs those in a racial caste can obtain, an ethnoracial caste system fixes an invisible ceiling firmly into place for most members of the population. The dominant culture's celebration of those who succeed is too often employed to create the myth that those who are pressed down have failed to show the "right stuff" for advancement.

The structural unemployment imposed by seasonal jobs further contributes to migrant families' economic precariousness. The Pew Research Center has shown that over the last two decades, Hispanics in America have fallen socioeconomically beneath African Americans. Between 2005 and 2009, the implosion of the housing market and lenders' unscrupulous mortgage-writing practices, such as targeting minority families for subprime lending, caused Hispanic families to lose 66 percent of their wealth (Massey 2011). Massey, the author of *Categorically Unequal: The American Stratification System*, argues that the fall in wealth is intimately linked to the failure—or refusal—to reform the immigration system. He says,

> Our immigration and border-control system has created a class of people cut off from traditional legal and economic structures and thus vulnerable to the worst depredations of the market system. . . . Thus the sudden creation of a new class of people, working low-wage jobs outside the legal labor markets. Not only was it difficult for them to safely accumulate wealth, but they were left uniquely vulnerable to economic exploitation—such as the promise of a mortgage with little documentation required at signing.
>
> When the Great Recession arrived, many Hispanics got hit with a double whammy: not only were many Hispanic homeowners left with negative equity, but the collapse of construction jobs, which had been a primary draw for immigrants beforehand, eliminated the very means by which they could continue making mortgage payments.
>
> And because many were working and living in legal gray areas, they had little recourse when they learned their mortgages came with ballooning fee structures and onerous penalties for late payments. What little wealth they had managed to accumulate simply vanished. (Massey 2011, A23)

Mexicans find themselves working several jobs and living in overcrowded conditions to help them get a toehold in the economy, with the hoped-for possibility of greater prosperity for their children and better survival of their family members in Mexico. This overworking is the common fate of underclass workers. How ironic it is that *lazy* was ever used by Anglos to describe Mexicans; these same people have had little choice but to work long hours for low compensation, most often doing so with energy and resourcefulness.

Achieving excess profits amid fierce commercial competition and fulfilling the desire for cheap consumer goods and services require cheap laborers. The presence of Mexicans in the United States is not wholly unwanted, despite the imposed illegality and exclusionary rhetoric that presently engulfs and isolates them. Indeed, outlawing workers without documents serves to keep their wages low and their workplace demeanor docile. Unfortunately, denying legal status to immigrant workers serves to lower the wages of citizen workers, too. This, too, is desirable for many with capital.

Education and Caste

During America's slavery era, many states passed laws forbidding anyone from teaching slaves to read and write. It was coldly calculated that uneducated slaves would be more amenable to the hard and menial labor they were required to perform. Their uneducated status was then used to argue that they were incapable of learning. Later, the illiteracy engendered by this rule was used to deny voting rights.

Restricting the quantity and quality of education that Mexican (and other) immigrants receive leaves most with little opportunity to move through the imposed occupational constrictions on their caste. Additionally, by eliminating a critical education, an education designed to help people think about the construction of the sociocultural and historical context in which they live, the ethnoracial caste system renders Mexican migrants and Chicanos unprepared to effectively pursue their civil and human rights. This effect is clearly intended by legislative design in Arizona, where ethnic studies was banned from public schools in 2010. Tucson school district administrators required teachers to avoid any teaching units where "race, ethnicity and oppression are central themes," even though 60 percent of their students were of Mexican descent and the majority of these were of low socioeconomic status.

In 2010, Arizona, despite being ranked fiftieth in education in the United States according to Morgan Quitno Press, decided to eliminate funding for early childhood education and adult education, including general education degree (GED) preparation—decisions disproportionately affecting Hispanics. Arizona's House Bill 2281 banned ethnic studies and excluded a number of books from the Arizona state curriculum, including Rodolfo Acuña's *Occupied America: A History of Chicanos*, Paulo Freire's *Peda-*

gogy of the Oppressed, and even Shakespeare's *Tempest*. This assault on ethnic studies was waged to erase the history of the Southwest and thus helps induce historical and cultural amnesia in both Hispanics and Anglos. The move clearly targeted Mexicans, for Chicano studies classes have been terminated, while Asian studies classes remain. Proscriptions of this particular kind of education contribute to what Adam Hochschild (1999) calls the "politics of forgetting," an enforced forgetting that weakens traditional cultures, dispelling their remembrance of the forces that first shattered them.

Young adults who were brought to the United States as children by undocumented immigrant parents have been fighting since 2001 to pass the DREAM (Development, Relief, and Education for Alien Minors) Act. This act restores states' option to determine residency for purposes of granting higher education benefits. It provides conditional permanent residency status to any individual who was under the age of fifteen when first entering the country, has been physically present in the United States for at least five years, has earned a high-school diploma or GED, is a person of good moral character, is not inadmissible or deportable under the criminal or security grounds specified by the Immigration and Nationality Act, and will be younger than thirty-two years of age when the law is enacted. These students would be able to obtain permanent resident status after two years of college or military service. This act, if passed, would allow students to be eligible for student loans and federal work-study programs; however, they would not be eligible for federal financial-aid programs, such as Pell Grants. Resistance to this bill is certainly not based on its financial implications, for the Congressional Budget Office and the Joint Committee on Taxation estimated in 2010 that the DREAM Act would reduce deficits by about $1.4 billion over the 2011–2020 period and increase government revenues by $2.3 billion over the next ten years.

Although they have been living in an American state almost their whole lives, most of these sixty-five thousand aspiring students, sometimes called "DREAMERS," are required to pay out-of-state tuition for community colleges, state colleges, and universities—an often untenable amount given their families' socioeconomic conditions. For instance, in North Carolina, undocumented immigrants can enter the system's fifty-eight community colleges only if they have graduated from a U.S. high school, pay out-of-state tuition, and do not displace a North Carolina or other U.S. citizen. As of 2012, thirty-nine states do not let undocumented students pay in-state tuition, and some deny them entrance to all state colleges and universities.

Section 28 of Alabama's anti-immigrant laws, passed in 2010, requires school officials to question children and their parents about their immigration status during the course of enrolling a child in public school and to record their responses. This law, coupled with a fear of deportation, led many families to leave the state or keep their children at home. It has been temporarily blocked by an appeals court, but it constitutes "the first step in a larger and long-considered strategy to topple a 29-year-old Supreme Court ruling that all children in the United States, regardless of their immigration status, are guaranteed a public education" (Robertson 2011). Arizona attempted to pass a law, SB 1097, that would require schools to document the immigration status of their pupils and would sanction the defunding of schools educating children without documents.

In 1982, in *Plyler v. Doe*, the Supreme Court overturned a Texas statute that allowed the state to withhold funds for educating children without documents, to bar them from enrollment, and to require them to pay tuition. The decision cited the Constitution's equal protection clause in arguing that the Texas statute imposes a lifetime hardship on a discrete class of children not accountable for their immigration status.

Alabama's laws seek to inflict this very hardship to force immigrants from the state. Collecting the names of undocumented children will pave the way for Alabama to circumvent the *Plyler v. Doe* decision by arguing that educating a high number of such children imposes a substantial financial harm on the state, the one loophole in the decision. Such an argument pushes aside the fact that educated residents increase a state's revenues through their higher salaries. Unfortunately, maintaining the caste system holds a higher value, as does the wish to rid the state of Mexican residents.

In Alabama, children came to school crying, fearful that they would be removed from the care of their parents. School absences and withdrawals increased. Bullying of Latino children by other children also increased as children carried their parents' prejudices into the schoolyard.

State statutes such as Alabama's and California's Proposition 187 (also subsequently struck down) further subvert the hope that public schools can be gateways to social mobility for children from humble origins. If these kinds of statutes and propositions are allowed to hold sway, school officials will become agents of the immigration system, and children without documents, through no fault of their own, will be consigned to a fate of illiteracy. These children, however, are not the only ones threatened by anti-immigrant legislative initiatives. Democrats as well as Republicans have launched state and federal efforts to eliminate birthright citizenship (thus subverting the Fourteenth Amendment) for children born in the United States to parents without documents.

Fear and Terror

Maintaining the imposed "caste" systems perversely invented by colonialism requires sowing fear and terror. If made widely known by a colonial power, practices such as lynching, torture, murder, the pursuit of those trying to escape, and imprisonment and the threat thereof enable relatively few police or troops to control a designated population for a while.

In the United States, Mexican immigrants are presently targeted in hate crimes committed by both young and old, white and black. There are over three hundred nativist extremist groups in the United States. The three largest are the Minutemen Civil Defense Corps; the Minuteman Project, with 38 chapters in 2010; and the Federal Immigration Reform and Enforcement (FIRE) Coalition, with 136 chapters in thirty-five states (Bierich 2011). These groups regularly take the apprehension of Mexicans without documents into their own hands, staking out encampments near the border. Many of these groups post pictures of terrified Mexicans they have captured. The leader of the U.S. Border Rangers, another such group, announced for the news media, "This is the Minuteman Project on steroids. We've got people with assault weapons. . . . We will use deadly force when appropriate" (quoted in Bierich 2011, 37). FIRE maintains a website where people can inform on employers who hire people without documents. They are also responsible for "aggressive protests aimed at the undocumented" (Bierich 2011, 36).

In one heartless online video made by older teenagers, migrants are picked up by people pretending to hire them for day labor. They are then driven to the door of Immigration and Customs Enforcement (ICE). When the workers realize their fate, they scramble terrified from the car, attempting to run away. The teenagers are filming while laughing hysterically. In North Carolina, a teacher videoed all the students in her class with Hispanic names while another threw a Latino student against the wall and told him, "Go back to your own country" (Southern Poverty Law Center 2011). On Long Island, New York, Latino immigrants "are regularly harassed, taunted, and pelted with objects from cars. They are frequently run off the road while riding bicycles, and many report being beaten with baseball bats and other objects" (Southern Poverty Law Center 2009). Tragically, in 2008, Marcelo Lucero, an Ecuadorean immigrant, was stabbed to death at a Long Island train station by seven young assailants who described their routine weekend pastime as "beaner jumping"—that is, assaulting Latinos. Suffolk County police have been faulted for not attending sooner to the climate of hate that endangers its immigrant residents.

Juan Crow Laws

The fear and intimidation that entrap people in a caste are engendered not only by self-appointed vigilantes operating outside the bounds of law but by duly appointed officials following duly passed laws. In the last decade, police have been enlisted to enforce the federal immigration agenda, weakening their mission to build trust in the communities they protect. Local jails have doubled as detention facilities, placing immigrants next to criminals and stressing the resources of local law enforcement. The 2010 passage of SB 1070 in Arizona set off more than 1,300 anti-immigrant legislative attempts nationwide, with hundreds passing in a wide variety of states.[1] The goal of these laws has been to make life so difficult that immigrants lacking documents will leave. In the words of the Arizona law, the intent is "to make attrition through enforcement the public policy of all state and local government agencies in Arizona." These laws attempt to criminalize all immigrants without documents, regardless of their history of work and community contribution and the immigration status of their family members.

SB 1070 required Arizona's law enforcement officers to verify the immigration status of anyone they arrested or otherwise detained, if they had a reasonable suspicion that the individual lacked immigration documents. Any officer who refused to carry out this action could be fined $5,000 a day. All immigrants were required to carry immigration documents. Failure to do so was designated a crime. It was also a "crime" for an immigrant without documents to apply for a job or to solicit work. Under this law, warrantless arrest is sanctioned "as long as an officer has 'probable cause to believe' that a person has committed a crime that could make him subject to deportation—even if that person is not wanted for the alleged offense and the federal government may not want to deport or even detain him" ("An Invitation to Abuse and Chaos" 2012, 10). The Arizona law is intent on criminalizing immigrants lacking documents far beyond the strictures of federal law, attempting to conflate undocumented immigrant status with criminal status. This is a serious devolution with tragic consequences for individuals and families.

The mayor of Phoenix has spoken out about the reality of this legislation and its enforcement, especially at the hands of Joe Arpaio, the city's notoriously draconian and anti-immigrant sheriff, as well as his posses:

> [He] sets up a press conference, brings in dogs, brings in helicopters, brings in SWAT teams, brings in horse patrols, and says that we are going after illegal immigrants in one sentence, and then the other sentence saying, no, we're just going after criminals.

His crime suppression is really nothing more than crime sweeps target-ing brown-skinned individuals. Stopping and arresting individuals in the middle of a block, for littering, for honking their horn too loud, for having broken tail lights, for riding a bike at night without a light, one case for driving a car with the thread of a tire too low—pretenses to stop individu-als who then have to prove they are here legally. (quoted in Smith 2010)

In 2010 the Justice Department filed suit in federal district court seeking to overturn SB 1070, claiming that in passing such statutes, states uncon-stitutionally assume federal powers; essentially, the suit argued that only the federal government may set immigration policy (Downes 2010). After hearing the case, Judge Susan Bolton ruled that Arizona police officers may not check a person's immigration status while enforcing other laws. She also concurred with the Justice Department's central argument, stating, "By enforcing this statute, Arizona would impose a 'distinct, unusual and extraordinary' burden on legal resident aliens that only the federal gov-ernment has the right to impose." The judge struck down the provisions that criminalized the mere presence of immigrants lacking documents in Arizona, that allowed for warrantless arrests, and that barred immigrants lacking documents from soliciting work in public places. This judgment was appealed to the Supreme Court, which in 2012 upheld the key pro-vision: the requirement that state law enforcement officers determine the immigration status of anyone they stop or arrest if they have reason to believe the individual may be in the country illegally. The Court struck down the parts of the law that made it a crime for undocumented individu-als merely to work or look for work in the state and that allowed police officers to conduct warrantless arrests if they had probable cause to believe people may have done things that would make them deportable under fed-eral law.

The struggle by a number of states to enforce such discriminatory legis-lation has won these measures the designation "Juan Crow laws," likening them to the segregation laws that states put in place after the Civil War. As of 2012, Alabama is "winning" this cruel race to intimidate families so fiercely that they need to pull up stakes and leave the state. The purpose of Alabama's HB 56, according to one of its cosponsors, Micky Hammon, is to attack "every aspect of an illegal alien's life so they will deport them-selves." A report by Human Rights Watch documented closing businesses, crime victims opting not to go to the police, and parents fearing to seek medical help for children.

Another cosponsor of HB 56, State Senator Scott Beason, clearly stated his intent to preserve Republican electoral dominance by running Latinos out of the state, saying, "[W]hen [Latinos'] children grow up and get the chance to vote, they vote for Democrats." He "urged fellow Republicans to 'empty the clip' to stop illegal immigrants" ("On the Rise in Alabama" 2011, A28). Such attempts to displace a racialized population in order to retain white power have a long, unjust history in the United States, leading to counties throughout the United States that today are almost wholly white. Diane McWhorter, the author of an op-ed piece entitled "The Strange Career of Juan Crow," notes, "In May the [Alabama] Legislature passed an 'improved' bill sponsored by Mr. Beason, even more severe than the original. It forced the police to obtain papers from passengers as well as drivers, and it ordered the state to maintain a database of known 'illegals,' recalling antebellum ads spotlighting runaway slaves. The law still exempts domestics, observing the plantation hierarchy of 'house Negroes' and 'field hands'" (McWhorter 2012, n.p.).

The Alabama law forbids those without documents to work or travel, to own or rent a house, and to enter into any kind of contracts. In the absence of federal immigration reform, the intimidation resulting from HB 56 is as harsh for the husband and wife who have labored for twenty years, and now have children who are American citizens, as it is for the newcomer. To do any business with the state—even to obtain a dog license—one must provide proof of citizenship or residency permission. Doing business with the state, city, or county without this proof constitutes a felony. The law even includes utility companies; they must demand to see immigration documents and deny water, gas, and electric power to anyone who fails to provide such proof of status. All contracts between those without documents and citizens are voided, with the exception of those for a night's lodging, food, and medical services. All employers are required to use E-Verify to ascertain that their employees have valid documents.

These laws have encouraged the free flow of hate speech and hate crimes and a dizzying myriad of injustices. From utility companies shutting off families' water, to a man displaying a gun to day laborers and refusing to pay them for their work, to the repossession of vehicles even though payments are up to date: families have been intimidated on all these and many other alarming fronts (Southern Poverty Law Center 2011).

In Alabama, many workers without documents have stopped performing their jobs in the agricultural and industrial sectors, resulting in fields of rotting produce, decreased production, reduced tax revenues, and most important, the overnight descent into severe poverty for families already awash in fear and insecurity. Food prices for all families have risen. The Southern Poverty Law Center (2011) estimates that even if the state were to lose only 8 percent of its migrant workers, its economy would contract by $40 million a year, and tax revenues would fall by $130 million. Citizens who look like police officers' stereotypic images of "illegal immigrants" are subject to racial profiling, unreasonable searches, and false and warrantless arrests. The passage of Alabama's HB 58 has lent fuel to vigilantes who intimidate immigrants by threatening to inform on them to local authorities; to those, mentioned earlier, who bully schoolchildren; and to the more general harassment of Latinos.

Communities across the United States that have passed harsh immigration laws are rethinking the burdens they have created, not only for immigrants, but also for citizens. Towns, cities, and states have incurred steep legal fees that have required the curtailing of needed services and higher taxes to fund the costs. Restaurants, beauty shops, convenience stores, and other businesses that previously had immigrants as clients have closed. State revenues have declined.

The federal wall at the border is swung into place many times over at the state and local levels. This long season of drafting discriminatory and exclusionary laws, which function in their own right as walls, seeks not only to create such an atmosphere of hostility toward Mexicans that they leave but also to "keep them in their place" if they stay, constraining them within a racial caste system.

The United States is currently undergoing an "Arizonification," with a flurry of exclusionary legislation intensifying oppression against Mexicans. It is reminiscent of the way Southern states acted after the Civil War, creating a network of laws that would ensure racial hierarchy and control. Vagrancy laws helped ensure the availability of convicts by imprisoning African Americans who did not have written proof of a job at the beginning of the year, and convict laws allowed plantations and companies to hire convicts as laborers. The two sets of laws, in tandem, created an effective double bind. Unlike the context of slavery, where the health of the slave mattered to his or her owner (since slaves constituted significant financial investments), convict contract labor entailed little to no concern with the well-being of the workers, allowing deplorable work conditions. The situation is much the same today with regard to migrant laborers, who are seen as replaceable. Their replaceability is communicated directly to them by many employers. Alexander (2010) describes how Jim Crow laws created and ensured a "low paid, submissive labor force," much as does our present state-by-state patchwork of prohibitions and penalties for immigrants without documents. To illustrate the parallels between Mexican immigrants and African Americans, with both groups consigned to the same caste system, we can cite the striking fact that after Latino agricultural workers fled Georgia when their employers were required to check their immigration status using E-Verify, the governor filled their places with jobless ex-convicts ("It Gets Even Worse" 2011, A18). Given Georgia's incarceration rate by race, this meant a workforce that is 80 percent African American and Hispanic.

In many cases, courts are overturning these laws, at least in part. Unfortunately, they have served to underscore the equation of undocumented immigrants with common criminals, exposing Mexicans to further marginalization into an all-too-American undercaste.

Withholding Enfranchisement and Due Process

Despite the courageous efforts to register African American voters in the South during the Civil Rights Movement, we find ourselves, a half-century later, battling multiple attempts to disfranchise—as well as the failure to enfranchise—people of color. Criminalization and disfranchisement bear a particularly pernicious relationship. In the case of African Americans, some five million citizens have been disfranchised through felony convictions and probationary status. Many other countries, however, allow convicts the right to vote even while serving a sentence, and still more let former inmates vote once they have served their sentences.

Whether by removing inmates and ex-inmates from the voting rolls, by erroneously yet intentionally classifying people as felons to deny them the opportunity to vote, or by requiring that people possess photo IDs, which poor people often have difficulty obtaining, there is a clear right-wing strategy to restrict the number of people of color who vote. The failure to provide a path to citizenship to the eleven million people who labor alongside citizens in this country is a part of this strategy. The nation encourages and accepts the cheap labor but refuses to share the right to participate in civil society as a voting member. The right wing's outrage about amnesty and the fury around the illegality of immigrants amount to little more than a smokescreen masking a push for a white Republican majority vote in the United States, harking back to the Nationality Act of 1790, which granted citizenship only to free, white persons.

Robert Allen "calls out" the present reality: "This diabolical disfranchisement insured that Florida's electoral votes would go to Bush. It also reveals that the right-wing plans to use a strategy of outright disfranchisement in a drive to prevent a multiracial progressive coalition from consolidating and winning political power" (2005, 9). Mexicans cannot be called even "second-class citizens" in the United States, for the denial of citizenship and voting rights are key ingredients to their permanent social exclusion. By refusing to reform immigration law in a manner that fairly treats those who labor here as citizens and soon-to-be citizens, we build a society with a caste of effectively stateless people who therefore possess little power to affect the destiny of the nation of which they have become a part. We add the modern migrant to the slave and the convict worker as those who are given no place and no political voice, while being used—and too often abused—by society.

Derision and Criminalization of Mexican Migrants

> Each of you came into this courtroom without a criminal record. Now, you have one.
>
> Magistrate Bernardo Velasco, speaking to
> Mexican migrants in an Arizona courtroom

As Anglos came to California in the latter part of the 1800s, they described Mexicans as "inefficient in enterprise," "an idle and thriftless people" who lacked the "enterprise and calculating mentality" of Americans (Takaki 1999, 171). William Dana lamented that Mexicans lacked the Yankee characteristics of industry, frugality, sobriety, and enterprise; if only the Mexican territory were in the hands of "enterprising people," he exclaimed, "what a country this might be!" (quoted in Takaki 1999, 171).

Stephen Austin put the situation as he saw it in stark terms: a conflict between the "mongrel Spanish-Indian and negro race" and "civilization and the Anglo-American race" (quoted in Takaki 1999, 174). Indeed, as Ronald Takaki, a pioneer in the field of ethnic studies, points out, Mexicans were described in terms similar to those slave masters used to describe their slaves. Takaki quotes the mine owner Sylvester Mowry: "My own experience has taught me that the lower class of Mexicans . . . are docile, faithful, good servants, capable of strong attachments when firmly and kindly treated. They have been 'peons' for generations. They will always remain so, as it is their natural condition" (ibid., 187). A Santa Fe Railway engineer averred that while the "Mexican cannot be driven like the Negro," anyone who knows "how to manage him" can get a lot of work out of him (quoted in ibid., 320). "The Mexican" was presumed to be a good railroad worker because he was held to be "fairly intelligent under competent supervision" (ibid.). Such an expression, "the Mexican," illustrates the too-common reduction of the individual to the speaker's stereotype of the group, what Memmi (1991, 85) called "the mark of the plural."

Before the Great Depression, Mexicans were valued for their labor and their purported attributes. They were compared favorably to Asians and Eastern Europeans on the grounds that they were not aspiring to become citizens and so would not drain the nation's resources. Their allegiance was seen to lie with Mexico. They were not seen as communists and thus not feared as instigators of political unrest. They were, however, consistently seen as inferior to Anglos, and their presence was viewed as threatening to the racial purity of a white America. The proximity of Mexico enabled American employers to draw on as much cheap labor as they wanted; indeed, having more immigrants than necessary would keep wages low. The golden solution to racist concerns about the Mexicanization of the Southwest was to freely expel laborers when they were not needed.

Once the Depression hit, the United States undertook a mass expulsion of immigrants. While Mexicans constituted only 1 percent of the immigrant population in the 1930s, they made up 50 percent of those formally deported and 80 percent of so-called "voluntary" departures, a term parallel to the current term "self-deportation" (Flores 2003, 363). Lisa Flores (2003) states that while the overt rhetoric for the deportation drive at that time invoked job scarcity, its underlying goal was to create an atmosphere of fear that would produce massive voluntary repatriation. Some have estimated that a half-million Mexicans and Mexican Americans repatriated out of fear of the hostile anti-Mexican climate that was cultivated during the 1930s by media and government. This number included many U.S. citizens of Mexican descent.

According to Flores (2003), the media of the early 1930s employed two prevailing narratives in portraying Mexican workers in the United States, one characterizing them as an asset fulfilling a national need and the other painting them as a national threat. When Mexicans were viewed through the lens of national need, they were seen as "peons," with qualities of docility, lack of ambition, ignorance, and agreeableness; they were, it was thought, easily controlled as workers, comfortable with submission to authority, timid, painfully eager to conform, and well behaved. They were thought to be interested in earning only a scant amount of money to provide for their own meager support and entertainment, after which they were eager to return home. "Taking over" the society was not on their minds, in contrast to both the purported "yellow peril" from Asia and the Eastern Europeans, who were presumed to be communists. The narrative of threat, on the other hand, emphasized that Mexicans were appearing in unexpected parts of the United States and beginning to settle there, challenging the sense that they were interested only in working here temporarily.

Mexicans, says Flores (2003, 373), had been able to live in a space "outside the national body" while in the United States. Increasingly, she says, the media seized on the narrative of threat, of the dangers posed by migrants, providing rhetorical arguments that served as a backdrop to the use of police and immigration officials. While Mexican laborers may have temporarily benefited from being positively compared to the Chinese, who were banned through the 1882 Chinese Exclusion Act, the same kind of racism that gave rise to that act soon bore its strange fruit in efforts to exclude Mexicans from the racial composition of American life. The same characterizations that had demeaned Chinese immigrants were now applied to Mexican immigrants: disease ridden, criminally disposed, drug dependent. The same Mexican laborers who had at times been lauded for their hard work and docility were transposed through the narrative of threat to "imported vermin," "mongrels," "alien dope dealers," communists, and dangerous and menacing criminals. Those promulgating such rhetoric seized the power to shape discourse about the permissible and impermissible roles for Mexicans in U.S. society and to figuratively reinscribe the border between "Americans" and "Mexicans"—without bothering to except the many U.S. citizens of Mexican descent.

Significantly, entry into the United States first came to be conceived as potentially criminal during this period. "The emphasis on criminality and the criminalization of entry combined to provide a rhetorical space in which the Mexican body became a criminal body," says Flores (2003, 376). Once a certain form of entry became criminalized by categorizing it as a felony punishable by fines and imprisonment, the terms "illegal alien" and "criminal alien" became more commonplace. Individuals without documents who had criminal histories were confused in the public imagination with Mexicans who had entered without papers but thereafter had worked hard and made many contributions to their local American communities. Flores reports how the Mexican immigrant was imagined as stealing into the nation as a burglar would steal into a home: "Their theft included the taking of jobs and other limited resources from deserving Americans"; this "conflation of criminality and immigration status positioned Mexicans as part of the problem and the solution" (2003, 377). Mexican American citizens were swept up in the Depression-era deportation drive and deported illegally. Social-service agents warned Mexican families to depart voluntarily before they were deported and barred from subsequent reentry. Cities passed legislation barring Mexicans from employment on state and federally funded projects. In the 1920s, poor Mexicans were seen as particularly prone to tuberculosis and parasitic infestations; those crossing the border were subjected to degrading rituals of public cleansings, line inspections while naked, and spraying with DDT. Other nationals and Mexicans who arrived in first-class train compartments were spared these humiliations.

One of the most successful ways to enforce an ethnoracial caste system is to criminalize large portions of the group. This redesignation feeds racist sentiment in the population and is used to justify enhanced control and surveillance of the population now placed under continuous suspicion.

Indeed, through criminalization, the entire racialized group becomes suspect, regardless of the faulty "evidence" that is used to justify this. Once in place, criminalization becomes normalized and naturalized. Presently, criminalization of Mexicans has become a pretext for a proliferating and profit-making detention industry. Criminalization is also used to justify economic and political disfranchisement.

Both Jim Crow laws and the mass incarceration of African Americans have to some extent succeeded in criminalizing people of color. Michelle Alexander (2010) explains that at the beginning of the civil rights movement, a new, ostensibly race-neutral language was developed to achieve and sustain the same racial hierarchy that had been accomplished under Jim Crow laws. The discourse of "law and order" was promulgated, and those opposing segregation were often described not as civil rights activists but as criminals. Those who resisted unfair laws were conflated with common criminals. "Indeed," says Alexander, "the stigma of criminality functions in much the same way that the stigma of race once did. It justifies a legal, social, and economic boundary between 'us' and 'them'" (16). The current intensification of efforts to criminalize Mexicans in the United States has the same function.[2]

We are here witnessing racism and xenophobia converging in a hateful manner. In 2011, Representative John Yates, of the Georgia state legislature, compared the threat of illegal immigrants in his state to the threat Hitler had posed to Europe, suggesting that border agents should be allowed to "shoot to kill." In 2010, the state representative Curry Todd, of Tennessee, compared undocumented pregnant women to "multiplying rats" that should be controlled by revoking the Fourteenth Amendment, which grants citizenship to babies born in the United States.

The United States has vacillated in its treatment with regard to Mexican migrants, sometimes criminalizing them and sometimes not, depending on varying interpretations of the nation's economic needs, as well as the need for a scapegoat. For instance, the complex questions of what caused the Great Depression, as well as who and what were responsible for the unemployment and misery it entailed, were often answered summarily: "Mexicans." This resulted in the criminalization and deportation of Mexicans, who just five years before had been seen as helping to satisfy the needs of Americans.

Similar things are happening now. Once again, since the Great Recession of 2008, Mexicans are being defined out of the national body by right-wing media, local legislation, and a corporate-state-run detention and deportation system. While Mexicans had nothing to do with the unscrupulous financial practices that led to the Great Recession and in fact suffered most from the mortgage industry, they were nevertheless blamed for the high unemployment that resulted. In a remarkable sleight of mind, Mexicans are once again seen as illegal intruders and aliens. Many Americans feel entitled to use migrant labor when it suits them but deny migrants the rights given to citizens, so that when economic downturns make it convenient, they can self-righteously argue for their forcible expulsion.

The United States more vigorously sought to secure its borders following 9/11, at least ostensibly as a response to a perceived threat of terrorist incursions. This reinforced efforts that were begun in 1994 in concert with the passage of NAFTA, the North American Free Trade Agreement. This agreement flooded the Mexican market with U.S. corn, made cheap by federal farm subsidies. It undercut the price of Mexican corn, the country's staple crop, and plunged millions of small farmers into bankruptcy. While Mexican government corruption has contributed to the hunger that millions of its citizens endure, Americans should know that their own government's policies have contributed substantially to the magnitude of the migration from Mexico that many now decry. By failing to legalize drugs or to implement adequate gun-control policies, as well as by insufficiently pursuing those who profit from the illegal export of arms to Mexico (which has strict gun-control laws), the United States has helped create much of the violence in Mexico from which many of that nation's citizens are now fleeing. Mexicans were also drawn to the border region to work in massive manufacturing plants that were set up in the newly created free-trade zone. As global capital shifted to areas of the world with cheaper labor, Mexican workers were stranded in a place far from home but close to the United States. It is hardly surprising that many came north to feed and sustain themselves and their families.

In the past, some have argued that each nation-state has the right to control its borders. In a world undergoing globalization, however, where one nation's policies and corporate activities destabilize the local economies of another country, causing forced migration, the right to control borders ceases to be absolute. To a significant extent, any nation that takes or supports actions that cause forced migration cedes its right to a tightly controlled border.

Following 9/11, the Immigration and Naturalization Service—do note the word *service*—was placed under the umbrella of the Department of Homeland Security. This created a category confusion that has caused much suffering for some and much profit for others.[3] This confusion arose when migrants and supposed terrorists were fused into a single category, criminalizing the nation's approach to migrants. The discourse that resulted from this fusion insisted that our borders must be tightened and further defended to protect us from terrorists. Note, however, that all those involved in the 9/11 attacks entered the country legally and on airplanes. After more than a decade following 9/11, not a single terrorist has been captured trying to cross the border between the United States and Mexico.

Nevertheless, Mexican immigrants apprehended crossing the border, who used to be released on the Mexican side on the same day, are now criminalized, placed in jail for 30 to 180 days, and then deported. Operation Streamline in Arizona (also known as the Arizona Denial Prosecution Initiative) is a federal initiative that parallels similar programs in Texas and California. It creates felons out of migrants. Each time a migrant is caught crossing the border, his or her jail sentence becomes longer. The felony designation makes getting work extremely difficult. Ananda Rose Robinson (2009, n.p.) says that the "trial for each of the accused lasts, on average, thirty seconds. One by one, shackled defendants are identified, asked if they are citizens of Mexico (or another, usually Central American, nation), if they understand their rights, and finally, how they plead to the charge of illegal entry (or reentry). One by one, they answer, 'Culpable.'" It matters little if there are children and a wife left behind. The further drop in societal status from being a noncitizen to being a felon is significant. Now brown bodies are a source not only for cheap labor or for the profits of the detention system but for profits from imprisonment as well. Ordinary citizens are paying for the imprisonment. Phone companies, vending machine franchises, prison uniform companies, Taser manufacturers, prison builders (such as Halliburton; Kellogg, Brown and Root; Corrections Corporation of America; Emerald; and Management Training Corporation), and for-profit operators are enjoying a prosperity that belies the difficult economic times for ordinary Americans.[4]

Detention and Deportation

The lives of ten million immigrants from Mexico are being turned upside down as the United States engages in what the deportation historian Daniel Kanstroom (2007, ix–x) calls a "large-scale, decade-long deportation experiment," an experiment that is "subject to minimal judicial oversight" and that is "grounded in 19th-century conceptions of sovereignty . . . marked by ideas about race, imperialism, and government power." These conceptions can be traced back to England and other European countries still earlier. They create a chord of forcible removals that has sounded steadily in American history.

The Detention and Removal Strategy for a Secure Homeland, also known as Operation Endgame, is a strategic plan put into place in 2003 by U.S. Immigration and Customs Enforcement (ICE). The Office of Detention and Removal Operations of the U.S. Department of Homeland Security set out to detain and deport all removable aliens and suspected terrorists by 2012 through aggressive enforcement and a reliance on detention.

Like African Americans, who find too many of their community members funneled into for-profit prisons, Mexican immigrants are now confronted with a burgeoning for-profit detention system. This detention-industrial complex flourishes on a failed immigration system—and largely on the apprehended bodies of Mexicans. These carceral systems, including prisons and detention centers, sustain the American caste system and profit from it through income earned by warehousing people. The families of those incarcerated or detained spiral further into poverty, failing to accumulate the modest wealth that could provide a measure of security.

In the United States, private, often multinational, companies are now controlling half of all detention beds. This continues even though many of these companies have received "scathing inspection reports" or have been named in "lawsuits and other documentation of widespread abuse and neglect, sometimes lethal" (Bernstein 2011, 1). The for-profit mission of these enterprises has led to understaffing and higher rates of human-rights violations and violence (Detention Watch Network 2011). Detention facilities are not required to comply with Freedom of Information Act requests and are protected by contractor immunity, which contributes to a glaring lack of transparency and accountability. According to the Detention Watch Network, abuses have included sexual assault, denial of medical treatment leading to death, and the intimidation or punishment of detainees who have complained of human-rights abuses; some detainees in the last group have been threatened with criminal prosecution, while others were placed in solitary confinement.

It cost $65 million to build Raymondville's Willacy County Processing Center in Texas, a surreal white-domed tent city surrounded by fences of razor wire that is the largest immigration "prison camp" in America, designed to house 3,000 people. Maria Hinojosa (2011) describes those warehoused there as having limited movement, no representation or due process, poor medical care, and little protection from sexual abuse. Women are advised by ICE employees not to report physical and sexual abuse. Men suffer beatings by guards and racial epithets. Maggots have been found in the food. Guards are accused of keeping detainees cold on purpose. Five years after it was built, the average census of 1,200 was deemed too low to justify the number of employees, and layoffs began. Poverty may be the industry of Brownsville, but detention is the leading industry in Raymondville. Higher profitability for stockholders of detention companies depends on sustaining or increasing the present level of detention for immigration violations. Moreover, there are few incentives for judges to act quickly in cases concerning deportation. Delays mean longer stays in detention facilities, and this adds up to profits for private contractors and corporations, whose line of work is detaining and deporting poor Mexicans. It is impossible to calculate what detention costs migrants in terms of separation of family members, loss of livelihood, and a daily dose of fear, anxiety, and uncertainty about almost certain deportation.

According to the Illinois Coalition for Immigrant and Refugee Rights, over ninety detainees have died while in ICE custody since 2003, many from severely inadequate medical care. Both national and multinational corporations in the detention business lobby Congress heavily, as well as arguing to their stockholders and state lawmakers that a tough immigration policy is good business—that is, that it yields high profits. Here neoliberalism's desire for maximal profits once again trumps human rights. Josiah Heyman (2008) describes the homeland security–industrial complex as a conjunction of corporate and bureaucratic entrepreneurs who when joined by allied congressional representatives constitute what he calls the infamous iron triangle, which powerfully influences budget allocation and public policymaking. They are supported by anti-immigration activists and the xenophobic atmosphere they cultivate.

In 2011 alone, ICE detained an average of thirty-three thousand immigrants a day in more than three hundred facilities, 49 percent of them privately operated. Two-thirds of the detainees are held in county and city jails, increasing local revenue. For the last three years (2009–2012), almost four hundred thousand immigrants have been detained each year, at a cost to taxpayers of $1.7 billion a year. This is six times the number of detainees that were being held a decade ago. Three million immigrants have been detained since 2003. At $95 to $135 a day per resident, this constitutes big business indeed (Detention Watch Network 2011).

Some counties have found detaining migrants to be an acceptable approach to balancing their failing budgets. In a report by Amnesty International (2009), California's Santa Clara County was found to have built detention facilities for this express purpose. Some counties whose city jails have unfilled beds can get federal funding if those beds—jail beds—are filled with immigrants on their way to deportation. The ICE field office in Chicago described three categories to sort through migrants rounded up in raids, the first described as being for "your rapists and murderers," the second for more minor offenses, and the third for those with no criminal record at all. Unfortunately, the more beds a municipality can rent, the more people in category 3 will be detained and deported—innocent people.

If you protest your deportation and request additional hearings, you must stay in detention facilities longer. The prison-like detention ends only when the detainee agrees to deportation—at which point the person is deposited on the other side of the border. In Chicago, the detainees are clothed in orange jumpsuits and placed in the Cook County jail along with criminals. When they are transported to the detention and deportation processing facilities or to the airport from the six states that house them in jail and detention facilities, they are shackled hand and foot and placed in small cells in a bus with painted-over windows. They are put on and taken off the bus at the processing facility in the dark of early morning, behind a fence that prevents any perception of what is happening to them. Corrections Corporation of America was at the table when the former Arizona state senator Russell Pearce drafted Arizona's SB 1070, the contested law that invites racial profiling. If those without documents who have agreed to be returned to their countries subsequently return to the United States and are apprehended for any reason, they are charged with a felony. They are then imprisoned, sometimes for three to seven years, before being deported. This is a lot of profit for those in the prison business, paid for by U.S. citizen-taxpayers.

The tidal wave against Mexican immigrants was set in motion by the passage of the Antiterrorism and Effective Death Penalty Act and the Illegal Immigration Reform and Immigrant Responsibility Act in 1996. These two acts sanction arresting undocumented immigrants without warrants and deporting them without recourse to a hearing before a judge. When a judge is involved, his or her discretion is limited. Without such discretion, the detainee's family status and length of residence are less likely to be taken into account.

People held in detention are not serving criminal sentences. They are awaiting decisions on their immigration claims. Nevertheless, most immigrants are held in jails and prisons, despite ICE's own determination that "the majority of the population is characterized as low custody, or having a low propensity for violence" (Schriro 2009, 2). Facilities designed for detention would be hard to distinguish from jails and prisons because they have been built and are managed on the same principles. In a Homeland Security overview of detention with recommendations for improvement, Dora Schriro writes:

> As a matter of law, Immigration Detention is unlike Criminal Incarceration. Yet Immigration Detention and Criminal Incarceration detainees tend to be seen by the public as comparable, and both confined populations are typically managed in similar ways. Each group is ordinarily detained in secure facilities with hardened perimeters in remote locations at con-

siderable distances from counsel and/or their communities. With only a few exceptions, the facilities that ICE uses to detain aliens were originally built, and currently operate, as jails and prisons to confine pre-trial and sentenced felons. Their design, construction, staffing plans, and population management strategies are based largely upon the principles of command and control. Likewise, ICE adopted standards that are based upon corrections law and promulgated by correctional organizations to guide the operation of jails and prisons. Establishing standards for Immigration Detention is our challenge and our opportunity. (2009, 4)

In 2008, the Department of Homeland Security launched the Secure Communities program, purportedly designed to "prioritize the removal of criminal aliens by focusing efforts on the most dangerous and violent offenders. This includes criminal aliens determined to be removable and charged with or convicted of crimes such as homicide, rape, robbery, kidnapping, major drug offenses, or those involving threats to national security" (U.S. Immigration and Customs Enforcement 2010, 2). A wide net was initially cast, including workplace and house raids,[5] rapid ways to satisfy quotas for Homeland Security regions. As noted in chapter 5, people stopped by a police officer for minor offences found their fingerprints taken and run through both an FBI criminal history database and a database of Department of Homeland Security immigration records. Having a broken taillight, changing lanes without signaling, or failing to produce a driver's license at a DUI checkpoint suddenly became events altering the integrity and destiny of entire families. The initiative allowed law enforcement officers to engage in racial profiling, stopping people under weak pretexts given the slightest suspicion of immigration ambiguities and thereby filling the deportation pipeline with immigrants who are noncriminals.[6] If lacking documents, the immigrant could be deported even if the original charge or suspicion for which he or she was stopped was dropped. More than half of those deported have no serious criminal record. Ninety-three percent of those arrested under Secure Communities were Latinos (Preston 2011a). A third of those arrested have a spouse or child who is an American citizen. According to the Center for Constitutional Rights, Secure Communities "is an immigration dragnet[,] not a program focused on 'high threat' individuals[,] as ICE has told local police departments" (Center for Constitutional Rights 2010, 2).

As abuses and misuses of Secure Communities were uncovered, some cities and states attempted to opt out of the program, a course of action they had been encouraged to think was possible. Illinois, for instance, tried to opt out of the program, citing a discrepancy between the Memorandum of Understanding it had signed and the actual daily operation of the program. Now, however, the Department of Homeland Security says there can be no opting out. Some cities and states are attempting to curtail the abuses of the program by passing bills to limit the harm inflicted on immigrants and their families.

In California, for instance, the Trust Act (AB 1081), introduced by Assembly Member Tom Ammiano, authorizes a local government to participate in the Secure Communities program (S-Comm) only if the legislative body of the local government authorizes participation. It requires that only the fingerprints of convicted felons be matched against federal databases. This would enable the stated purpose of the Secure Communities program to be executed: the deportation of serious criminals. It allows local communities to tailor their participation in Secure Communities to their local needs and values. "The bill would set safeguards for municipalities that do elect to participate in S-Comm to guard against racial profiling and would ensure that children and domestic-violence survivors are not swept up by S-Comm. The Trust Act also upholds the right to a day in court by only reporting for deportation individuals convicted—not merely accused—of crimes" (Phelan 2011, n.p). Supporters argue that S-Comm's "over-broad reach and lack of transparency eroded trust between police and immigrant communities, making victims and witnesses to crimes reluctant to come forward" (ibid.). S-Comm was instituted in many communities without any public debate and without citizens "buying in."

In 2011 and 2012, the Obama administration attempted to reintroduce the earlier stated priorities of the Secure Communities program, advising ICE to detain "high priority" individuals and to release "low priority" individuals. The former are defined as those who pose a serious threat to national security, serious felons, repeat offenders, known gang members, and those with a record of repeated immigration violations. Low-priority individuals include veterans; longtime lawful residents; DREAMers and others brought to the United States as children; pregnant women; victims of domestic abuse and other serious crimes; and spouses, including LGBT spouses. Unfortunately, agents in the field have not yet begun to fully follow this directive, resulting in another year of record deportations.

Children Up Against the Wall

As the immigration war continues in the United States, the price for children of immigrants—citizens and noncitizens—is too rarely empathically felt and calculated. Nina Rabin's 2011 report "Disappearing Parents: A Report on Immigration Enforcement and the Child Welfare System" documents how the rise of detention and deportation of parents has led to the abrupt separation of children from their parents and extended stays in foster care for children who are American citizens. Children are not the only ones who don't know where their parents are. Attorneys, judges, and caseworkers also report difficulty in locating parents within the detention system. Immigrant parents in detention can lose their parental rights because they are unable to comply with timelines for regaining custody while in detention, and responsible parties are often unable to reach them or transport them to hearings. In *Immigrants Raising Children* (2011), Hirokazu Yoshikawa considers children born to immigrants without documents in New York City, a supposedly "immigrant-friendly" city. Within the first two years of their lives, their parents' documentation status registered its effects in these children's language skills and cognitive development, which were significantly lower than those of children whose parents were legal immigrants or native-born citizens (Semple 2011). Many such children have less access to learning materials and stimulating preschool environments. Because their parents fear deportation, they are less likely to apply for needed food and child-care subsidies. The parents' economic and emotional hardships can limit their engagement with their children, as well as their warmth and responsiveness. Yoshikawa points to a causal chain of relationships that begins in early childhood. Poor cognitive development can lead to lower school performance. The latter affects school dropout rates. This in turn leads to a less educated workforce and lower economic productivity. Such limited educational opportunities thus harm both the deprived individuals and the larger society. The health and well-being of children similarly affect all, in the present and in the future. Children are aware that their parents and families are portrayed as criminals. Given that young children have an extremely limited understanding of immigration and nationality, this stigmatization must be quite confusing. These children grow up feeling the stigma of being unwanted by many in the larger society. Ethnoracism and classism leave their indelible marks on the child's psyche. Without the prospect of citizenship ahead, fantasies of future vocations are severely narrowed, and the usefulness of school is thrown into question. Mexican young people are aware that their parents make daily sacrifices to offer them greater opportunity, and yet the larger society prevents them from freely and fully fulfilling their promise.

As deportations have increased, children must increasingly cope with a daily fear that one or both of their parents will disappear from the home because of a workplace raid or apprehension by ICE. The increased stress on the family increases the risk and reality of domestic violence, depression, anxiety, and substance abuse among parents. Between 2005 and 2010, three hundred thousand children who were American citizens left the United States with their parents who were deported or who chose to move back because of harsher laws (Cave 2012).

In a study of immigrant families affected by detention and deportation, Brabeck, Lykes, and Hershberg document parents' descriptions of the psychological and psychosocial toll these things take on their children: "academic problems (e.g., failing grades); depressive symptoms (e.g., sadness, crying, sleep, and appetite disturbance and lack of pleasure in previously enjoyed activities); anxiety symptoms (e.g., insecurity about the future, worry, fear, nightmares, and separation anxiety); developmental regression (e.g., speech difficulties); and behavioral difficulties (e.g., withdrawing and increased tantrums)" (2001, 9).

Immigrant children are forced to navigate their wider communities' failures to embrace and value them and the feelings of marginalization that result from this social exclusion. All the while, they have no choice but to fear for their parents' and their own safety and the integrity of their families. The psychological burdens of immigrant children can result in predictable mental-health outcomes of depression, anxiety, substance abuse, and suicidality.

More than five thousand children—most of them U.S. citizens—are currently living in the child welfare system because their immigrant parents have been either detained or deported. Many will not be reunited with their parents because the parents cannot meet the requirement for custody while in detention. Individuals who are themselves immigrants without documents are not allowed to take responsibility for the children of relatives. In the United States today, we are witnessing the re-creation of institutional orphanages for children of deported parents, an occurrence many had hoped was far in the past.

Each year, thousands of children make a perilous passage to the United States by themselves from Central America in search of one or both of their parents. So many have lost limbs traveling on the top of trains that there are shelters in Chiapas for the young amputees. Despite a ruling in Texas, the Flores Settlement Agreement, that immigrant children should be housed in state-licensed child-care facilities, some children have been housed at Lackland Air Force Base in Texas without access to counsel, and others, at a former YMCA in San Antonio. In any given year, licensed shelters in the Southwest will house seven to eight thousand children who have migrated across the border, usually to find a parent. If the Southwest were designated a war zone, these children would receive more aggressive aid, for the United Nations and other organizations would help to reunite them with their parents. Sadly, as a nation, we have largely ignored or accepted the collateral damage done to these children's lives.

PSYCHIC PERILS OF THE DISPOSSESSED

What are the psychological perils of being dispossessed? Of finding oneself devalued and expendable, of being required to exist as invisibly as possible so as not to bring harm to oneself and one's family, of looking to the future and clearly seeing signs that hard work will not appreciably change one's degraded social status? These things are the legacy of our history and our current practices. Our system requires self-erasure by poor Mexicans and Mexican Americans, punishing many of those who shed anonymity to try to advance their cause and secure their rights.

Can we imagine the psychic perils of knowing you are valued only for your labor and understanding that your labor increases the riches of others while you yourself have few opportunities to leap past the clutches of poverty? Lisa Yun (2009) describes this as feeling oneself to be a disposable person, to be used at will and then criminalized at will and deported, thrown out like trash. She calls the migrant laborer "the indispensable yet disposable body"; as people without papers, migrants live in fear of being discovered and separated from their loved ones and the place they now call home.

At a school north of New York, a white schoolgirl refused to trade postcards with her African American classmate, W. E. B. DuBois. In later reflection, he described the pivotal incident: "Then it dawned upon me with a certain suddenness that I was different from the others; or like, mayhap in heart and life and longing, but shut out from the world by a vast veil" ([1903] 1989, 2). The Negro, says DuBois, is gifted with "second-sight in this American world,—a world which yields him no true self-consciousness, but only lets him see himself through the revelation of the other world. It is a peculiar sensation, this double-consciousness, this sense of always looking at one's self through the eyes of others, of measuring one's soul by the tape of a world that looks on in amused contempt and pity" (5). As measured by the contempt they receive, Mexicans also find themselves on the far side of a vast veil. Mexicans find themselves "a problem" to Anglos in much the same way as, DuBois said, African Americans were a problem to European Americans. Frantz Fanon, a psychiatrist and a theorist of African liberation, described his own parallel experiences of this in France. Singled out by a child, he found himself to be an object causing fright. "Look! A Negro!" the child repeats to his mother. "*Maman*, look, a Negro; I'm scared." Fanon felt fixed by the child's white gaze, epidermalized, reduced to his skin. He found himself a being-for-others, rather than a being-for-himself. "I wanted to kill myself laughing," he said, "but laughter had become out of the question" (1967, 91–92).

Figure 14. Representation of discarded fragments of migrants' bodies, *2501 Migrantes*, Alejandro Santiago, Museo de Arte Contemporáneo, Oaxaca, Mexico. Photo by Mary Watkins.

Fanon described colonialism as a "systematized negation of the other, a frenzied determination to deny the other any attribute of humanity" (2005, 182). Sadly, Mexican migrants in the United States also find themselves derided and reduced in the eyes of others; they are called "lazy," "stupid," "docile," "dirty," "aliens," "invaders," "squat little Indians,"[7] "animals," "vermin," "cockroaches," "criminals," "lawbreakers," "diseased," "parasitic," "mongrels," "half-breeds," "ignorant," "peons," "bastards," "greasers."

Indeed, poor Mexicans are subjected by too many to what the anthropologist Nancy Scheper-Hughes calls "pseudo-speciation," where members of one group consider another group to be a different species. The negative judgments arising from this are used to refuse "social support and humane care" (Scheper-Hughes 2007, 178). Indigent Mexican migrants try to stay safe by becoming invisible but are then forced into the light of surveillance and control through raids in the workplace and at home and other forms of harassment. The more they attempt to be invisible (e.g., by remaining silent about labor and human rights abuses), the more they are tolerated. When vocal, as in the national immigration reform rallies of 2006, they often experience retaliation, detention, and deportation.

Scheper-Hughes describes a continuum from everyday violence to outright genocide, all of which depend on "the capacity to reduce other humans to nonpersons, monsters, or things which give license to institutional forms of mass violence" (2007, 169). The current degradation of poor Mexicans in America could be considered what she called a "peacetime crime," an "invisible genocide."

The term *trauma* is often associated with the psychological treatment of soldiers who have witnessed or perpetrated violence at close range. It has been absorbed into a mental-health treatment system that relies on a highly individualistic paradigm of the self, often depriving psychological symptoms of their cultural, historical, and political contexts and meanings. The term "collective trauma" has been proposed to help us acknowledge the kinds of psychologically destructive events and conditions that whole groups endure.

Epidemiological studies show an increased incidence of psychopathology in contexts marked by a variety of factors: poverty (particularly with large gaps between the poor and the wealthy), rapid urbanization that leads to inadequate infrastructure, population mobility, forced migration, familial fragmentation, poor and inadequate housing and education, gender inequities, racism, homophobia, torture, rapid social change and social disintegration, war, genocide, chronic violence, unemployment, failures of social and community support structures, and ecological degradation (Kleinman 1988). Most of these collective traumas are in full sway for those undergoing forced migration, and they can be found in intensely concentrated forms at the border and in the internal colonies to be found throughout the United States. Losses of home places, family members, friends, community, and culture compound the effects of the original traumatic contexts. All that was previously familiar and that provided a measure of security and continuity is sacrificed when one is forced to move to address basic life necessities for oneself and one's family. Racist treatment, detention, and deportation reinscribe earlier traumas for immigrants, deepening their psychic wounds and often creating a sense of fatalism. They also, however, fuel a struggle for survival, cultural identity, and justice that can result in political and cultural action (Bada, Fox, and Selee 2007).

Once one realizes that others see one as wanting, one begins to read the signs of this derogation everywhere in a racist society. To find oneself as the "other" in a racist society often leads to malformation of identity, leading to a woeful absence of self-esteem. Alcoholism, drug use, depression, and domestic and horizontal (in-group) violence may be added to the burdens. But if one can begin to understand how one has internalized societal oppression, one can begin to perform the painstaking psychic tasks of separating the toxic self-perceptions that have permeated the intimate spaces of one's psyche from a sense of self that has arisen in the context of loving and caring relations.

The path is perilous. Many people spend their lives unconsciously identified with toxic self-images that have been inflicted on them and thus live as victims of the modes by which dominant others have seen them.[8] Their families, too, may be poisoned by an expectation of limitation and deficiency, and the very familial love that is necessary to metabolize societal hatred may be compromised by a variety of tragic challenges that prove too difficult to be wholly surmounted. Bitterness, hatred, violence against members of one's own group, a sense of futility, silence, hopelessness, and fatalism are all poison fruits of being "othered" in a society plagued by racism. Mexican migrants suffer the "vast veil" of racism pulled against them.

Systematic dispossession, however, has psychic effects other than the internalization of racist representations. When one's voice cannot be raised without punishment, when one's consent is not invited, when one's interests are negated, one will often come to resist. Robert Allen says, "As the social crises generated by market globalization intensify, the conditions are created for the emergence of a new oppositional consciousness, a consciousness that can spark resistance to unregulated market globalization and the racial and national privileging that it promotes" (2005, 7). He projects that those racially subjugated in the most developed countries will join with marginalized populations throughout the world to create a counterforce to neoliberal hegemony. While colonialism accounts for much of the presence of whites in the Western hemisphere, Allen notes that the "neo-imperialism of market globalization" has greatly increased the presence of individuals from indigenous groups in the United States through the immigration of millions of displaced workers. These workers, were they to organize, could become a potent force for change.

Their encounter with U.S. racism has a radicalizing effect on many of these new immigrants, especially the youth, who discover that their hope for a better life in the United States is fundamentally constricted by the reality of racial discrimination. The offspring of these new colonial immigrants—the racialized, transnational children of globalization, many of whom are now young adults—will be especially critical agents in the struggle for global social justice. These millions of new colonial/racial subjects, . . . along with the millions of descendants of earlier forced migrations caused by colonialism and slavery, constitute a potential force for progressive, democratic change. Malcolm X recognized this[,] and in the last year of his life he proposed building political coalitions between black people and other people of color within the U.S. and in the European nations, and allying these formations with the counter-hegemonic force of marginalized peoples in Asia, Africa and Latin America. (Allen 2005, 8)

While many whites do care deeply about the victims of forced migration, the tipping point in the project of profoundly revisioning immigration in the light of globalization has not yet been reached in the United States. Examining mass incarceration and the maintenance of a racialized underclass in the United States, Michelle Alexander argues that whites' failure to care across color lines "lies at the core of this system of control and every racial caste system that has existed in the U.S. or anywhere else in the world" (2010, 222). She agrees with Martin Luther King Jr. that indifference and turning a blind eye to the plight of other races—even more than hostility toward them—creates the foundation for racial caste systems.

We must come to understand the treatment and mass detention of Mexicans in this larger context of the U.S. racial caste system, seeing it, too, as deeply analogous to the mass incarceration of African Americans and other Latinos. Only in this way will we understand that what has been presented to us as issues of immigration control and enforcement, particularly oriented to the deportation of serious violent offenders, is more precisely a program to aggressively maintain an undercaste—and a frank humanitarian disaster (Lakoff and Ferguson 2006). The sufferings of Mexicans, as well as those of others caught in this system, accrue at the door to the conscience of our nation. In particular, they congregate at the gate of the Anglo soul—our next topic—where they deserve sustained attention.

CHAPTER 7

The Souls of Anglos

I cannot be if others are not; above all, I cannot be if I forbid others from being.

Paulo Freire, *Pedagogy of the Heart* (1998)

One cannot deny the humanity of another without diminishing one's own: in the face of one's victim, one sees oneself.

James Baldwin, "White Man's Guilt" (1961)

Temo que la verdadera frontera la trae cada uno dentro. / I'm afraid that each of us carries the real frontier inside.

Carlos Fuentes, *The Old Gringo* (1985)

Looking Both Ways at the Border

When we travel south toward Mexico, the wall at the U.S.-Mexico border stops our vision into life on the Mexican side. It protects citizens from taking in the disturbing vistas and intimate scenes that would otherwise readily display the relative poverty, insufficient infrastructure, drug-war violence, and militarism that plague border cities and towns. The wall acts to separate daily realities, placing the experiences of many out of Americans' sight.

Within American towns and cities, where internal colonialism thrives, social conventions between Anglos and Mexican migrants, usually marked by disparities in economic class, also function as walls, leaving few Anglos knowledgeable about the Mexican communities in their midst. To prevent these "walls" from deflecting the Anglo gaze, we must create windows and doors in them so that one can look both ways at these borders.

To rend the veil of racism that DuBois described, Anglos must locate themselves, find *themselves* as "others" on the other side of the "vast veil" of racism (DuBois [1903] 1989, 2). Here, on the far side, many whites enjoy the privileges of relative power and profit by virtue of inherited whiteness.

This is not to deny the vast and unjust socioeconomic divides among whites themselves, although this is not our current focus.

W. E. B. DuBois begins each chapter of *The Souls of Black Folk* with a bar of a Sorrow Song, spirituals that "welled up from black souls" during slavery and described the sufferings, resilience, and hope of those forced into servitude ([1903] 1989, xxxii). These songs are resonant with many Mexican *corridos*, ballads expressing oppression, difficulty, courage, and romance. When Anglos open their hearts and minds to the Mexican American borderlands, they begin to hear a needed lamentation, a "sorrow song" of their own, born of shame and long-delayed regret for grievous wrongs. Recovering the souls of Anglos has everything to do with listening for these tragic notes, slowly assembling them in one's being until almost wholly new modes of relationship are created and offered to those who have been racialized by Anglos. As Anglo authors, we include ourselves as we speak about Anglos and address white consciousness.

In the previous chapter, we described the shadows that fall over the Mexican psyche in the United States by dint of internal colonialism and the racist "othering" that is its main ingredient. In this chapter, the focus shifts to the psychic and social toll this "othering" exacts from Anglos. We describe the psychic landscape of Anglos as they turn to find themselves as "others" in the Mexican imagination. Insofar as Mexican stereotypes of Anglos can provoke an honest self-examination of one's stance toward Mexican migrants, as well as that of one's own racial group, how might resulting feelings of shame be creatively metabolized? We want to draw attention to the psychic and social metabolization necessary for emerging from a self-serving collusion with dominant and dominating interests into a greater solidarity with those forced to leave their native homes to survive. We need to focus on a path of psychic decolonization for whites, one that moves from turning a blind eye to the sufferings of those deemed nonwhite to developing a color consciousness that allows whites to understand the racializing dynamics that undergird the misery so many of Mexican descent experience in the United States. The path we will plot begins at the point of finding oneself ashamed in the eyes of others or in one's own eyes and the possibilities for using this shame in a restorative manner. In this chapter, we directly address Anglos such as ourselves.

DOUBLE VISION: SEEING ONESELF THROUGH THE EYES OF OTHERS

Malintzin, a Nahua woman, became Hernán Cortés's translator, interpreter, intermediary, and intimate as the explorer conquered Mexico for Spain. To survive, she needed to learn "to look both ways": the way of her indigenous people and the way of the conquering group. Under conditions of duress, she gave birth to the kind of double consciousness W. E. B. DuBois was to describe in *The Souls of Black Folk* almost four hundred years later. Malintzin could see how she and her people saw the conquerors, and she could see how the conquerors saw her and her people. Malintzin came to collude with the colonialist forces, and she both survived and suffered by dint of this collusion. We can try to imagine Malintzin's thoughts and feelings as a way to see into the psychic, moral, and social challenges we face as (post)colonial exploitation displaces masses of people all over the globe.

How must our path toward consciousness and the retrieval of our soul differ from the kinds of paths for those trapped on the other side of the veil of racism, those whom we outlined in chapter 6? Whereas Mexicans, African Americans, and Native Americans cannot escape from seeing themselves through the eyes of the dominant society, developing the double vision DuBois describes, Anglos must commit themselves to developing this vision. Just as Mexicans experience the sudden intrusion of an Anglo gaze that finds them wanting, Anglos, too, can find themselves cast as stereotypic "others" in the Mexican gaze. But Anglos can more easily defend against this. We can turn away from totalizing stereotypic assessments of ourselves, or our group, which only periodically break through the powerful wall of privilege that protects us. I acknowledge that many of us find ourselves on both sides of various kinds of divisive veils. At this historical moment in the United States, when we consider the veil that divides citizens from migrants without documents, we must acknowledge the differences between citizens who enjoy the full range of privileges within the United States, those who are in the process of losing their access to many of these privileges, and those who have been largely locked out because of conjunctions of race, ethnicity, and class.

To address "Anglos" is for the moment to give priority to race over class as a construct. Our overarching intention, however, is not to separate race and class, since Mexicans without documents suffer both from their relative poverty and from a history of being racialized in the United States.

It is easier to rest in one's own positive view of oneself than to turn toward the other and ask, "How do you see me/us?" Indeed, the mere thought that others can have an opinion of us can be surprising. Those who possess privilege have psychic barriers dividing them from those who view them negatively. Conversation is structured to protect them from others' negative views of them. We reconstruct history so that the parts that would betray the shortcomings of our group are left out.

To understand the "souls of white folk," or the souls of Anglos, we must understand how we arrange things to obtain advantages pernicious to others. How do we arrange our eyes to look at history from a certain angle, occluding those parts that would give rise to shame and discomfort? How do we arrive at a narrative about our nation, city, or town that makes it seem as though Anglos have been here forever, dropping from daily memory and acknowledgment those who preceded us?

Too often, the white person occludes the experience and history of others by looking through the narrow lens of individualism. If we allow our gaze to widen, we find ourselves thrown into question by others—or, frankly, condemned. We find we need to deepen our perception—or perhaps discover for the first time—that we are, to borrow DuBois's words, "a problem" to others. "Disappearing" the means by which Anglos got economic advantage naturalizes affluence, rejects reparative possibilities and responsibilities, and allows the unjust and harsh divisions of rights and resources to go on. Our greed must be problematized so that its grasp on us can be loosened and others in turn can be freed from being seen and treated only as cheap labor.

LOOKING IN THE MIRROR "THE STRANGER" HOLDS: HOW DO MEXICANS SEE ANGLOS?

Richard Rodriguez shares how Anglos are seen by Chicanos:

> We didn't have an adequate name for you. In private, you were the gringo. The ethnic albino. The goyim. The ghost. You were not us. In public we also said "Anglo"—an arcane usage of the nineteenth century—you-who-speak-English. If we withdrew from directly addressing you, you became *ellos*—They—as in, They kept us on the other side of the town. They owned the land. They owned the banks. They ran the towns—They and their wives in their summer-print dresses. They kept wages low. They made us sit upstairs in the movie houses. Or downstairs. (1992, 64–65)

Shortly after 9/11, something promising happened in America. For a brief period, some Americans acknowledged their profound ignorance about Muslims, the range of Muslim religious and social beliefs, and the causes for the resentment some Muslim groups felt toward the United States' policies and actions. This attempt at understanding how we are seen was short-circuited when the United States began waging war in the Middle East. Once the wars got underway, linking 9/11 with foreign-policy missteps was seen as unpatriotic. But seeing it this way did not make it so. To hold on to the question "Why do they hate us?" has been fertile for many. It has led them to learn more about Islam and its diverse practice, as well as the American pursuit of self-interest in Muslim lands, and given them a greater understanding of the geographical and cultural diversity of Muslims; it has further led to some solidarities among Muslims, Christians, Jews, and atheists.

The question that comes right before "Why do they hate us?" is "How do they see us?" The answers to this question lead back into an examination, appreciation, and recuperation of history that is painful and necessary to the path I am outlining. To ask how Mexicans see Anglos opens us to generalizations: Which Mexicans? Which Anglos? But while stereotypes paint in broad strokes, they also bear lessons. Although some Mexicans who have the economic means to adopt Anglo lifestyles may be less critical of Anglos, even venerating and imitating them, those thrown into the scramble to survive in America as immigrants will—if it is safe to do so— voice a number of critiques. Who am I, as an Anglo, to Mexicans?

As we have discussed in chapter 5, U.S. history in the Southwest has gained Anglos a reputation for land grabbing, terrorization, and exploitation. Who moves onto others' lands by invitation, but does so in large numbers, with the intention of stealing the land and displacing its residents? Who offers citizenship and the freedom to practice their religion to those trapped within the new national borders but then lynches and robs some of them? Who is this "other" who builds walls in people's backyards? Who consumes drugs even when it brings murder and terror to one's neighbors? Who exports guns, even to a neighboring country whose government has outlawed them?

While Anglos saw themselves as a civilizing force, as members of a God-blessed superior race, many Mexican Californios saw the Anglo frontiersmen moving westward in the 1840s as "grimy adventurers," "exiles from civilization" (quoted in Takaki 1999, 167). The Mexican government had prohibited American immigration. Those who came anyway were seen as plunderers and likened to the bears, *los osos*, that preyed on the rancheros' cattle (Takaki 1999).

One Mexican newspaper likened Americans to a "horde of banditti, of drunkards, of fornicators[,] . . . vandals vomited from hell, monsters who bid defiance to the laws of nature[,] . . . shameless, daring, ignorant, ragged, bad-smelling, long-bearded men with hats turned up at the brim, thirsty with the desire to appropriate our riches and our beautiful damsels" (quoted in Takaki 1999, 175). And even the man heading the forces that captured Mexico City, General Winfield Scott, admitted that American soldiers had "committed atrocities to make Heaven weep and every American of Christian morals blush for his country. Murder, robbery and rape of mothers and daughters in the presence of tied-up males of the families all along the Rio Grande" (ibid.).

One hundred and sixty years later, I ask my Mexican friends what they think of Anglos. When I asked Cecilia, she blushed and paused, and then she leaned over to me and asked, with a mixture of anxiety, doubt, and attempted humor, "Are you a CIA agent? It is dangerous. I could be made to leave." She is afraid that to communicate a negative impression of the so-called "hosts" could be grounds to deport even someone here legally. While this may sound paranoid, American history is strewn with efforts to get "others" (such as French Canadians) to pledge their fealty and harsh retaliations if they did not. With hearty reassurance and coaxing, Cecilia and others have shared with me what the Anglo shadow today looks like to the Mexicans over whom it falls.

Some of those I asked pointed to character traits, calling Anglos *cuadrados* (rule driven and square minded); *infelices* (wretched); *malditos gringos* (damned, cursed, wicked gringos); *cursis* (vulgar, crude, ridiculous, exaggerated); *sosos* (insipid, dull, uninteresting, bland); *estúpidos, egoístos* (stupid and selfish); and *falsos* (deceitful). Others mentioned a status, attitude, or practice they viewed as common to the group: "The gringos take everything from the poor to crush them." "Gringos think their race is best." "They are rich." "They have an ambition for expanding." "They are greedy and they are liars [*mentirosos*] and abusive." "They are bastards, *hijos de la chingada* [sons of bitches]." "They are *ventajosos* [unscrupulous], taking advantage of whatever they have." "They are people who have misused their power [*quien ha abusado del poder*]." "Gringos do things that are inhuman." "Their history is a series of abuses." "They deserve the narcotics we bring them."

Gringos are thieves, swindlers, invaders, and usurpers. We crucify and we swindle. We are the kind of people who make others aliens and strangers in their own land when we are the newcomers. We outlaw the languages of those who were here before us. We are racists and slave drivers, marked by greed, egotism, and selfishness. We are self-centered opportunists, parasitical to the body of the people, *el pueblo*. When it suits us, we suck the blood of migrants. When it does not, we clean them off our streets and throw them away without care, separating family members and depositing people in Mexican locations they have never been and where they know no one. At the border we act crazy and drunken, without moral principles.

In a transborder art project with children in Tijuana, Norma Iglesias-Prieto (2012) asked, "If the United States were an animal, which animal would it be?" One child answered, "A lion, because it wants to be the king of the jungle." Another, "A donkey, because they are stubborn and foolish."

In *The Cultural Politics of Emotion* (2004), Sara Ahmed explains that whereas guilt generally springs from the violation of common standards, shame relates to some quality of the self. Ahmed says, "In shame, more than my action is at stake: *the badness of an action is transferred to me* such that I feel myself to be bad" (2004, 105). The one who is ashamed often tries to evade the eyes of those who see him or her as shameful. Indeed, walls of relative privilege can be slid into place to avoid the direct gaze of others. For Anglos, it is the exception when a Mexican looks at us and speaks his mind about us. We can look at workers in an agricultural field, but we do not experience their gaze back at us. If they were looking at us, we might experience ourselves as lazy, as people who avoid the hard work necessary to grow our own food, build our own roads, and even maintain our own homes.

Becoming a Problem to Ourselves: Soul Mutilations

Many of the defenses against others that we regularly employ and normalize not only cause great misery to those who are "othered" but diminish us as well. Those on the side of privilege in the current age of globalization suffer soul wounds of their own, injuries not dissimilar to the psychic mutilation Fanon and Memmi described for those who participate in colonialism. These wounds require their own phenomenological analysis.

To be in the present without rooting ourselves in the past, to amputate our history: Having imposed the "melting pot" on others, we have come to suffer it ourselves. Many of us are paradoxically not unlike the descendants of slaves insofar as we are hard pressed to know where our families originated, how they got here, and what they sought to accomplish in coming here. We meet each other in the present, with little sense of our familial and cultural pasts. While some may search for their roots through tourism and genealogical research, roots discovered in these ways are far from those felt through direct family narratives and attention to history. We have some interest in history but no real devotion to it, for the histories we would encounter are deeply problematic.

To turn our backs on our neighbors: Whether we define Mexicans as not belonging here or we more simply follow social convention by avoiding conversations that would require us to recognize and witness their struggles and needs, we leave holes in many of our daily interactions, in our consciousness, and in the social fabric.

To assert false stature, to raise oneself through the diminishment of others: For Anglos, the long-ensconced and largely accepted diminishment of Mexicans results in a diminishment of ourselves as well. Every false note of assumed superiority carries an unconscious note of inferiority; every unjust action, a submerged sense of guilt and shame. The resulting inner cacophony puts Anglos ill at ease with themselves. The contradiction they impose on the Mexican, their habit of severing a person's labor from that individual's personhood, is of necessity mirrored by a fragmentation of their own selves. They are left with a fragmentary self-identification reproduced by mass culture, that of the "hearty consumer." The finer threads of discerning conscience and empathic connection are locked away from easy access.

To seal the situation, confining themselves and others into this unhappy state of affairs, many Anglos refuse to create paths to citizenship for those on whom they depend, thereby consigning millions to an underclass with little political representation and themselves to more of the same faulty self-evaluation.

To engage in excessive appetites and the abuse of "others": Consuming the labor of others to enhance convenience and comfort ultimately leaves us in a discomfiting world. We cannot solve this discomfort by claiming others' illegality while disavowing our own unexamined and often petty appetites. It is striking that, as we Americans watch the heightening violence in Mexico out of the corners of our eyes, few call for drug abstinence as an expression of solidarity with the Mexican people. Presumably, the relatively easy availability of marijuana balances out a situation where beheadings are used to terrorize a population, stray gunfire takes innocent lives, and ordinary places are turned into war zones. Individualism leaves unquestioned the shadow side of our appetites, increasingly removing the miseries of sweatshops and industrial plants to the other side of walls that make sight more difficult.

To take refuge in exaggerated outrage rather than accept responsibility for the shadows our actions cast on our neighbors: Even as we deny any responsibility for helping extend the human rights to adequate shelter, food, health care, and education to our neighbors who have come without legal sanction, we wantonly enjoy the fruits of our neighbors' labor. Split against ourselves, we take refuge in exaggerated and simple-minded outrage, wiping aside all the complexities of the situation. The frequent cry, "What don't you understand about the word 'illegal'?" does not acknowledge how U.S. policies help displace millions from Mexican farms.

To defend the right to profit, severing our own conscience regarding the means employed and the people exploited to create the excess gain: "Free" trade that depends on labor exploitation ends up bearing little freedom for Mexican workers at the border or for the conscience of Anglos. Two hundred years ago, the Quaker John Woolman asked that "we look upon our treasures, and the furniture of our houses, and [our] garments . . . and try whether the seeds of war have nourishment in these our possessions" (1989, 255). Our neat lawns, clean houses, good foods, finely stitched clothes, and emptied garbage cans must also be considered as we calculate the human price paid to achieve them.

To take refuge in scapegoating blinds us to the deeper causes of our dilemmas: The wall, along with the rhetoric that accompanies it, encourages citizens to believe that the harms they face come from the outside rather than from the inside. This is particularly pernicious when people who have lost their jobs or fear unemployment in the currently precarious market are led to imagine that immigrants are stealing their potential jobs and job security. This misreading deflects their attention from the actual causes of the unemployment and economic instability.

To minimize the pain of displacement for others and thus for oneself: The Mexican sees the Anglo as a lonely person. Having left our own places, we have moved others off the land to which we came, erasing their history. We settle in places that we have severed from the past, doubly orphaning ourselves. We try to live as though it doesn't really matter, but we are afraid to put any root too deeply into the earth beneath us, as though touching the buried shards of Indian pottery and Mexican adobe would awaken us from our simple-minded dream that we own the land on which we dwell.

An Anglo man passes a Mexican's yard on Sunday afternoon and sees him surrounded by family and friends. There is laughter; music blares. A cold beer, a piñata atmosphere. The Anglo goes home, too often alone. His mother and father are divorced, living far away; his children live far apart, as though thrown from a spaceship into different states or even countries. What the Mexican enjoys in his postage-stamp yard seems unavailable to the Anglo. The Mexican looks more at home than the Anglo. The Anglo tries not to give it a second thought.

The archetypal psychologist James Hillman says, "When we refuse the historical aspect in our complexes," ignoring "how history reaches us through our complexes, . . . we create orphans" (1998, 143). While saving ourselves from feelings of guilt and shame, we end up orphaned in the very world where we want to feel at home. We need to become a problem to ourselves and feel the shame of our situation.

Re-Visioning Shame as a Potentially Fruitful Emotion

Allowing Shame, Inviting Shame

While psychologists offer ways to manage anger and navigate the stages of grief, they often omit shame from emotional literacy, implying that it is to be avoided, as though it were only a psychic sinkhole. We need to begin to differentiate the psychic landscape of shame so that we can better see how it affects our relationships to and public policies regarding migrants and others who are denigrated in our societies.

The dominant American ethos can be characterized as both guilt- and shame-avoidant. It is slow to acknowledge wrongdoing and even slower to acknowledge "wrongbeing." The public space in which shame could be allowed and examined is almost nonexistent. Instead of feeling shame, we are prone to try to remove—even through violence—the presumed source of the feeling. One way of attempting to avoid shame is to remove the people who have suffered as the victims of shameful acts. For a stunning example of this, consider the white-led push to return former slaves to Liberia, Africa, after the end of the Civil War. Presently many want to return Mexicans to Mexico and erase the history of their treatment here through the removal of ethnic studies from school curricula. We must be empathic with the psychic dynamics that occasion such efforts of removal: upwelling feelings of shame, inadequate resources for establishing self-esteem, and paranoia. When we treat others badly, we suffer the "paranoia" of knowing that our actions may be turned back on us. The shame caused to others inevitably seeps back toward the self.

Certain sociocultural dynamics mitigate the ability to acknowledge shame. In considering Hannah Arendt's work, Elisabeth Young-Bruehl (2009) underscores how shame can be blocked by the overcertainties of ideology. This is clearly the case in the United States today. For many, the phrase "what don't *they* [immigrants without documents] understand about the word 'illegal'?" blocks a deeper examination of the complex causes of migration. For others, an ideology of completely open borders can preclude taking up citizens' legitimate concerns about employment and the management of state and local resources.

We need to find the means for nonviolently addressing shame, to appropriately acknowledge and apologize for wrongdoings, and to make restitution for harms committed. Acknowledgment, the bearing of shameful feelings, apology, and restitution will provide the material for building authentic self-respect, for retrieving a sense of worth. They are the steps of reconciliation that can begin to reweave torn social fabrics. To lock one's door against a neighbor's need causes shame for those on both sides of the door.

Metabolizing Shame

Not all cultures cut themselves off from the learning that can happen when there is a psychic and social space for shame. The Maori people consider shame to be one step removed from heaven. According to the Jungian analyst Joan Chodorow, the Korean system of understanding emotions casts shame as a "differentiated feeling" rather than a basic emotion. "The *capacity to experience shame* 'in recognition of one's error' is the first of four noble qualities leading toward the development of compassion" (Chodorow 2009, 5). We are unfamiliar with what it looks like and feels like to allow oneself to be suffused with shame in order to move toward greater compassion. Too often shameful feelings cause us to look away from those whom we have harmed rather than to reengage with them in ways that allow us to be seen as the cause of others' suffering. As long as we avoid shame, our compassion is like a shriveled or amputated limb. To learn to work with our shame would allow us to experience shame not as an emotion that we loathe and avoid but as a differentiated feeling that can be used to inform our basic stance toward others. Indeed, for shame not to predispose us to defensive rage and violence, we need to bring consciousness to it, so that we can use it as a path to appropriate guilt, meaningful remorse, empathic connection, and concern for others. Hopefully, then, our actions will reflect our shifts in awareness, eventuating in more caring, compassionate, and just treatment of others.

Hannah Arendt addressed shame in 1945, before the end of the war:

> For many years now we have met Germans who declare that they are ashamed of being Germans. I have often felt tempted to answer that I am ashamed of being human. This elemental shame, which many people of the most various nationalities share with one another today, is what is finally left of our sense of international solidarity; and it has not yet found an adequate political expression. . . . For the idea of humanity, when purged of all sentimentality, has the very serious consequence that in one form or another men must assume responsibility for all crimes committed by men and that all nations share the onus of evil committed by all others. (2003, 154)

We need to learn how to bear a double dose of elemental shame: first, for having helped to so greatly disrupt local economies that people are forced to migrate; second, for imposing on migrants the constant threat of a second dislocation through detention and deportation. We must write shame into our vocabulary for communal and psychological health, seeing it as a step toward living with others with more compassion and integrity.

Reintegrative Shame

John Braithwaite, in *Crime, Shame, and Reintegration*, focuses on the use of shame to "provoke personal obligations to others within a community of concern" (1989, 84). Societal conditions that favor communitarianism at the societal level and interdependence at the individual level of analysis are most conducive to this use of shame. The interdependencies "must be attachments which invoke personal obligation to others within a community of concern. They are not perceived as isolated exchange relationships of convenience but as matters of profound group obligations" (85). If shame is to be reintegrative, however, one must denounce the offense but not the offender. Crucial opportunities must be provided for shame to be removed or transformed.

As Braithwaite carefully describes it, shame need not foreclose people from human relatedness. To avoid this, we must create rituals for remorse and repentance and paths of restitution and reparation that will facilitate integration into the common human family.

The psychiatrist James Gilligan, who spent decades working with violent offenders in the Massachusetts prison system, has drawn on his professional experience to illuminate the link between shame and violence. He found that those who are most vulnerable to debilitating feelings of shame have no nonviolent means to ward off or diminish these feelings and little if any emotional capacity to experience guilt and love in ways that might inhibit violence. In the face of shame, they are more likely to use violence as a means to establish their personhood and demand "respect" (1997, 112).

Let us turn first to those Americans who suffer the burden of low social status and the shame that can arise from that, those who do not altogether blame themselves, for they understand that the hurdles facing them have been largely imposed by others. Gilligan points out that this combination of shame and innocence in members of low-status groups makes homicide more likely than suicide: "Those who are primarily exposed to feelings of shame and innocence would primarily blame and punish others, and thus would be more likely to commit homicide than suicide; whereas those who are statistically more likely to be exposed to feelings of guilt (and pride) would have a higher rate of suicide to homicide" (1997, 207).

On Staten Island and Long Island; in Phoenix; in Richmond, Virginia; in Coeur d'Alene, Idaho; in Boulder, Colorado—in all these places, hate crimes against Mexicans and other Latinos are on the rise. Some perpetrators pretend to offer their victims jobs but deliver them to a Homeland Security office; others carve racist death threats in high-school cafeteria tables; still others stalk migrants, beating them while yelling racist slurs and sometimes even murdering them. These are not rare occurrences. Most racist incidences go unreported for fear of deportation.

Gilligan argues that all violence has as its aim the achievement of justice for oneself or those on whose behalf one thinks one is acting. For many men, it is also about the "maintenance of manhood." The assaults on Staten Island have been carried out largely by poor African American teens and young adults. Gilligan describes poor whites' discrimination against African Americans as "one of the few forms of self-esteem insurance that they are allowed" (1997, 199). In the present case, some African American youths are themselves attempting to rescue their own self-esteem by perpetrating hate crimes. The absence of nonviolent means of maintaining self-respect, such as education and employment, leaves violence as a last resource. Gilligan underscores that envy is itself a form of shame, causing us to feel inferior to those we envy. When jobs are in short supply, harassment and violence against the objects of one's envy—in this case, the employed—is a sad self-defense. What these young people need is not a community free of Mexicans but a community that offers opportunities for self-respect through education, training, employment, and community leadership, the latter something rarely allowed youth.

Some African Americans accept the conservative right's claim that their joblessness results from the presence of Mexicans and other Latino immigrants. What could be more convenient than for some in the black underclass in America to blame poor Mexicans for having created their problems? Horizontal violence—violence, that is, against those in one's own or a similar group—keeps people in submission to ruling-class authorities who appear mainly in their absence. Histories of oppression become dissolved and invisible. Those whose self-love and self-esteem are most diminished are chilled by shame and humiliation before coming to reside in psychic numbness, that state in which violence fails to register its woeful cost. Gilligan describes the intentional strategy of dividing those without substantive power into groups of predators and prey, relieving some of the need for policing and suppression from those in control. This is a common strategy in American prisons, where some prisoners are allowed to suppress and abuse others.

Working-class and poor whites have been tutored by right-wing media and politicians to think in racial rather than class terms, to identify with their racial status rather than their working-class status, which they share with many people of color. Many are convinced that their interests are pitted against those of color in a zero-sum game. Some such whites have used a sense of racial superiority to mitigate the psychic and very real daily assaults of working conditions and poor economic status. At the end of the march from Selma to Montgomery in 1965, Martin Luther King Jr. asserted that "the Southern aristocracy took the world and gave the poor white man Jim Crow. . . . And when his wrinkled stomach cried out for the food that his empty pockets could not provide, he ate Jim Crow, a psychological bird that told him that no matter how bad off he was, at least he was a white man, better than the black man" (2002, 124). "Time and time again," says Michelle Alexander, "poor and working-class whites were persuaded to choose their racial status interests over their economic interests with blacks, resulting in the emergence of new caste systems that only marginally benefitted whites but were devastating for African Americans" (2010, 243).

This has led to voting patterns and to racial discrimination and isolation that have served to worsen the situation of poor whites. Where this racial identification has been even partly overcome, emerging transracial solidarities have improved the working and economic conditions for poor and working-class whites. Alexander (2010) urges us to remember Martin Luther King Jr.'s insight that we must move from a focus on civil rights to one on human rights. This shift helps us recognize that the economic insecurity of poor and working-class whites can be tragically harnessed to racial animosities even as we embrace the human-rights needs of Mexican migrants.

Indeed, in a globalized economic system, the causes of forced migration significantly overlap the causes of under- and unemployment, job insecurity, poor working conditions, and low wages. We must understand these common causes if we are to create a human-rights paradigm that is relevant to poor and working-class whites, Mexicans, and African Americans. Alexander argues that when the civil rights movement failed to adequately promote the link between the poor and working-class whites and African Americans, efforts at affirmative action were "like salt on a wound as African Americans leapfrogged over working class whites to Harvard and Yale and jobs in police and fire departments" (2012, 246).

But it is not only the poor and minorities who confuse the causes of their difficulties. Members of the white middle class, which is itself falling into an economic abyss, too often blame Mexicans for their own problems: rising unemployment, bad schools, inadequate health care, and poor policing and emergency services. This conservative right-wing account fuels several groups of citizens in their attempt to scapegoat Mexicans by intensifying a climate of hatred and division. According to this line of rhetoric, Mexicans are taking away Americans' jobs and using up municipal revenues for their medical and educational needs. In short, it blames the current economic recession on Mexicans, who are seen as invaders and parasites. This scapegoating is a skillful sleight of hand that deflects attention from the excessive greed of many whose actions have caused millions to lose their life savings, housing, retirement, and jobs.

Gilligan understands collective violence, exemplified by the Holocaust, as resulting from many of these same factors. Hitler rose to power in 1933 on the heels of the Depression and promised to reverse the "shame of Versailles." According to Gilligan, members of the lower middle class supported Hitler in an attempt to free themselves from the shame that unemployment, loss of homes, and downward social mobility had left them feeling. "The members of this group felt in danger of losing their capital and suffering a loss of social and economic status, a degradation, by becoming part of the humiliated, inferior, poverty-stricken lower class, or felt they had already suffered that humiliating sea-change into something poor and strange, and were eager for revenge—for a way of re-establishing their status or power" (Gilligan 1997, 67). Jews were the scapegoat, seen as the cause of this threatening situation. They were envied, falling prey to those who felt diminished and thus sought to diminish others in their stead. The claim of cultural superiority and an imagined racial superiority appear to alleviate the threat of shame. We see it in the United States and throughout Europe, where foes of immigration fear a loss of the host culture and language. Some Anglos fear the Hispanization of the United States. The fear of finding one's group a minority fuels their xenophobia. The call to restore honor, engineered by individuals such as the conservative radio talk-show host Glenn Beck, bespeaks the loss of self-respect that is an ingredient of xenophobic racism. Too many Anglos feel frustrated, invisible, and devalued in their own country.

They can alleviate some of these feelings not only by seeing the Mexican migrant as a stupid, lazy parasite but also by exerting unconscious pressure to make the migrant feel this about him- or herself. Shame itself migrates into the migrant. As shame is transferred from citizen to noncitizen, particular others—lovers, husbands, fathers, sons, daughters, mothers, and friends of the newly shamed subject—are conglomerated and reduced to lawbreakers.

Sadly, many in the United States now occupy a position similar to that of lower middle-class Germans in the 1930s. They have lost their homes and their jobs or fear they stand on the brink of doing so. They and their children may lack adequate education and health care. They no longer have adequate retirement funds or even the hope of obtaining them. They no longer feel that an adulthood of success, security, and self-respect is achievable, and for this they feel ashamed. This shame, moreover, largely stems from the trope of American individualism, the notion that all are solely responsible for their own success or failure, however the playing field might tilt.

So scapegoating can indeed temporarily address shameful feelings, but unfortunately it always moves toward greater violence. The atrocities committed against the victims of scapegoating are themselves shameful, but they must be justified by rhetoric that falsely elevates the crime to a virtue, as in the notion that one is "cleansing" the population. Scapegoating also distracts us from seeing where our troubles are actually rooted. It is utilized and fueled by leaders who have hidden motivations and intentions that are more likely to succeed if groups are divided from one another.

We need a conjunction of psychology and history to understand why many Anglos experience the Mexicans in their midst as interlopers who are causing high unemployment and dwindling local and state budgets. Those who are victims of history have come to be seen as perpetrators of fraud, abuse, and violence. Nowhere in this narrative is it acknowledged that Anglos were themselves interlopers in the mid-1800s, that their nation's policies have substantially contributed to the present mass migration, that Anglos have profited from the presence of low-cost labor, and that many Anglo businesses have colluded with and even encouraged false documentation. In part, these gaps in the narrative are due to historical and social amnesia—to a failure to examine the shadows our walls cast, to address racism, and to make the study of history essential to our efforts to know ourselves.

Scapegoating is understandable in such a situation, but we need to see through it and disrupt it. Failures in education, health care, and employment opportunities do not occur simply because "others" have taken up residence in a new homeland. Getting rid of these "others" will not solve these problems. The complex global forces and unbridled greed that have caused forced migration of unprecedented proportions are the same as those that have eroded the self-confidence and self-respect of the people involved in scapegoating. In the present case, scapegoating is a diversion from critically attending to the massive betrayal of ordinary Americans by those who use their power and position for excessive personal gain. The economic catastrophes wrought by the exercise of excessive greed have so disrupted the lives of ordinary Americans that our possibilities for hospitality are tragically overwhelmed by fear of inadequate resources for ourselves. The illegality of the Mexican crossing the border is far easier to protest than the illegality of money schemes within the banking system that even regulators don't sufficiently understand.

Encouraging Collective Shame and Remorse

> But the day that people will have understood who you were, they will bite the earth with sadness and remorse, they will water it with their tears, and they will build temples to you.
>
> Vercors (pseudonym of Jean Marcel Bruller),
> inscription on the Mémorial des Martyrs de la Déportation, Paris

A group or culture that can begin to practice historical memory instead of social amnesia, that can collectively acknowledge and sincerely apologize for events in the past that have harmed others, that can make amends, and that claims its shadow of exclusion and abuse is a culture that is creating nonviolent ways for people to live together, to be reconciled as neighbors rather than polarized as enemies. Margaret Gilbert (2001, 231) points out that collective remorse does not rule out individual remorse, but it also does not require it. One may feel no personal responsibility for offenses that harmed others yet still acknowledge membership in the group that was responsible.

Gilbert describes membership remorse as a group member's remorse over the act of a group of which he or she is a member. The group member need not have participated in the acts or even known about them at the time. Gilbert says that group "members all bear some relevant relation to the act of their group" because of their "participation in the underlying joint commitment" (2001, 227). Group remorse may be suffered secretly, she says, with others not knowing. Membership and group remorse pave the way not only for "backward-looking forgiveness" but also for "a renewal of forward-looking trust" (218). Moving from shame to remorse allows a shift from defensive and hostile relations to the possibility of a desire for making amends, restitution, and reparations.

Engaging History

The borderlands theorist Gloria Anzaldúa (1999) urges us to take an inventory of the histories that have shaped us and then to put them "through a sieve" so as to "winnow out the lies" (104). James Baldwin put the dilemma bluntly in his essay "The White Man's Guilt," printed in *Ebony* magazine:

> People who imagine that history flatters them (as it does, indeed, since they wrote it) are impaled on their history like a butterfly on a pin and become incapable of seeing or changing themselves, or the world.
>
> This is the place in which it seems to me, most white Americans find themselves. Impaled. They are dimly, or vividly, aware that the history

they have fed themselves is mainly a lie, but they do not know how to release themselves from it, and they suffer enormously from the personal incoherence. (1965, 47)

Arizona's recently passed law banning ethnic studies in that state is bad for those of Mexican descent and bad for Anglos.[1] A sensitive Anglo reading the books on Arizona's banned list might well feel a sense of shame at the history of land grabs, violent displacements, lynchings, rapes, and exploitation that has marred Anglos' presence in the American Southwest. The removal of Chicano history from American schools is akin to the removal and deportation of Mexican migrants themselves, for both involve removing a source of shame from the American landscape.

In order to avert hostile defensiveness, which distorts and perverts history, school authorities must craft educational environments that allow for respectful dialogue and eschew false histories more consoling to those in power. Otherwise, those who suffer from a heritage of inequality and violence are perversely presented as criminals, as aliens attempting to undo the society they are seen as invading and exploiting. Sensitively allowing for shame and providing ample ways for students to live more equitably with their Mexican neighbors help ensure that defense against shameful feelings does not lead to rage and violence. The reduction of what Gilligan calls "shame-provoking inequalities" is crucial, for shame accrues on both sides of the veil.

Restorative History, Restorative Shame, Restorative Justice

Sadly, our challenge is not to reintegrate those who were once part of our common fabric and then expelled. It is to decisively build relationships with those neighbors who have never been included, relationships distinguished by justice and respect. It is also to realize that we ourselves are on the outside of the common, in need of integration.

We have a choice regarding how we treat the immigrants who enter our communities. America has successfully integrated many immigrant groups, allowing them to climb the ladder of success and to enter professional jobs. We have failed with respect to other groups. Do we make an internal colony of those who come, or do we learn from our history and commit ourselves to extending human rights to those who labor in our communities? With forced migrations reaching unprecedented proportions, the right to live in particular places has become ever more contested, sometimes with history rewritten to justify present claims. Others may become defined not simply as in the way but as out of place, in the wrong place. As multiple claims on the same place intensify, those in one group may believe they would be better off if the other group were eliminated. This may be the case, even if the latter group had prior claim to the place and a history of habitation in the area. Unfortunately, ill-treatment and even violence may be used to displace a group from the place they now call home.

America has used brute power not only to legitimate its interference in other people's homelands but also to define others in terms that justify expelling them from a land that we have conveniently claimed as our own place, forgetting that it belonged to ancestors of these same others. Across the globe, uprooted by the effects of transnational globalization and its attendant violence and ecological devastation, people are being forced to become migrants, leaving their homes, communities, and often families. Our hope is that engendering restorative shame at a history remembered and taken to heart can help heal the ways we greet and treat our neighbors.

A discourse based on shame also has perils. One may feel better after apologizing, but the victim may derive no real benefit from it. Indeed, apology without altered behavior serves to further disrupt the possibilities of trust and repair. Reflecting on white Australians' creation of "Sorry Books," which apologized for abuses against Aborigines, Sara Ahmed warns that we should apologize only to help those who were harmed and not principally to feel better about ourselves by relieving our guilt and shame—or worse, to bolster our self-image with pride in our new insights. Only when the acknowledgment of shame is paired with a new mode of being with others that seeks to repair what can be repaired, and that commits us to never again causing the sufferings previously caused, does shame bear restorative fruit.

To address our soul loss, we must begin to look carefully at the images in the mirrors that our Mexican neighbors hold up to us. How are we seen? What truth is there? We must grapple with these starkly negative—though often hidden—assessments. We will need to acknowledge that the actions of our people—and perhaps our own actions—have sown this derision, mistrust, and disdain. We must desire to act in ways that will give rise to more just realities. In time, these seeds will generate wholly different images, though this is not to be sought as an end in itself. This is a place to begin walking toward being a neighbor, a place to start anew in full awareness that the past will not be erased and that generations of undue hardship thrust on people in the past will require generations of integrity to gain the trust of those in the present and the future so that we can make common cause. Over a century ago, DuBois said that "the nation has not yet found peace from its sins" ([1903] 1989, 5). Indeed, it is still a peace we need to seek.

May we want to reckon up our debts, acknowledge them, create formal apologies, and commit to reparations and remembrance. These restorative actions will not only help us retrieve the Anglo soul but also, and more important, help grace the world of which we are but one part with increased justice and peace. By walking these pathways, Anglos can cease holding themselves apart from the arms of the world in which they were born.

DuBois says,

> Through all the sorrow of the Sorrow Songs there breathes a hope—a faith in the ultimate justice of things. The minor cadences of despair change often to triumph and calm confidence. Sometimes it is faith in life, some-times a faith in death, sometimes assurance of boundless justice in some fair world beyond. But whichever it is, the meaning is always clear: that sometime, somewhere, men will judge men by their souls and not by their skins. Is such a hope justified? Do the Sorrow Songs sing true? ([1903] 1989, 186)

Will Anglos find access to their own lamentations and sorrow, so that hope for those consigned to racial and economic castes and for Anglos themselves can be justified?

The Mexican migrants who struggle with poverty know they enter a foreign and hostile land. The wall announces the United States' will to assert control over their movements. They will soon learn that their labor is desired, but not their personhood—if they have not already fully learned this in Mexico. They will be treated as entirely expendable. They discover that they are to express no needs, and certainly no demands to meet those needs. If they are to remain, they must attempt to be invisible while seem-ingly tireless in the service of others. Even so, this unjust arrangement can-not be trusted, for their newly constructed home can be dismantled at any moment. Indeed, the system keeps an eye on them, even far from the border. It keeps them on edge. Such a situation does not merit the word *hospital-ity*. It is exploitation, pure and simple. Is it any wonder that the children of these migrants grow up to carry a resentment and bitterness in their hearts that is equal to their sense of futility about rising to a place of personhood in the eyes of Anglos? How dark the shadow we have cast; how arbitrary the diminishment they find themselves born under.

In colonialism, those settlers who found colonial arrangements inhu-mane could leave the colony. In the neocolonialism wrought by globaliza-tion, colonial arrangements happen all around us in our own community, so that our transformation of relationships and arrangements of power must begin here. As Americans, the wall we encounter is of our own mak-ing. We see the door we have shut on others. We can notice how we turn away from it and look elsewhere.

To restore our souls, we "norteamericanos" need our own medicine history, to put this in Aurora Levins Morales's (1999) language. This is a bitter herb, but without it we are doomed to repeat a savage history of exploitation and self-aggrandizement at the expense of others. Without it, we cannot develop the "double consciousness" of which DuBois spoke. It will be acquired through effort. When we hear how others see us, we will feel shame, and we must be ready to bear it, understanding that it will be the humus of another form of consciousness, more empathic, more soulful.

We must suffer becoming "other" to ourselves, a problem to ourselves. This will place us as kin to Malintzin. We will be seen as "race traitors." We will find there is a hidden room in the heart of our house. We have been locked out. The stranger shows us that we are locked out of the inside of our home (Derrida 2000). He provides us a necessary reorientation that should elicit our gratitude. This is a reorientation to our neighbor. We would cease to demand his invisibility, cease to throw him out, to blame him for inequalities and lack of opportunities that have nothing to do with him. This reorientation allows us to see him with respect—indeed, with gratitude as well. The migrant has come a long way. Being more aware of his history and his burdens, let us welcome him in and in so doing come closer to the heart of our home.

Soul Retrieval

Let me now consider the kind of neighbor each of us is to the migrant, to the stranger. The psychoanalyst Eric Santner argues that "it is precisely [our] answerability that is at the heart of our very aliveness to the world" (2001, 9). While Freud was oriented to the "various ways we remove ourselves from the midst" of life, defending against aliveness, says Santner, we need to create a psychology of the possibility and the actuality of encounter, to open to "the uncanny presence" of our neighbors (ibid.). To nourish our imagination about such encounters, we can turn to the Bantu principle of *ubuntu*, which guided many South Africans during the proceedings of the post-apartheid Truth and Reconciliation Commission (TRC). In traditional African society, a person may have some riches and authority, but if they do not have *ubuntu*, they are not respected. *Ubuntu* is hospitality; it is a welcoming and open attitude, a generosity and caring, a willingness to share. *Ubuntu*, says Michael Battle, is the "development of a person who proves to be a neighbor to strangers and welcomes them as friends" (1997, 65). I become a person through you, as you do through me. Bishop Desmond Tutu, who presided over the TRC, says that "in the spirit of ubuntu, the central concern is the healing of breaches, the redressing of imbalances, the restoration of broken relationships" (2000, 54). The South African psychologist Pumla Gobodo-Madikizela, speaking from her experience working on the TRC, clarifies how we can go about dissolving "the apartheid of the mind" from which our societal apartheid ensues: "To humanize the other and to act in ways that humanize us for others are the corollary acts that are needed" (2003, 109).

When we fail to focus on our broken relationships, we trigger an autoimmune attack. In our failure to grasp the deep level of our interbeing, the pursuit of what appears to be our own self-interest compromises our existence. For this reason, the philosopher Jacques Derrida described our current inhospitable and unjust approaches to immigration as autoimmune attacks, destroying the common body by turning mistakenly on one part.

The kind of restorative and generative shame at issue in this chapter calls us to a new self, one that acknowledges the poverty of hoarding, the ignorance born of separation, and the lovelessness bred by overattachment to self-interest. This self is enlivened by protest and resistance to that which undermines *ubuntu*, understanding the risk of loss of soul and connection. It responds to the psychic gravitational pull that the migrant's forced movement away from his or her home exerts on us, causing us to cross our own borders of reserve and alienation and create forms of mutuality that are graced by an integrity we have almost forgotten is possible.

The pilgrimages required of us are both intrapsychic and interpersonal, for they must entail those shifts that enable us to enter into relations with those whom we have previously ignored, minimized, derogated, denied, or forsaken. Once disturbed by finding ourselves "others," we who enjoy many fruits of privilege must breach our group's social conventions in order to inquire further, leaving the safety of the walls—metaphorical and literal—that we have within and around us. That which has been cast out is now encountered anew. Without our knowing the history on which our present moment rests, we cannot ask ourselves the questions we need to address. We sacrifice the possibility of knowing ourselves, of finding our true roots. Without finding our place in history, we cannot wholly forge our integrity. When we amputate history so that it comes out just "right," we also amputate our hope for forming a community that is graced by bridges connecting its member groups. We condemn ourselves to the alienation, loneliness, and paranoia that accompany all apartheid-like arrangements between groups.

It is not just Mexican migrants who are "up against the wall"; Anglos are as well. Paulo Freire, the Brazilian pedagogist and leader of Brazil's literacy movement, describes phenomena such as the literal and psychosocial walls at stake here as "limit situations." He reminds us of Alvaro Vieira Pinto's definition of a limit situation as not "the impassable boundaries where all possibilities end, but the real boundaries where all possibilities begin; [they are not] the frontier which separates being from nothingness, but the frontier which separates being from being more" (quoted in Freire [1970] 1989, 89). The limit situations we confront require our careful and sustained critical reflection so that we can begin both to see how situations that seem inevitable and fixed are actually constructed and to determine who and what they serve so that they can be reimagined and created otherwise. This decade has delivered us to another dark chapter in the history of Mexican migration to the United States, where the physical wall at La Frontera has slid into place behind people who had anticipated being able to move more freely across the border. Ironically, the wall has trapped people who might otherwise have gone home, because for now, the wall and the impediments to crossing it creates have blocked the self-regulating flow of migration. Freirean pedagogy would have us critically decode the limit situations in our lives and encourages us to imagine more humane possibilities. This process of annunciatory or prophetic imagination guides our actions in the present as we together remake the problematic aspects of our shared world. The following chapters of this book will address the creative options that have arisen from such processes. While some may argue that we are further than ever from a wider adoption of any of these alternatives, it is vitally important to keep our imagination alive at this difficult juncture, for otherwise we will lose the vision of what will be possible and merely react to the stricter limits that have been more recently imposed.

For shame to become generative and restorative, we must undertake alternative actions that play a role in setting relationships right. To open our imagination to these alternatives is to engage the work of what has been called alterglobalization, an altogether different form of globalization, for its *teloi* are the spread of justice and sustainability. An adequate alterglobalization must address psychic decolonization and work toward forms of global citizenry that reject policies that diminish our humanity with one another while creating forms of transborder solidarity that begin to release us from the walls we have created. Such decolonization requires us to engage in an intentional set of practices that succeeds in placing us into direct relationships with those who have been separated from us. Only then can the empathic linking of communities proceed, and the valuing of each human being—whether Anglo or Mexican—become unquestioned.

CHAPTER 8

Border-Wall Art as Limit Acts

Something there is that doesn't love a wall,
That sends the frozen-ground-swell under it,
And spills the upper boulders in the sun,
And makes gaps even two can pass abreast.

Robert Frost, "Mending Wall"

Often, a sense of futility or defensive violence overtakes us when we are pressed against a wall; at other times, however, the experience engenders an explosion of creative imagination. Deploying imagination in the face of oppressive fixity exemplifies what the Brazilian pedagogist Paulo Freire calls a "limit act," an act that both resists the imposition of destructive limits and creates anew in the face of them. The building of the wall at the U.S.-Mexico border has paradoxically yet predictably called forth the rupturing swells that Frost knew eventually undo imposed divisions, that spill "the upper boulders in the sun." Indeed, as we, the authors, have engaged with the destructive human and ecological ramifications of the wall, we have been soothed and inspired by witnessing and participating in some of the many transborder initiatives that function as limit acts. Quickened by the aggressive "securing" of the border, creative counteracts have gained focus and resolve. As xenophobia and racism have gained ground, these actions of resistance have attained the force of prophetic imagination.

In the end, every wall will come down, a theme first broached in chapter 1, which characterized the wall at La Frontera as a "leaking vessel" that will eventually deteriorate and become useless. Even while the wall is still being secured, however, we can take actions to hasten this moment in the future, at the same time pushing back against those less literal walls between ourselves and others over which we have day-to-day control. Each time we undertake a limit act against the apartheids in our midst, we reawaken and nourish a wider possibility of solidarity. Part of the alchemy of border work is the ability to move fluidly from a level of organization that has proved temporarily unsuccessful to another level where limit acts can reach their goal, paving the way for a successful return to the earlier impasse.

When I, Mary, first encountered the wall, I was on the U.S. side at Friendship Park. The monotonous military green of the landing strips from the Persian Gulf War used to make up the wall blocked a full view of the Mexican beach on the other side. The next day, while on the other side, in Tijuana, I discovered creative and vibrant wall art transposing the drab military backdrop. Studying this art, talking with some of the artists, and linking the wall art in Mexico with border-wall art in Derry, Belfast, Palestine, and Berlin have greatly helped galvanize my capacity to see—to envision—alternatives. Learning about the transborder and international collaboration of wall artists was already a counterforce to the divisiveness of the wall itself.

This chapter concerns the initial site of our study: the wall itself. Whereas it analyzes border-wall art as limit acts at the literal border, the next chapter addresses limit acts at the metaphorical borders in the relations between Mexican migrants and citizens, acts that point us toward a different way of living together. In this chapter, we consider border-wall art's power to undermine the wall's functions, to transmute the impeding material surfaces into a gallery that nourishes critical consciousness, memorializes losses, and sparks prophetic imagination. Border-wall art portrays marginalized points of view, critiques dominant messages, and not only posits alternate possibilities but creates them. Such are the functions of limit acts. While the wall stands, it is put to different uses—indeed, to tasks most often antithetical to its intended purposes and meanings. Performative border art also defies the limit of the wall, rehearsing transgressions that allow imagination to transcend the wall's brute technologized and material limit.

The art on the wall at the border is like a healing salve placed on an open wound. To encounter images on such a forbidding surface is to remember Nietzsche's insight: "We have art in order not to perish from the truth." In building the wall, the U.S. government violently thrust a foreign object into and onto the earth, intruded into aquifers, and incised fragile and unique terrains. As Part 1 revealed, the wall divides people from their backyards and animals from their habitats and migratory ranges. It slashes through the hearts of nature preserves, a university, and the streets of people's towns and cities. It stands as a powerful contradiction to the welcome we strive for in our homes and communities. It is ugly, and indeed, it repels and repulses.

Conversely, the art on the wall invites one in and brings one up close, creating an intimacy with the wall. In the midst of wall art, one feels not pressed "up against the wall" but invited to altogether other vistas and ways of thinking. Transgressively, the art uses the wall to begin to undo the wall itself.

Some say the Berlin Wall fell from the weight of the paint used for graffiti and murals on the West Berlin side. The East Berlin side of that wall remained sterile except for a few marks. The U.S. side of the wall at the U.S.-Mexico border similarly bears no wall art. A single exhibition in Brownsville curated by the artist Mark Clark, of Galeria 409, was attached to the fence-like wall in Brownsville for a few hours and then removed as planned. Any graffiti placed on the U.S. side of the wall has been erased or blacked out. Artists' proposals have been rejected by the Department of Homeland Security. On the Mexican side, however, the arts of contestation, protest, memorial, outrage, and prophetic imagination thrive.

GRAFFITI: GENERATIVE WORDS AND IMAGES

Paulo Freire's popular education method is employed not only for teaching literacy skills but also for helping people learn to read, to decode, and to analyze the situations in which they live. Proceeding in this spirit, we can begin our critical analysis by bringing into dialogue generative words and phrases that help us claim and focus on what is important in our realities. These words name both what is problematic and what is valued (e.g., femicide, militarization, clean water). Those who create separation barriers and walls tend to name them in ways that obscure their functions. For instance, the East German government called the Berlin Wall the "anti-Fascist protection rampart." The wall that separates Catholic and Protestant neighborhoods in west Belfast is called the "Peace Wall." Graffiti art often functions to descriptively name a wall from the perspective of those whom it prevents from moving freely. The first graffiti on the Berlin Wall read "KZ=DDR," equating East Germany (the Deutsche Demokratische Republik) with a "concentration camp" (*Konzentrationslager*), a chilling and insightful summation attempting to crystallize the function of the wall as keeping people in, not out. While the government talked about protecting its citizens from the decadence of capitalism and fascism, the wall actually functioned to create a prison-like existence for most East Germans. German graffiti also posed the question of how much longer the wall would be allowed to divide: "Wie lange noch?" (How much longer?), a question that introduced fragility and uncertainty to what was presented as powerfully solid and durable. Similarly, the word "GHETTO" is written across the Israeli separation wall, ironically linking the ghettoes in which Jews historically suffered to the environments being created for Palestinians in the occupied territories.

Similarly, some of the graffiti on the U.S. wall incisively sum up the situation from the Mexican side: The brief exclamation "Go home, Yankee!" underscores the vexed history wherein the original inhabitants were labeled interlopers, destabilizing the position of the wall and contesting the placement of the border itself. The graffito "Deportan a la Migra" ("Deport the Border Patrol") reverses the demand, made by 51 percent in the United States, to deport Mexicans without documents. "Yankee, Fuera Irak/Fuera México" ("Yankee, Get out of Iraq, Get out of Mexico!") draws attention to the U.S. government's propensity to intervene in other people's lands. This graffito interrogates the wall's tacit claim that Mexican interlopers should be forcibly restrained. It turns the tables on present understandings, leading us to ask who the real interlopers are and where the real border lies.

Many graffiti artists are trying to establish the larger context of which the wall is a part, for instance, by linking the wall to U.S. military interventions in other parts of the world. This parallels how the art on the International Wall in west Belfast tries to link the struggle in Northern Ireland to that in the Basque Country, to the embargoes against Cuba, and to slavery in the United States. These links create international solidarities. For instance, the phrase "Fronteras: Cicatrizes en la Tierra" ("Borders: Scars in the Earth"), often used as graffiti, by implication links the U.S.-Mexico border wall to other international border walls. Even brief graffiti statements can have the power to transform the very thinking out of which the wall first arose. On the Nogales wall, one reads "Las paredes vueltas de lado son puentes" ("Walls turned on their sides are bridges"), indicating that overturning walls can create bridges.

Such mottoes are joined by single generative images that attempt to show some of the meanings of the wall. Some individuals simply paint or sculpt money signs (see figure 19), pointing not only to the money migrants hope to make in the United States but also to the profits made by trapping people at the border and shunting them into low-paying jobs in the maquiladoras, industrial factories on the Mexican side. One of the most powerful generative images of the border and its wall is that of "una herida abierta," an open wound.

The border wall clearly differs from garden walls, which protect restorative places. It is another variety of wall, one that is imposed on an open and dynamic landscape, forcibly separating peoples and families. This sense of the wall as an open wound was captured earlier in a project by the Berlin artist Peter Unsicker, who wrapped a portion of the Berlin Wall outside of his window with surgical gauze. On the Mexican side of the wall, in Tijuana, someone has painted a gaping wound with clumsy sutures. It is

Figure 15. Graffiti on the U.S. wall, "Fronteras: Cicatrizes en la Tierra" ("Borders: Scars on the Land"), Nogales, Mexico. Photo by Mary Watkins.

Figure 16. Mural of the border as a sutured wound, *una llaga*, U.S. border wall, Tijuana, Mexico. Photo by Mary Watkins.

not a delicate painting but a rough and jagged one, evoking the destructive tear in the landscape and the pressing need for repair and healing.

Separation walls have given rise to a lexicon of imagery recognizable across particular situations. The Palestinian side of the Israeli separation wall bears a particularly poignant image of a weeping face, expressing the grief and tragedy this wall has occasioned. Upon seeing Jews intensely praying at Jerusalem's Western Wall, Europeans dubbed it "the Wailing Wall." This Palestinian face evokes a different sense of a wailing wall, one where the wall itself cries, as though witness to the separations and injustices that it starkly imposes. This face could easily be imagined on the U.S. wall.

MEMORIAL

Much of the art on the wall memorializes the deaths of those trying to cross into the United States. The very wall that has caused these deaths is used to name and remember them, as though to bring to the wall itself a sense of conscience and consciousness. Crosses with names and caskets with numbers of migrants who have died each year since NAFTA's passage dot the wall. Each is a solemn assessment of the wall's tragic and deadly outcome. These images commemorate all the migrants who, because they were traveling without identification when they met their deaths, will remain unnamed, leaving behind families who lack any way of knowing whether they have disappeared into America or perished on their way there. It is a slow and steady death count of those who have perished on their way north, often about equal to the numbers of young American men and women who have died in the wars in Afghanistan and Iraq. We are reminded that, at our border, we are involved in a war of a different kind. The artist Carmela Castrejon prophesied as much when she hung blood-soaked clothes on a thirteen-mile stretch of fence built at the border in 1991, coinciding with the first year of the Gulf War.

One of the most moving memorials to both the living and dead who are touched by migration is Alejandro Santiago's *2501 Migrantes*. Upon returning to San Pedro Teococuilco, his hometown near Oaxaca, Santiago was shocked and saddened by the migration of 2,500 residents because of poverty, lack of schools, and chronic unemployment. Like hundreds of other Mexican towns, it has been depopulated by 50 percent or more because economic need has pushed its residents to look for work in El Norte. Many of Santiago's friends and relatives had also left for the United States, heightening his intimate sense of abandonment.

Santiago had a dream in which his community was repopulated. When he awoke, he undertook the project of creating ceramic representation of

Figure 17. Detail, *2501 Migrantes*, Alejandro Santiago, on exhibit at the Museo de Arte Contemporáneo, Oaxaca, Mexico. Photo by Mary Watkins.

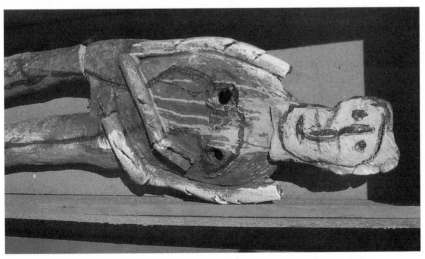

Figure 18. Detail, *2501 Migrantes*, Alejandro Santiago, on exhibit at the Museo de Arte Contemporáneo, Oaxaca, Mexico. Photo by Mary Watkins.

all those absent from his village (Casanova, n.d.). His vision was to create a tribute that would offer dignity to those who had to migrate. He hoped that the project could draw individuals back to Teococuilco, as well as help to keep its young people at home by creating jobs and offering creative activity. Santiago enlisted a local team composed of the sons and daughters of local farmers struggling to support their families, training them to become ceramicists, in order to accomplish this project. The late Santiago understood emigration as signaling a loss of connection to one's community and the land. To foster these connections, he introduced farm animals into Teococuilco and initiated projects for water conservation and agriculture, hoping to create a self-sustaining ecosystem (Johnson 2006).

Although he could traverse the border legally, Santiago arranged to cross with a coyote so that he could experience what those in his village had endured to find passage to the north. He became the 2,501st migrant. That harrowing experience taught him that his clay figures should be naked to express the utter vulnerability migrants suffer in leaving their homes, risking their lives crossing perilous deserts and mountains, and struggling to succeed in a country where they are deemed aliens. The nude ceramic clay figures, set at roughly three-quarters life size, display the migrants' uprootedness, the marks and scars of their journey imprinted on their flesh, their weary gazes, and broken bodies, all testifying to their desperate pilgrimage.

2501 Migrantes is Santiago's "tribute" to those who cross borders and must begin their lives anew, as well as to those whose lives are taken by borders. These figures have been placed in the desert near the border, at the Museo de Arte Contemporáneo de Oaxaca, and ultimately they will be displayed in Santiago's hometown. In schoolyards and churches, at the town's zocalo, and near shops and fields, these figures will mark the absence of those who have gone north to feed their families, to secure funds so that they can come back and build a home, or to pay for the medical care of an ailing mother or father. As you walk among these figures and stand beside them, you are gifted with tender encounters. Made of earth, these figures possess a fragile, vulnerable, naked, ghostlike presence that makes a strong appeal to viewers. Those who stand among them are led to imagine what it would be like to wait for a stranger to lead them into completely unfamiliar and inhospitable terrain, to be at that stranger's mercy as they cross a passage that threatens them with death, and to enter a land that forbids them. These "mutely expressive" (Johnson 2006) figures have a profound impact on those who experience them. The viewer is transformed from bystander to witness, pulled into the situation by the imploring and lost faces. One part of the installation includes multiple rows of open coffins, each portraying a migrant in his or her final resting state, having succumbed to the inhospitality of the desert. One of the most moving parts of the installation is a refuse pile where parts of broken figures lie waiting to be thrown away. The migrants are used up, broken, and discarded.

BORDER DYNAMICS

Instead of displaying relatively focused generative words and images, more complex border-wall art often depicts the dynamics of the border from the perspective of those who live in its shadow. Until 2010, on Calle Internacional in Nogales, Mexico, anyone walking along the wall would find *El Paseo de Humanidad* (*The Parade of Humanity*), by three artists from both sides of the border: Guadalupe Serrano, Alberto Morackis, and Alfred Quiroz. Their transborder partnership reflects efforts to link artists from both nations who defy, through their artistic collaboration, the separation that the wall attempts to impose.[1] Inspired by the border art of Tijuana, Quiroz says that making the art was "like a rebellion, because people are not supposed to touch the border" (personal communication 2011).

This transgressive 2004 installation of sixteen giant *milagros* by Quiroz and nineteen metallic human figures by the Taller Yonke Arte Público artists Morackis and Serrano warn migrants of the dangers they will face as they cross the border.[2] It borrows from Mayan, Aztec, and Catholic iconographies, asserting the generative power of Mexican peoples' cultures and traditions.

Milagros are religious folk charms illustrating the object of a person's prayers or gratitude. They may be held in the hand while praying, attached to statues of saints, nailed or pinned to crosses, or suspended from altars and shrines by ribbons. A particular milagro is held to help quicken the supplicant's prayer for such things as a recovery from an illness or a heartbreak. It also helps the person to focus his or her attention on a specific ailment during prayer. They are carried for good luck and protection.

Quiroz uses the popular iconography of healing in Mexico to offer both blessings and warnings. These charms, central to popular healing rituals, are fixed to the separation wall as though to the wall of a church. While they are intended to help heal the sufferings of those who are on the way to cross the border, it seems as though they might also act to heal the wall itself. Placing the milagros on the wall transforms it from a structure that reinscribes economic and national divides into a site of supplication and prayer. On the very wall that asserts power, control, and inhospitality, Quiroz suggests a different way to be with the border: treating it as a holy place, a place to pray for well-being and health. In the face of a wall that negates what migrants bring to their "host" culture, Quiroz celebrates the

Figure 19 (left). Giant milagro, detail of Milagros series, Alfred Quiroz, *Parade of Humanity/Paseo de Humanidad*, U.S. border wall, Calle Internacional, Nogales, Mexico, 2004–2010. Artwork funded by an Artist Project grant from the Arizona Commission on the Arts; © 2004 by Alfred J. Quiroz. Photo by Mary Watkins.

Figure 20 (below). Milagros series, Alfred Quiroz, *Parade of Humanity/Paseo de Humanidad*, U.S. border wall, Calle Internacional, Nogales, Mexico, 2004–2010. Artwork funded by an Artist Project grant from the Arizona Commission on the Arts; © 2004 by Alfred J. Quiroz. Photo by Alfred Quiroz.

healing images of their folk traditions. For instance, at one milagro one can pray for the traveler, symbolized by a milagro in the form of a leg.

Quiroz uses the milagros "to tell the story of the border." *Tucson Weekly*'s art critic, Margaret Regan, says,

> They're meant to be read in sequence. One set begins with a flaming heart, a conflagration that sends the wanderer away from home. Next is a snarling coyote head, a stand-in for the human coyotes who smuggle migrants across the border for a fee. Then there's a big leg, another traditional milagro icon, but this one is equipped with border-crossing jeans and a sneaker that is on the run. Ahead are a truck laden with skulls, two gallon-size water bottles lying uselessly next to a skull in a now equally useless hat, and finally, the trio of skulls lying at the foot of a saguaro. Yet others address the economic aspect of the situation: one depicts a retail bar code on a saguaro. Everything is up for sale. (2004, n.p.)

The central portion of this work depicts the dynamics of exchange operating at the border, combining, says Morackis, Aztec iconography with contemporary sensibility (Regan 2004). The artists present the border as a red revolving door through which migrants both depart and return. Using the male and female symbols familiar to us from the doors of public restrooms, the artists symbolize the mass nature of the migration underway. Above is the map of Mexico before the Mexican-American War, reminding us of the fact that what lies on the other side of the wall was not long ago a part of Mexico.

What do the migrants bring to the United States? One figure carries mariachi instruments on his back; another, the Virgin of Guadalupe in his backpack. They bring not only their labor but also their culture, their music, and spirituality. We are introduced to cultural figures, such as Juan Soldado, who according to many was wrongfully executed in Tijuana for a crime he did not commit. He symbolizes failed justice, an experience all too many migrants will encounter as they cross the border. Another is the legendary Jesús Malverde, known as the saint of narcotraffickers, a folk hero in Sinaloa and analogous to Robin Hood in being a champion of the poor (Alvarez 2008). One figure represents a Border Patrol agent, *la migra*. He is chasing the migrants with a big stick. His chest and heart area are constructed of the same corrugated metal as the wall is. He is speaking something that resembles Latin, an unintelligible language to those he addresses. Above his head is a credit card logo: from one point of view, he is an agent of the free-market capitalism that has forced these travelers to take flight from their homelands and is now intercepting them at the border.

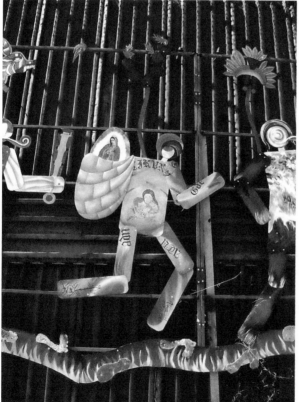

Figure 21 (above). Detail, *Parade of Humanity/ Paseo de Humanidad*, Guadalupe Serrano and Alberto Morackis, U.S. border wall, Calle Internacional, Nogales, Mexico, 2004. Photo by Mary Watkins.

Figure 22 (left). Detail, *Parade of Humanity/ Paseo de Humanidad*, Guadalupe Serrano and Alberto Morackis, U.S. border wall, Calle Internacional, Nogales, Mexico, 2004. Photo by Mary Watkins.

What are the migrants bringing home? A bomb and weapons are painted on the body of a woman, for the United States is the largest exporter of arms to Mexico—which has strict gun-control laws. A shrouded body, a victim of the crossing itself, is carried back to its homeland. Manufactured goods, from screws to a washing machine to women's boots, are depicted, items migrants bring back to their families, who would otherwise not have them.

The desert itself, often called a "road of fire," is depicted as a flaming path that burns the travelers' shoes and feet, a trail of footsteps marking their travels. Indeed, the journey leaves a variety of imprints; a body covered with eyes, for example, points to the lasting effects of being closely watched by the Border Patrol. This figure, reduced to someone who is seen and tracked, is doubly visible, for his organs are exposed to show the effects of dehydration from the desert heat. A woman traveler bears sign-language symbols on her body that spell what she desires: "vida," life. One female figure holds a child by the hand while in her belly she carries an unborn child into the dangerous terrain.

The sculptors Serrano and Morackis planned an installation called *Border Dynamics* for both sides of the wall, the United States and Mexico (figures 23 and 24). Although U.S. border authorities initially approved the project, they later reversed the decision, purportedly because they feared Mexican migrants would slide down the backs of the figures and that children might hurt themselves climbing on them. All four figures were temporarily placed on the Mexican side and then later installed at the University of Arizona campus in Tucson in the arrangement that had originally been intended: two figures on each side of a wall.

Border Dynamics leads viewers to meditate on both the action and the inattention that keep a wall in place. In this installation, the artists draw our attention past those maintaining the wall through their intentional force and invite us to acknowledge how, by turning our backs, we all create and sustain the walls we live within and impose on others. The work urges us to acknowledge the degree to which our weight has often silently sustained the walls in our communities, as well as at the border, while our eyes are focused elsewhere.

PROPHETIC IMAGINATION

The assaultive power of separation walls constellates prophetic imagining as an essential form of limit act. Developing a critical understanding of border dynamics by demystifying the past and present opens a creative space in which people can begin to dream of a future that is more deeply aligned with what is desired. Envisioning images of the future can help us move

Figure 23. *Border Dynamics,* Alberto Morackis and Guadalupe Serrano, University of Arizona, Tucson, 2005. Photo by Mary Watkins.

Figure 24. *Border Dynamics,* Alberto Morackis and Guadalupe Serrano, University of Arizona, Tucson, 2005. Photo by Mary Watkins.

past the restrictions and curtailments of the present, giving life to images of liberation, justice, and peaceful coexistence. These images act as seeds for actions in the present and future. Utopic images of a world without destructive separations appear on many separation walls around the globe and are an essential part of the lexicon of wall art.

In 2005 the street artist Banksy contributed nine images to the Israeli West Bank barrier. One of the nine depicted a little girl floating over the wall, drawn up by freely soaring balloons. In another image, children are digging, as though at a beach, next to what looks like a rip in the wall through which an idyllic beach is visible. In yet another, a ladder simply goes all the way up, leading to the other side. Similarly, a painting on the Berlin Wall represented a large zipper opening the structure to reveal a lush natural world right behind its stultifying presence.

In Tijuana, doves have been released over the wall, birds that can freely fly across human-made walls and fences. They presage a freer passage for the humans and animals below. As noted earlier, performance artists have been shot by cannon from Tijuana to Friendship Park, transgressing the limit situation of the wall. The wall in this city bears a mural of an open door, signaling hospitality and freedom in lieu of exclusion (see figure 27, in the epilogue). In 2010, Alfred Quiroz collaborated with Grupo Yonke to make a portion of the wall at Nogales invisible; Quiroz photographed an area of Nogales, Arizona, transposed the image onto vinyl, and installed the result on the border wall on the Mexican side exactly opposite the location the photo depicted. A viewer looking at the life-size photo of trees and vegetation would experience the area as if the wall were no longer present. It gave viewers a glimpse into both the past and the future, the border without the separation wall.

The Life and Dreams of the Perla Ravine (*Vida y Sueños de la Cañada Perla*) is a mural painted on the Mexican side of the wall in Nogales. This mural was originally painted in 1998 in Chiapas, Mexico, to celebrate the inauguration of the autonomous municipality of Ricardo Flores Magón,[3] one of the Zapatista communities. The leader of the artistic team was the artist Sergio "el Checo" Valdez. Fourteen hours after its creation, on April 11, 1998, paramilitary forces destroyed the mural; the artist and others were imprisoned. Subcomandante Marcos, the spokesperson for the Zapatistas, called for it to be repainted throughout the world, and this has now happened in San Francisco, Toronto, Munich, Barcelona, Madrid, Bilão, Ruest (Germany), Bortigiadis (Sardinia), Florence, Mexico City, Brussels, Paris, and Oakland. The mural depicts Mayan indigenous communities in Chiapas as living in peace after five hundred years of assault by colonialism and neoliberalism. In 2005 Guadalupe Serrano invited Valdez to oversee its replication on the border wall in Nogales.[4]

We experienced this mural as a healing salve placed on the wound of the wall and the border. It functions as the Sabbath does in Judaism, bringing messianic time into ordinary time, transforming the place of the present with its divisive struggles into a temporary sacred space of enacting and manifesting what is most desired (Heschel 1951). The mural, then, lets us imagine a time when peace and justice will prevail, a place where people will live in the fullness of creation, where women can safely gather, and children are free to swim in refreshing waters. The inspirational leaders of this Mayan community, Ricardo Flores Magón and Zapata, watch over the peaceful scene. Through the multiple incarnations of this mural in many communities, we are encouraged to experience a solidarity of diverse peoples that contradicts the wall's stark commitment to division.

You, the reader, may find it worthwhile pausing here to invite your own images of a time when the border region will be transformed into a place

Figure 25. Detail, *The Life and Dreams of the Perla Ravine/Vida y Sueños de la Cañada Perla*, replica of mural painted in Taniperla, Mexico, by Sergio Valdez, Calle Internacional, Nogales, Mexico, 2005. Photo by Mary Watkins.

Figure 26. Detail, *The Life and Dreams of the Perla Ravine/Vida y Sueños de la Cañada Perla,* **replica of mural painted in Taniperla, Mexico, by Sergio Valdez, Calle Internacional, Nogales, Mexico, 2005. Photo by Mary Watkins.**

where people and environment thrive together. What do you imagine it could look and feel like? What are the ingredients for this flowering?

RECONCILIATION ARTS: THE SEARCH FOR COMMON UNDERSTANDING AND GROUND

On the path to peaceful coexistence, images that transgress, resist, and subvert separation walls must at some point be joined to images that seek to promote mutual understanding, empathic connection, and dialogue for reconciliation. At the U.S. border wall, the desire for reconciliation has most often been expressed through binational performance and rituals. At Friendship Park, before the strangulation of an area where people from the United States and Mexico could speak through the fence, binational choirs sung together. Holy Communion was shared; communion wafers were passed through the gaps in the fence. The binational Border Arts Project took to the road one summer, winding its way back and forth across the border in a caravan of cars and vans to symbolically suture the wound imposed on the ever-widening terrain accompanying the border wall. In Texas, an international kayak competition, Laredo's RioFest, was created to "take back" the Rio Grande from the Border Patrol and restore it, even if temporarily, to the communities on the two sides of the river. Also in Texas, binational faith groups have joined together in a project called "Hands across the River," showing solidarity for communities and families that have been bisected by the wall. Participants from both countries gather on bridges between the United States and Mexico and join hands, connecting what has been separated by U.S. border policies.

Performances of unity in the face of division, however, are not enough.

Reconciliation art begins from a position of compassionate listening to those on both sides of the division. It seeks, through the presentation of images, to build understanding, with the hope that fruitful dialogue can be stimulated. The Israeli artist Ruthe Zuntz, the German artist Michael Reitz, and the Israeli architect Anat Moshe undertook one such project in 2007 at the Israeli separation wall in Abu Dis. The wall became a screen for a multimedia project, *Challenging Walls: Life beyond the Walls.* Life-size photographs of people from both sides of the wall were projected to Palestinian and Israeli audiences, attempting to bring the two sides closer together through their common witness of the visual displays. The photographers had grown up next to separation walls in their home communities in Germany, Cyprus, Northern Ireland, Israel, and Palestine. The photos from these four walled-off conflict zones show the daily lives of people on both sides of such walls. Zuntz said, "The goal of the project is to draw attention to the lives of the people on either side of the wall. If we succeed in removing the mental walls between the two sides, we will be able to overcome the fear and despair that separate the two peoples, as well as the physical wall itself" (quoted in Belarmino 2007).

If arts and imagination are to be used for reconciliation, to heal the open wound of the border, they must attend to the lived realities on both sides of the wall, communicate these to both sides, and search for the common ground that could once again be exposed to allow for fertility and hybridity. If we face the U.S. side of the wall, we find an absence of art and image.[5] It is as though the brute materiality of the wall is mute beyond its literal expression of power and control. The imagination of Americans is needed so that the American side of the wall can begin to voice the concerns of various U.S. groups that express serious reservations concerning the existence of the wall. Not all images, however, lead to transformations for the common good, a fact too easy to forget in a naive romanticization of image. In Derry, Northern Ireland, for example, some fear that certain

Figure 16. Mural of the border as a sutured wound, *una llaga*, U.S. border wall, Tijuana, Mexico. Photo by Mary Watkins.

Figure 17. Detail, *2501 Migrantes*, Alejandro Santiago, on exhibit at the Museo de Arte Contemporáneo, Oaxaca, Mexico. Photo by Mary Watkins.

Figure 19. Giant milagro, detail of Milagros series, by Alfred Quiroz, *Parade of Humanity/Paseo de Humanidad*, U.S. border wall, Calle Internacional, Nogales, Mexico, 2004–2010. Artwork funded by an Artist Project grant from the Arizona commission on the Arts; © 2004 by Alfred J. Quiroz. Photo by Mary Watkins.

Figure 20. Milagros series by Alfred Quiroz, *Parade of Humanity/Paseo de Humanidad*, U.S. border wall, Calle Internacional, Nogales, Mexico, 2004–2010. Artwork funded by an Artist Project grant from the Arizona commission on the Arts; © 2004 by Alfred J. Quiroz. Photo by Alfred Quiroz.

Figure 21. Detail, *Parade of Humanity/Paseo de Humanidad*, Guadalupe Serrano and Alberto Morackis, U.S. border wall, Calle Internacional, Nogales, Mexico, 2004. Photo by Mary Watkins.

Figure 22. Detail, *Parade of Humanity/Paseo de Humanidad*, Guadalupe Serrano and Alberto Morackis, U.S. border wall, Calle Internacional, Nogales, Mexico, 2004. Photo by Mary Watkins.

Figure 23. *Border Dynamics,* Alberto Morackis and Guadalupe Serrano, University of Arizona, Tucson, 2005. Photo Mary Watkins.

Figure 24. *Border Dynamics,* Alberto Morackis and Guadalupe Serrano, University of Arizona, Tucson 2005. Photo Mary Watkins.

ɟure 25. Detail, *The Life and Dreams of the Perla Ravine/Vida y Sueños de la Cañada Perla*, replica of mural inted in Taniperla, Mexico, by Sergio Valdez, Calle Internacional, Nogales, Mexico, 2005. Photo by Mary Watkins.

ɟure 26. Detail, *The Life and Dreams of the Perla Ravine/Vida y Sueños de la Cañada Perla*, replica of mural inted in Taniperla, Mexico, by Sergio Valdez, Calle Internacional, Nogales, Mexico, 2005. Photo by Mary Watkins.

Figure 27. Painting of an open door, affixed to the U.S. border wall, Playas de Tijuana, Tijuana, Mexico, 2004. Photo by Mary Watkins.

murals from both Catholic and Protestant sides are so highly partisan as to feed division and further violence.

During the last decade, I, Mary, have met with various groups in U.S. communities and shared the art on the Mexican side of the wall. I have inquired into and imagined images that might be painted in a mural or shown in a slideshow on the U.S. wall (were it legal to do so), images that could provoke reflection on the lives of people living in the shadow of the wall on each side of the border. On the U.S. side, I have wondered, how might the daily lives of Arizona ranchers, Border Patrol workers, and migrant workers be depicted? What are the core concerns of those who have advocated for the wall? What generative words could portray the concerns of citizens who want the wall to extend the full reach of our border? What generative words and images can help us see more clearly the motives that drove the building of the wall and that contribute to its sustenance? What historical border dynamics must Americans more deeply recognize and address? What must Americans acknowledge, memorialize, and mourn with respect to the border? What are *our* prophetic images for how the border region could flourish in the future?

In Arizona, some ranchers are not simply angry that migrants cut their fences to pass through and slash their water lines to assuage thirst brought on by the arid terrain; they are also afraid for their lives, for armed drug smugglers and human traffickers have joined the traffic of migrants. The present economic stresses bring additional concerns. On the one hand, many fear not having enough resources for education and medical care in their communities and worry that an influx of immigrants will overstretch the available systems. On the other, many citizens worry that unemployment will erode their way of life, the security of their families, and even their senses of themselves; in view of this, some blame immigrants for taking jobs they feel should be reserved for citizens. Beyond that, others fear that the English language and the nation's European cultural heritage are threatened as the United States moves steadily away from a white majority.

As we have worked to listen sympathetically to the concerns of people who favor the wall, we have tried to follow the peace-building practices of the Vietnamese Buddhist teacher Thich Nhat Hanh (2004, 2005) by noticing their common ground with people who are migrating: human desires for adequate housing, education, health care, security, and employment and for the preservation of one's culture and language. If the art on the wall looking south were to be an art of reconciliation, it could show this shared ground that points to a common humanity. Collectively thinking about ways in which people across borders can jointly meet these needs is essential work for this coming century.

We have asked what history Americans need to acknowledge if we are to understand the U.S. dynamics that built and sustain the separation wall at the border. How might historical images be linked to images of present lived realities so as to illustrate their interconnectedness? For instance, might images of the slave housing on the plantations in the antebellum Deep South, where four people lived in quarters measuring eighteen feet by eighteen feet, be placed beside images of the miserably cramped housing for migrant laborers throughout the United States and of what Mexicans call "pigeon housing" for maquiladora workers?

Understanding the border wall requires seeing the border as part of a historical lineage of displacements that were perpetrated to create the United States: displacements first of indigenous groups; then of Africans from their tribal kingdoms; and then of Mexicans from their lands in what are now Texas, Arizona, New Mexico, and California. These displacements are interlinked with the forced displacements of peoples increasingly occurring throughout the contemporary world. Finally, we have asked what form our "Perla ravines" might take, what prophetic images we might use to envision how to live in a way that confers more humanity on the U.S.-Mexico borderlands.

Participants in the groups working with the images on the U.S. wall have also inquired into the history of analogous, although metaphorical, divisions in their towns and cities. Most often, the group members have identified legacies of racism and classism and developed images that capture the divisions currently marring most of the places Americans live. They have imagined the history and associated realities painted in murals on the walls of their towns, working against tendencies of historical amnesia.

Americans do not have to go to the border with Mexico to practice the arts of reconciliation. As the Santa Barbara playwright Leo Cabranes-Grant says: "We are each transportable borders, enacting a separation or challenging it" (2004, 4). We are faced each day with living inside or resisting the borders that we have created or that have been imposed on us. Like border artists, we too can name these walls, question the dynamics that birth them, and bring forth images to express what they are really about. We can look into their history and mourn what is lost in the face of them. We too can pay tribute to those who resist the meanings imposed on them by such powerful walls. We too can rehearse for a daily life where doors are made in these walls, where we use our bodies and our hearts to hold them open and walk more freely back and forth as we work to forge a hospitality that is crucial to our own souls.

The art and graffiti on separation walls use the surface of the walls themselves to undo the exclusionary logic that created them. The words and images on these walls direct our attention to what such walls would have us *not* see. They offer both the history and dynamics that negate the walls' flat and brute command to stop and go no further. The art begins to work out in advance how the border could be lived differently. And yet it is just one part of necessary resistance, the building of critical consciousness, and necessary re-imagining. Re-imagining the U.S.-Mexico border, the inspiration of this volume, must occur also at closer range, where citizens and migrants live as neighbors, though often in separate worlds. It is in our relationships that we each have the power to transgress social conventions that act as walls and to embody—in advance of or alongside any immigration policy—our own transborder ethics.

CHAPTER 9

Creating Communities of Hospitality

Growing Connective Tissue between Immigrants and Citizens

Once relations between two peoples, communities, and governments have deteriorated to the point that physical walls are built between them, the road back to relationships marked by mutual trust and respect and shared human rights becomes long. If a long history of continuing injustices accompanies those divisions, as the history of the United States and Mexico does, any rapprochement will require formal and public efforts of acknowledgment, apology, and reparations. We must seek to repair matters at many levels and to restore human rights long withheld if we are to establish equality and ensure that the lives of all members of a community are held as sacred and granted dignity.

Each time ordinary people in either of the two divided groups create a connection, constructing a "bridge" between them, or go off their ordinary segregated paths to understand and appreciate one another, they poke a metaphorical hole in the walls that have marked their separation. In lieu of walls, tissues of connection begin to develop, knitting together members of the two groups. These informal relationships must be matched by joint actions of advocacy and solidarity, so that the formal structures that replicate inequality are dismantled.

Physical separation walls call forth almost unfathomable creativity. The art on the Mexican side of the U.S. border wall and the border activism about which we, the authors, learned have been our inspiration and guide to the kinds of transgressions, resistance, and reconciliation that are creating a different manner of relationship between Americans and Mexicans. There is no definitive map to this work in progress, for ingenuity in devising new strategies is one of the basic ingredients in successful resistance. Nevertheless, we can begin to draw inspiration and instruction from all the processes undermining "the wall" now happening at every possible level of organization. This activity has given us the hope to continue studying what is otherwise a tragic chapter in the life of the United States—tragic, that is, for both citizens and Mexican migrants. We clearly see that we should not merely respond to the discourse and actions surrounding current anti-immigration legislation, for if we do so, we will fail to imagine the bold steps necessary to create an approach to forced migration marked by compassion, justice, wisdom, and integrity, an approach that places Mexican migration within the larger framework of the global forces fueling forced migration. As Michelle Alexander (2012) has argued with respect to the prison abolition movement, we should not remain chained to our historical moment or caught within the bounds of what we currently see as possible or impossible.

Beginning with the international framework of the United Nations International Convention on the Protection of the Rights of All Migrant Workers and Members of Their Families, this chapter sketches a blueprint regarding the kinds of things citizens can do or support that will make their communities immigrant friendly, with particular attention to immigrants without documents. Such steps will help cities and towns avoid destructive internal divisions. We will look at sanctuary cities, police officers' resistance to deputization as ICE (Immigration and Customs Enforcement) agents, the provision of driver's licenses and identification cards to migrants, migrant-worker centers, migrants' access to education, enfranchisement of migrants to allow political participation, living-wage initiatives, language *intercambios*, immersion education initiatives for nonmigrants that educate them about the challenges migrants live daily, and reconciliation between migrant and citizen communities where members of those communities acknowledge the kinds of painful history we have described (in chapters 5 and 6) in order to engage the present and the future in more just and empathic ways. It is hoped that this mosaic—while exemplary and suggestive rather than comprehensive and encyclopedic—will whet our desire to live borders differently in our psyches, neighborhoods, schools, towns, and cities and between nations, as well as provoke our imagination regarding how we might do this. We place our hope in the actions that grow out of such desires and acts of imagination.

TRANSBORDER ETHICS

The best available map for creating a transborder ethics is the International Convention on the Protection of the Rights of All Migrant Workers and Members of Their Families, which operates under the umbrella of the UN's Office of the High Commissioner for Human Rights. It is a comprehensive international treaty that provides a detailed ethical response to a world where forced migration is increasing and where the nation in which one happened to be born need not come to determine all one's prospects in life—including, at times, even the continuation of life itself. While this convention stops short of proclaiming open borders and the rights of human beings to live in countries outside the ones in which they were born, it does stake out a moral terrain that, if universally accepted, would improve the lives of millions of forced migrants.

Like the Universal Declaration of Human Rights, the UN's migrants' rights convention proceeds on the assumption that the dignity of each life and the right to life should be respected and upheld. It recognizes that human rights should be approached as indivisible, the rights of one person and group inextricably linked to those of others, regardless of differences in ethnicity, gender, class, race, and nationality. A migrant is not simply a worker but a human being and should have rights comparable to a citizen's in terms of working conditions and equality of treatment. The convention proclaims that each person has the right to liberty and to security. Each person has the right to leave a country and to reenter his or her country of origin. The host state, it says, should provide effective protection against violence, physical injury, threat, and intimidation: "Any verification by law enforcement officials of the identity of migrant workers or members of their families shall be carried out in accordance with procedure established by law." Migrants should not be subject to arbitrary arrests or detention. If a migrant or family member is arrested or detained, they are entitled to court proceedings. If they are detained or arrested unlawfully, they are entitled to compensation. If detained, they "shall be treated with humanity and with respect for the inherent dignity of the human person and their cultural identity." If a migrant or member of the family is deprived of liberty, he or she should be held separately from convicted persons or persons pending trial.

If juveniles are imprisoned, the convention states, they should be accorded treatment appropriate to their age and legal status. If a migrant worker is deprived of liberty, "competent authorities of the State" should pay attention to problems posed for members of the family. Indeed, if detained or imprisoned, the migrant worker deserves the same rights as a citizen, including the right to a fair and public hearing.

Migrant workers and their families should not be subject to measures of "collective expulsion." Each case of expulsion should be examined and decided individually. No migrant or member of his or her family should be subjected to torture or to cruel, inhumane, or degrading treatment or punishment. They should not be subjected to forced or compulsory labor. They have the right to freedom of thought, conscience, and religion; to hold opinions; and to freedom of expression. They should not be subjected to arbitrary and unlawful interference with their privacy, family, home, or correspondence and other communications.

The UN General Assembly adopted the convention in 1990, but it was not ratified until 2003, for this required its adoption by twenty states. Unfortunately, this convention has been adopted only by countries whose citizens have been forced to migrate in great numbers. To date, the United States and European countries that receive migrants have not ratified it. Were the United States to ratify and follow this convention, many of the deleterious actions taken against immigrants without documents in this country would be thrown into relief and, it is to be hoped, curtailed and stopped: abuse and intimidation by the Border Patrol, collective expulsion, degrading treatment by police and detention personnel, arbitrary arrest and detention, lack of due process and adequate representation, lack of compensation for unlawful arrest and detention, the intermixing of immigrants without criminal records and criminals in jails and detention facilities, and inappropriate care of juveniles in the event of their imprisonment—and also in the event of their guardian's detention or imprisonment. In the absence of national ratification, this document can still act as a moral compass for counties and municipalities.

CITIES AND SITES OF SANCTUARY

Many cities in Europe and the United States are reviving the idea of increasing municipal sovereignty so that they can offer hospitality to those forced to migrate from their homelands. In protest against harsh national immigration and asylum policies, they have worked to establish themselves as cities of refuge or cities of hospitality. Scores of U.S. cities have passed referenda to create more hospitable conditions for immigrants. In particular, they have sought to reject national initiatives that would require local police departments to help enforce immigration laws and have drafted directives stating that authorities should not ask the immigration status of those who require police services, medical care, or social services (unless federally mandated for particular programs). At the same time, as was discussed in chapter 6, other cities have moved to greater inhospitality, intimidation, and outright harassment of their immigrant neighbors.

Moreover, as these U.S. and European cities work to extend their sovereignty and autonomy so as to enhance justice for immigrants, they are linking with others, nationally and transnationally, that are similarly working to imagine a world without walls. The philosopher Jacques Derrida argued that new cities of refuge could reorient the politics of the nation: "If we look to the city, rather than to the state, it is because we have given up hope that the state might create a new image for the city" (2001, 6).

This kind of initiative—a politics of hospitality—exemplifies a different political strategy, one that is oriented more laterally than vertically, one that decenters centralized power. When the politics of the nation-state loses its ethical compass, civil society must forward initiatives at both the local and the transnational levels to counter the consequent abuses while maintaining and increasing leverage for reforms at the state level.

Whereas some cities and states strive to make life so unlivable for immigrants without documents that they will leave ("attrition through enforcement"), efforts to offer sanctuary and refuge act to welcome immigrants as new neighbors. Individuals involved in these efforts, who generally attempt to understand how conditions in immigrants' home countries could be improved so as to make forced migration unnecessary, operate as citizen-neighbors to these immigrants, helping immigrants to meet their human needs. Provision of sanctuary can occur at multiple levels of organization: at a national level, as in accepting and placing those designated "refugees"; at a state level, as in resisting federal mandates targeting immigrants without documents; at a local level, as in establishing the municipality as a city of refuge, a sanctuary, or immigrant-friendly city; at a neighborhood level, as in offering forms of support similar to Jane Addams's original conception of a settlement house and in the multiple gestures of welcome and support that neighbors are capable of providing to one another.

In the Old Testament, God asks Moses to create six cities of refuge, three in Canaan and three in Jordan. "These six cities shall be a refuge, for the children of Israel, and for the stranger, and for the sojourner among them" (Numbers 35:15). In an address to the International Parliament of Writers, Derrida traced this idea of "open cities," or refuge cities, places where migrants can seek sanctuary from the pressures of persecution, immigration, and exile. In European medieval traditions, according to Derrida, the city had a certain degree of sovereignty by which it could determine its own laws of hospitality. The International Parliament of Writers, including Derrida, became interested in these laws of hospitality as migrants and asylum seekers were either turned away from borders or, once inside, treated as inferior because they lacked papers or legal status.

In the United States, the Sanctuary Movement began as a movement of conscience in response to a million people fleeing persecution, civil conflict, and state-sponsored violence in Central America during the 1980s. It arose, that is, as a compassionate and ethical response to the tribulations of new neighbors whose experiences in their home countries had already traumatized them and who desperately needed to find a safe place to lead a tenable life. The refugees were unable to gain asylum in the United States even though their lives depended on it; for its part, the U.S. government was reluctant to acknowledge the direness of the situation given its complicity with the repressive governments responsible for the exodus. It was, for example, providing arms and military training to the Central American governments from which the asylum seekers were fleeing. Churches and temples began to declare themselves sanctuaries so that those needing asylum would not be deported to their home countries, where they might well be tortured and killed. In doing so, faith communities attempted to follow God's commandment to Moses that Israel set aside cities as places of refuge where the persecuted could find asylum.

The provision of sanctuary by faith communities expanded to municipalities as they declared themselves sanctuary cities.[1] This usually meant that city funds could not be used for enforcing immigration laws. In most cases, police officers and other city employees were directed not to inquire about a person's immigration status. Presently, the New Sanctuary Movement is invigorating and extending this history. Some communities that have historically declared themselves "cities of refuge" or "sanctuary cities" have reaffirmed their status.[2] Meanwhile, a backlash against sanctuary cities and those providing sanctuary is taking place in the Department of Homeland Security, the U.S. Congress, and some state governments and city councils. Tennessee has banned sanctuary cities. Federal legislators have proposed bills to disallow sanctuary cities from receiving federal funds.

As we, the authors, traveled along the border, we witnessed many efforts to provide sanctuary, but none was as moving as Annunciation House, a safe house in El Paso a few blocks from the border fence. Ruben Garcia founded it in 1978 to provide support, education, financial help, and temporary housing to Central American refugees. The day we visited, the welcoming room was filled with Mexican and Salvadoran mothers and children who had recently arrived across the border. Thousands are currently fleeing Ciudad Juárez, Mexico—on the other side of the wall—seeking to escape the sustained and escalating violence brought on by the war waged against drug cartels. ICE's detention facilities, to which asylum seekers are brought, are overrun, so ICE itself often asks Annunciation House to accommodate those fleeing the violence, particularly pregnant women, widows, and those with medical needs. Garcia, named a 2012 Teacher of Peace by the international peace organization Pax Christi, has steadfastly believed in the "rightful place of the immigrant as a working part of this country" (quoted in Bracamontes 2012). Annunciation House accommodates sixty-plus immigrants who, with the help of a caseworker, formulate goals and a plan to reach them as they start their life in a new country. We met volunteers who, on hearing of Annunciation House and the moral and humanitarian crisis at the border, had traveled halfway around the world to offer their help.

Dayton, Ohio, chose to focus not on undocumented immigrants per se but on welcoming all immigrants to its city. It did so to combat declining population, to improve its own economic viability, and to create a place where all people are treated kindly, fairly, and humanely. The Welcome Dayton plan, passed unanimously by its city commissioners in 2011, provides a blueprint for an immigrant-friendly city, establishing recommendations in the following areas: business and economic development, government and justice systems, social and health services, community, culture, arts, and education ("Welcome Dayton," n.d.). It is dedicating an area of the city to immigrant entrepreneurship, helping newcomers to establish small businesses.

The Utah Compact also acknowledges immigrants' value as workers and taxpayers. The compact is a statement of principles forged in 2010 by conservative Republicans to provide a framework to the state in the face of a morally rudderless federal impasse on immigration policy reform. It is not legislation, but it has influenced policy decisions. While it acknowledges that immigration is principally an issue between the federal government and other countries, not one between a U.S. state and other countries, it underscores that police officers should not be diverted from their principal mandate of fighting crime and made to address civil violations. It also insists that families should not be separated. The signatories to the compact agree that "Utah should always be a place that welcomes people of goodwill." The compact began a movement in a number of other states; this movement seeks to create similar comprehensive frameworks for articulating how national values can inform immigration practice.

In 2004 we were inspired by the National Immigration Law Center's "Annotated Chart of Laws, Resolutions, and Policies Instituted across the U.S. against State and Local Police Enforcement of Immigration Laws." This list documents an inspiring array of approaches for states, cities, and towns to establish solidarity with and support for their immigrant residents. Sadly, the momentum of these initiatives was dampened, as was documented in chapter 6, both by federal initiatives such as the Secure Communities program and by state- and municipal-level efforts to make life so difficult for immigrants that they would "voluntarily deport" themselves. Even though the courts are gradually overturning these laws, the rash of anti-immigrant legislation has succeeded in shifting the national discourse further to the right. In this climate, we would do well to remember what is possible when a community rouses itself to protect its most vulnerable members. While municipalities that had designated themselves sanctuary cities or towns also lost ground during the last decade, they had developed not only an infrastructure of support for immigrants without documents but also a keen ethical discernment regarding the plight of forced migrants. The proclamations of mayors and city councils announcing that they recognize, appreciate, and welcome the participation and contributions of their immigrant residents contribute to creating an atmosphere of inclusion.

Separating Community Policing from Federal Immigration Initiatives

For migrants, perhaps the most practically important effect of living in a sanctuary city—or at least a city that is not "at war" with its undocumented residents—concerns policing. If their daily lives are to be viable, migrants need to be relieved of the constant fear of apprehension and concomitant separation from their family members. Otherwise, the simplest errand can become a terrifying journey filled with uncertainty and anxiety. Saying goodbye to your children when you take them to school becomes an anxiety-ridden daily experience in which any misstep could result in detention and deportation.

In addition, the public safety of all residents is enhanced when community policing is not diverted from its mission. Those without documents need to feel safe to come forward to report crimes, without fear of detention and deportation. This is critical in cases of domestic violence, where calling for help can too often turn into a nightmare of detention and deportation for the one who needed and sought protection.

Los Angeles's police department was the first to pursue this direction in the United States. Its Special Order 40 directs its officers not to initiate actions to discover immigration status or to arrest or book people on charges related to immigration status.[3] It instituted these measures to increase crime reporting and to encourage those in the immigrant community to aid police investigations.

During the last decade, police departments have been under great pressure to widen their duties, making their officers into deputies of immigration enforcement, as was outlined in chapter 6. Some police chiefs, however, have long provided a more compassionate and wise mandate to their officers, for they recognize how the fear of detention and deportation undermines immigrants' trust in police officers; when that occurs, immigrants tend not to report crimes, which means that more criminal activity, including domestic violence, goes undetected. Still, ordinary citizens must let their police chiefs know that they want policing efforts kept separate from immigration issues. To do otherwise not only increases police officers' workloads but also forces county jails to misuse space, detaining immigrants in cells that should be employed to house criminals. Further, both practices—involving police officers in immigration and housing immigration detainees in jails—increase the public's propensity to think of immigrants without documents as criminals, a woeful confusion of categories with dangerous and demeaning repercussions (see chapter 6).

Safeguarding community-policing efforts from federal immigration initiatives is necessary so that residents are not afraid to call on the police when they need protection. Police officers who know residents personally are empathically aware of their challenges and needs. Deputizing officers as Immigration and Customs Enforcement agents contradicts the premises of community policing, which relies on the cultivation of basic trust.

PROVISION OF IDENTIFICATION CARDS, DRIVER'S LICENSES, AND AUTOMOTIVE INSURANCE

Lacking identification, immigrants without documents cannot do basic things that citizens take for granted, such as opening bank accounts, cashing paychecks without paying often exorbitant rates, getting automobile insurance, and traveling on airplanes and trains. Cities such as New Haven, Trenton, Cambridge, and San Francisco have created municipal identification cards that enable immigrants without documents to navigate daily living more easily.

Not having a driver's license limits people in the jobs they can take. Those without documents often spend long hours using public transportation; if they are stopped by police officers while driving without a license, they may be arrested and possibly deported. In addition, automotive insurance is more easily available to licensed drivers. Broadening insurance coverage benefits all drivers, whether citizens or immigrants without documents. For one thing, it decreases the number of hit-and-run accidents. Permitting undocumented drivers to get licenses also makes roads safer, since drivers have to pass tests before the state licenses them. Finally, allowing undocumented immigrants to obtain driver's licenses means they will not be criminalized simply for driving, which is a necessary activity for most working people in the United States. One immigrant described it this way: "For many of us, [the provision of I.D. cards has] given us a certain sense of tranquility"; "We can live as integrated citizens, and not isolated ones" (quoted in Costantini 2011, n.p.). When he was New York's governor, Eliot Spitzer suggested that immigrants without documents should be allowed to use their passports to obtain a driver's license. Hawaii, Maine, Michigan, New Mexico, Oregon, Washington, and Utah already grant driver's licenses to people without documents.

LABOR RIGHTS AND PROTECTIONS

Immigrants without documents exist in an extremely vulnerable state within the U.S. workforce. Their wages are often below the federally mandated minimum and less than those of citizens performing comparable jobs. Many are victimized by unscrupulous employers who withhold their wages or charge unjustifiable expenses against their wages, resulting in minimal income. They are often not afforded the same basic workplace safety standards as citizen workers and have no health care and disability provisions for health issues that arise in the course of employment. Daily life in labor lines proves extremely stressful and is often dangerous, for immigrants are picked up by strangers and taken to unfamiliar locations (and even, as mentioned earlier, delivered to ICE offices).

Worker centers for immigrants have been created in towns and cities to mitigate these stresses and dangers, and they act to safeguard both workers and employers. By establishing living wages and providing access to liability insurance, such centers protect workers against abuses and help them if they are injured on the job. At such centers, workers can gain access to English classes, computer classes, and legal aid to support paths to legal residency and citizenship. Those at the bottom of the occupational ladder are enabled to enter a path of education and training toward more sustainable livelihoods.

Labor unions can use their political power to make a space for their immigrant brothers and sisters, refusing to divide citizen workers from immigrant workers. Linda Alcoff (2011) describes the work done by the Service Employees International Union (SEIU) to develop "a historically groundbreaking policy of non-differentiation between documented and undocumented workers for the purposes of organizing, and deciding where their organizing resources will be allocated." Such a principle not only increases the union's power in relation to management but also shows a needed solidarity between citizen and noncitizen workers.

In addition to helping to provide organized workers' centers and undertaking formal participation in labor unions, citizens need to interact ethically with immigrant workers with regard to fair recompense for labor, making sure that employers do not use the immigration status of their workers to compromise workers' earnings, benefits, and safety.

POLITICAL PARTICIPATION

Most Americans would be surprised to know that, before the 1920s, noncitizens in forty state and federal territories voted in local, state, and federal elections and that at present, over forty countries worldwide permit non-citizens to vote (Hayduk 2006). In the United States, only a small handful of municipalities allow noncitizens to vote in municipal and school-board elections. While some municipalities have approved such an ordinance, such as Cambridge, Newton, and Amherst in Massachusetts, the state legislature has failed to pass it. New York City is currently considering a bill ("Voting by Non-Citizen Residents") that would allow municipal voting by noncitizens who are residing in the country legally and who have lived in New York City for at least six months. Proponents argue that the constitution calls for no taxation without representation.

When people have no possibility of citizenship and are excluded from enfranchisement, they are relegated to living in a place where everything is determined by others. The philosopher Hannah Arendt warned that when we render people within our nation *stateless*, without a political voice and life, we move closer to totalitarianism. Crimes against humanity, she said, are crimes against the possibility of politics. When we deprive people of a political voice, there is an assault on the concept of the human being.

In *The Rights of Others: Aliens, Residents, and Citizens*, the political scientist Seyla Benhabib (2004) considers the political membership of aliens, strangers, immigrants, newcomers, refugees, and asylum seekers to be an aspect of domestic and international justice. She asks us to not leave political membership to be defined by state sovereignty and national citizenship alone. We need to look for multiple ways for migrants to participate politically at local and global levels, softening the divide between citizen and immigrant neighbor through the pursuit of a common goal of political participation.

PUBLIC HOMEPLACES

The development and sustaining of ethnic, racial, cultural, and linguistic pride in the face of discrimination and ethnoracism is key to psychological and community health. What Mary Belenky and bell hooks describe as public "homeplaces" are critical to creating a social and psychic space where such work can occur. The social critic hooks (1990) defines homeplaces in the African American community as spaces that provide the "warmth and comfort of shelter, the feeding of our bodies, and the nurturing of our soul. There we claimed dignity, integrity of being; there we learned to have faith" (41–42). In these homeplaces, one can learn to read history critically, and to seek an understanding of the oppression that one's group has been subject to. Arts are crucial components that help individuals and groups express their experiences, retrieve and communicate their histories, and develop together an imagination of what is truly desired, using it as a North Star by which to orient. The shame that has been induced by the discriminatory and unjust circumstances under which many immigrants are forced to craft their lives is challenged, critiqued, and, one hopes, dispelled. Yet precisely as one learns to see who and what has profited from diminishment and abjection, one can recover and claim one's rightful stature; indeed, one can achieve a nobility of stature that is often recognizable and remarkable.

Informal and formal opportunities to pursue ethnic and cultural studies are important activities in public homeplaces, given how frequently the history and cultural values of a marginalized group are distorted, or not represented at all, by mainstream public education in the United States. At the same time, native languages are disparaged in the public-school system, with cultural centers required for their valuing and maintenance.

In the fall of 2012, I met several teachers from the Tucson ethnic-studies program who were giving a teach-in at Occupy Wall Street's Free University. These teachers had lost their teaching jobs when the Mexican American studies program was closed down after the passage of Arizona House Bill 2281 in 2010. This bill prohibits classes that advocate for ethnic solidarity instead of treating each student as an individual, that are designed primarily for a particular ethnic group, and that are believed to promote resentment toward a race or class of people. Despite studies that show such programs to improve students' school success and graduation rates, those who voted against them could not tolerate classes where instructors taught the history of the Southwest, riddled with racism against Mexicans, and of Chicano resistance to the poor treatment they have received.

Like the repainting of the destroyed mural of *Life and Dreams of the Perla Ravine* in many places throughout the world (see chapter 8), the Arizona ethnic-studies teachers have been traveling through the United States, not only sharing the present demise of the program, but also teaching others how the program worked, what its successes were, and its basic vision. They hope that these seeds will take root, so that new programs will help to create an atmosphere in which Mexican, Central American, and Mexican American children can understand the history into which they have been born. In this way, these children will be able to take pride in their own cultural—and often indigenous—heritage and gain an understanding of the patterns of racism that too often distort their sense of themselves and their families.

For people who have been forced to migrate, one of the human rights they are too often forced to cede is the right to community—"both to live in communities of their own creation and to be part of the broader community around them" (Bacon 2005). Stripped of their family and home communities, they are expected to migrate as individuals, for the purpose of work. Nevertheless, Mexicans in the United States have created a vibrant nexus of relations that ties their current affiliations with other migrants from their hometowns and regions to affiliations with those back home. David Bacon underscores how they bring to the United States a rich tradition of social rights and of organizing, which enables them to experience themselves as "social actors with a right to acceptance both in Mexico and the United States" (16). A strong sense of community and communal responsibility often leads to the establishment of hometown associations. These serve as a source of resistance to the pernicious realities against which migrants struggle. Within these associations, people pool their money together to benefit their towns of origin. Money is sent back not just to their own families but to their hometowns for projects such as the construction of a football/soccer field, playground, or school. Nuria Ciofalo (personal communication, November 15, 2012), a community psychologist working with indigenous Mexican communities in the United States and Mexico, says this is based on indigenous forms of community organizing and mobilization in which people who are earning higher incomes than others contribute to the community as a whole.

Creating Zones of Encounter and Sites for Reconciliation

While many citizens and new immigrants come into daily contact with one another, that contact is most often one in which the latter is serving the former in some manner or in which the citizen is supervising the work of the immigrant. There are very few places where citizen and immigrant meet to get to know one another, to enjoy and understand each other's cultures, and to engage together in civic activities. In the United States, there is a situation of virtual apartheid between Anglo and Mexican communities. To create cities and towns where hospitality and mutual understanding thrive, zones of encounter and sites for reconciliation must be intentionally nourished.

Over a hundred years ago, Jane Addams and others created Hull House in Chicago, the first settlement house in the United States, to address the separation between recent immigrants and those more settled. Middle- and upper-class women, whose families had settled earlier, and immigrant women suffering poverty and displacement were welcomed to develop mutual relationships and to better understand the problems facing their city. The women met together not to create a melting pot but to explore how connective tissue could be formed between different communities, holding a vision of America as alive with the hybridity of different cultural experiences. Here they developed friendships, strategized about how to address community problems, joined in arts projects with one another, and celebrated the crafts of cultures represented by the women. While the less recently arrived often provided the function of what Mary Pipher (2003) has more recently called "cultural brokers," helping with practical issues of getting settled in a foreign land, the initiative was not seen in missionary or service terms. Instead, an interdependent sensibility guided the vision. For Addams (1912), it was clear that "without the advance and improvement of the whole, no man can hope for any lasting improvement in his own moral or material individual condition" (126).

In *Bowling Alone: The Collapse and Revival of American Community*, Robert Putnam (2001) asks what the settlement houses of the twenty-first century will look like in America. The early settlement houses were intended as meeting places for both immigrants recently arrived in the United States and those who had been here awhile, those struggling with poverty and those comfortably stationed in the middle class or above. The well-being of one group was not imagined as possible without the well-being of the other. The descendants of these early zones of encounter between immigrants and citizens are now largely driven by grants and run by helping professionals. Settlement houses today, while trading on some of the founding ideas of Jane Addams, are no longer largely a voluntary association of those seeking to create bridges between communities. The helping professions now staff them, gala balls fund them, and the human miseries associated with forced migration are too often psychopathologized, so they can fall under the rubrics of the mental-health system's individualistically oriented diagnoses and treatments. Such settlement houses no longer appear to meet the need to grow sufficient connective tissue between recently arrived immigrants and those whose families have been here for a generation or more.

The past can be better metabolized, and a more just future created, through informal exchanges in the present between individuals from groups that have been historically divided. In most towns and cities, meetings between migrants and citizens happen only on top of economic and ethnic divides. Immigrants without documents are reluctant to speak of their difficult experiences out of fear of racism and deportation. There is a collusion of silence that keeps citizens ignorant of the challenges and heartaches borne by many of their fellow immigrant townspeople.

To create sites of reconciliation requires insight into the need for them and sustained effort to build bridges across separations established over a long history. Learning each other's languages is a first step toward more personal communication. Neighborhoods, workplaces, adult education centers, and religious congregations can set up *intercambios*. *Intercambio* is the Spanish word for "exchange," and it is used to describe language-learning situations where a dyad splits the conversational time, using the primary language of one partner in the first half and the language of the other partner in the second half. Trying to express themselves in a language other than their mother tongue humbles both individuals. Each turns toward basic descriptions of everyday life to facilitate communication. Beyond the awkwardness, it can be a touching and humorous exchange, marked by surviving an experience together, whereby each partner suffers some vulnerability in the lack of mastery of the other's language. Through this kind of simple sharing, language-learning partners find themselves in a situation that is strikingly more equal than what they find in the workplace and in most other social spaces. Partners learn about each other's background, childhood, family, and personal aspirations. Indeed, the regular sharing fosters a mutuality too often lacking elsewhere. Knowing how unsafe migrants feel in the larger community, citizens can offer their support to community centers, where migrants go for information about housing and health care, help with immigration issues, and assistance in learning English.

Such intercultural meetings spawn relationships that can transcend delimited normative notions of hospitality by opening "spaces and forms of exchange that *allow* for mutual obligation, engagement, and civic participation" (Friese and Mezzadra 2007).

In the face of legal and civil initiatives that are hostile to immigrants without documents, it is especially important to create and sustain alternative spaces and places that kindle a different manner of relationship. While these places may appear merely ameliorative, their very existence can catalyze a mode of being that is currently in short supply. Initiatives such as Welcoming America provide resources to community groups that desire to create a more respectful and cohesive community where all neighbors, immigrants and long-term residents alike, thrive.

Such bicultural or multicultural centers can create multiple opportunities for Anglos and those of Mexican or Latin American descent to build relationships and to address any needs for support and solidarity. In addition to instituting language and cultural *intercambios*, and other exchanges that foster relationship and dialogue, they may also create educational and arts initiatives, support for small businesses, housing for those in transition, and needed political initiatives. Simply accompanying migrants to meetings at schools, medical appointments, and immigration appointments, as well as including them in holidays and community rituals, are actions deeply appreciated by many newcomers.

Zones of encounter must intentionally be created so that citizens can learn about the experiences of immigrants, experiences that are often hidden from them. BorderLinks, a nonprofit organization that creates immersion programs for citizens at the Arizona-Mexico border, has also offered immersion experiences in other cities, including Chicago and Santa Barbara, so that citizens can be educated by Latino groups about their experiences, initiatives, needs, and vision. Because of the divisions between Anglo and Mexican communities, such planned encounters are an important place to begin and can be organized by faith and other community groups.

Given the degree of historical amnesia in the United States, such immersion opportunities are needed to educate American citizens about the history of their own country with respect to a given immigrant group. The "ethnic studies" that educate particular groups about their histories need to be attended by *everyone* in the culture. The content of the ethnic-studies program in Arizona that has been presently outlawed should be integrated into the teaching of American history in public schools, and also taught in public homeplaces and in bicultural or multicultural centers, so that it becomes common knowledge.

REPARATION AND RECONCILIATION

Once the history of the Southwest and the treatment of Mexicans in the United States is more widely understood by Americans, it will be clear that formal and informal processes of reconciliation need to be put into place in our communities, as apologies and reparations are pursued at a national level for injustices such as the deportation of U.S. citizens of Mexican descent that occurred in the early 1930s, for labor abuses, lack of legal representation, illegal detention, and avoidable deaths during detention stemming from a lack of adequate medical care. Reconciliation dialogues are needed between migrant and citizen communities where members turn toward the weight of their community's history in order to engage the present and the future in more understanding and empathic ways. Might the settlement house of the twenty-first century be a site for cultivating conversations that have been long delayed in the United States, conversations informed by issues of reparations, truth, and reconciliation?

In the wake of apartheid and the violence, injustice, and racism that sustained it, a process of truth and reconciliation was created in South Africa; that development has spawned similar efforts to heal the gaps between official histories and the experiences of those excluded from these histories in many other nations. In 2004, the first Truth and Reconciliation Commission (TRC) in the United States was begun in Greensboro, North Carolina (Clark 2006).[4] It sought to heal an interracial community wound that occurred in 1979, when five anti–Ku Klux Klan demonstrators were murdered: a deadly symptom of a larger structure of racial injustice flowing from the times of slavery in the United States.[5] The second TRC is now being convened in Maine to address the treatment of Native American children in government-sponsored boarding schools. Such attempts at reconciliation will seed other such attempts. They will expose the walls that are so widely present in communities, inquire into their history and function, address grievous wrongs that have been hidden, and begin a process of imagining and embodying multiple means of reparations for the past, reparations that create connective tissue between historically alienated communities for the future.

The Slave Reparations Movement is a similar effort now underway in the United States (Eisler 2004). The newly opened debates concerning reparations for slavery publicly address not only the almost 250-year-old history of slavery in America but also the legacy of slavery for the continuing economic servitude of many African Americans. Historians and economists working in this area are clear that, in general, African Americans are paid less than whites for the same job. Despite affirmative-action initiatives, the economic capital base of whites that was built on the labor of slaves and "convicts"—particularly through textile manufacturing, coal mining, railroad building, and tobacco farming, where slaves were treated as material property—continues to give whites unjust advantages. This automatic inheritance of economic privilege by whites happens regardless of their families' length of stay in the United States, because it is an inheritance based on skin color. Freed slaves were never given the compensatory forty acres and a mule that General Sherman promised as part of Reconstruction. Instead, they were kept out of neighborhoods that accrued value, denied mortgages, and excluded from the Homestead Act of 1862, even as economically prosperous African American areas were destroyed, as happened in Tulsa, Oklahoma, in 1921; all this has led to continuing inequality. The historian Manning Marable and others have called for a national commission whose aims would be the erasure of racialized deficits through the provision of such things as equitable health care and education for African Americans, as well as more access by African Americans to managerial roles. This movement is important in generating insight into the fact that migrant Mexican labor, too, has functioned to fuel white economic privilege while not providing those who have labored with the economic rewards they would need to move out of poverty.

These various movements of reconciliation and reparation bring into dialogue aspects of American history many would prefer not to know about and reflect on. For whites, not knowing or not remembering leads to a false sense of entitlement, an unquestioning assumption of economic privilege that distorts their image of themselves, their labors, and their rights. Keeping the past at bay allows privilege to continue to accrue, balancing economic gain with soul loss.

Such zones of encounter and sites of reconciliation pave the way for commitment by philanthropic organizations to consider their community investments as part of a reparative legacy. This reframing of philanthrophic action helps to repair intercommunity wounds by acknowledging the crucial contributions immigrant groups have made to their cities and to the United States generally, while also acknowledging the harms inflicted on immigrant groups.

It is not too early to begin to imagine the kinds of acknowledgment of human-rights abuses and frank human misery that recent U.S. history has imposed upon many Mexican migrants. It will be necessary to create forms of restorative justice to heal the historical injustices that migrants have suffered in the United States. We know that reconciliation between communities marked by historical injustices must both proceed along a path of witnessing, acknowledgment, apology, and reparation and begin with multiple daily efforts to reconcile among individuals and communities.

The Education of Immigrant Children

While not always rising to the challenge, public schools are crucial to creating welcoming communities for both immigrant children and parents. The school can serve as the first place to involve immigrant parents in community decision-making—though, sadly, it often is not. We need sustained efforts to encourage the involvement of immigrant parents, particularly those who fear deportation over inadequate documents. It is crucial that schools do not assume the role of immigration policy enforcement but rather provide a sanctuary where the concerns of education are central.

The integration of ethnic studies into the curriculum can help all children understand their histories and societal dynamics, as well as affirm cultural pride and self-esteem. Bilingual education can be an opportunity for all students to prepare themselves for living in a multicultural society.

The action of some states to try and outlaw education for immigrant youth without documents contradicts basic human rights and contributes to an atmosphere where youth do not feel a sense of belonging within the only community they have to call home.

It is unfair for immigrant children of undocumented parents to suffer for their parents' life choices. This is what happens, however, when those children are denied work permits, access to secure government-sponsored educational loans, the ability to pay in-state tuition, and a path to citizenship. The courage of "DREAMers," those young people in support of the DREAM Act, in advocating for the reforms that would redress these deprivations has begun to move the heart and conscience of the nation. Communities can support them through creating scholarship funds and advocating for in-state tuition assessments and scholarships while supporting the national passage of the DREAM Act, which would allow qualifying undocumented youth to apply for federal financial aid for higher education and open a pathway to citizenship that requires completion of a college degree or two years of military service.

BORDER PEACE PARKS

Border peace parks are part of efforts now called environmental peacebuilding. Establishing transfrontier conservation zones where an ecosystem falls across multiple jurisdictions helps to allow animals and humans to range freely. In some instances, as when two bordering countries have a conflict at an international border, it can even help to maintain peace (see Ali 2007).

Peace parks are about coexistence between humans and nature, "about promoting regional peace and stability, conserving biodiversity and stimulating job creation by developing nature conservation as a land-use option" (Peace Parks Foundation, n.d.). When there are shared efforts to preserve an ecosystem, both human and other-than-human nature prosper. Those who live in and near peace parks can gain economic stability, both through the stewardship roles that are necessary and from any ecotourism that ensues. The resulting mutual cooperation and trust, combined with greater economic prosperity, contribute to regional peace and stability. There are presently 188 transboundary protected areas in the world, including the border between Ecuador and Peru, where establishing a peace park has helped to quell border conflict and contributed to the support of the peace accords and the building of a culture of peace in the region. It is an inspiring integration of a peace plan with a binational conservation effort. The establishment of this peace park was coupled with financial investment in projects such as job development, transportation infrastructure, education, healthcare, education around domestic violence, and conflict resolution.

In the early 2000s, several Texan and Mexican mayors and environmental groups proposed the establishment of peace parks and binational ecozones along the U.S.-Mexico border. Instead, the border wall sliced through conservation areas, disrupting the migratory pathway of animals. The proposal of peace parks in the area was not a new idea. In 1935, right after Big Bend National Park was authorized in Texas, a joint U.S.-Mexico commission was appointed to explore the creation of an international park aimed at preserving the integrity of this remarkable bioregion. Indeed, in 1933, the Chamber of Commerce in Alpine, Texas, in the Big Bend region, commissioned a landscape architect to begin designing such a park. In 1944, when President Roosevelt welcomed Big Bend into the National Park system, he said that he imagined "one great international park" on both sides of the Rio Grande. The vision of such a park had already been realized on the northern U.S. border with Canada: the Waterton-Glacier International Peace Park. Nor are such cooperative projects limited to past efforts. In 2010, U.S. and Mexican Presidents Obama and Calderón signaled their joint interest in pursuing the dream of a binational park.

Border peace parks and binational integrated conservation zones attempt to employ the people at border zones so that their own migration is not necessary. They also provide important freedom for animals to range. In south Texas, wildlife advocates have worked for decades to integrate Sabal Palm Sanctuary, Bentsen–Rio Grande Valley State Park, Lower Rio Grande National Wildlife Refuge, and the Lennox Foundation Southmost Preserve (Leskiw 2009) (see chapter 4). The U.S.-Mexico border includes remarkable bioregions that need conservation, as well as large cities teeming with population. Peace parks could well be part of a larger strategy of bringing jobs and education to the border regions so that migration becomes less tempting—and less necessary.

CODA

A border peace park treats the terrain as the integrated, fluid, dynamic, and interdependent ecosystem it is. It respects the natural flows of rivers and streams, as well as the migratory paths of animals. It leaves the landscape unmarred by artifical and imposed political divisions. It does not deny the fact of the borderline that formally indicates where two nations meet, but neither does it raise the significance of this line to a level that negates and even destroys the shared life of the terrain.

In our communities, we can imagine border peace parks of a different kind, where citizen and immigrant neighbors' lives crisscross and interact in ways that contribute to the vitality and well-being of the whole. To the extent that such ventures and others like them succeed, borders will be reclaimed as places for creativity and regeneration, and as sacred sites where hybridity of many kinds can thrive.

Prophetic imagination helps us to imagine past the scars of division that have been imposed not only on the earth and its animals but also between parts of the human community. Freire described this kind of imagination as annunciation, an imagination that announces another way of being beyond violent divisiveness. Prophetic imagination announces itself not only in sweeping visions for the future but also in small incarnations in the present, nourished by those in the past. Through these embodiments, we can see into a future with one another that is graced with inclusivity and mutual respect, where each is granted dignity and the fulfillment of human rights.

In this last decade, as ethnic hatred and xenophobia have been reignited in the United States, thousands of such embodiments have been created and sustained, nourishing a different vision of the borders between the United States and Mexico and their peoples. It is here that we place our hope.

Gaining Access to the Heart of Our Home

> When an alien lives with you in your land, do not mistreat him. The alien
> living with you must be treated as one of your native-born. Love him as
> yourself, for you were aliens in Egypt. I am the Lord your God.
>
> Leviticus 19:33–34 (NIV)

In Part 2, we have tried to delineate what is psychologically and ethically at stake for migrants and citizens when citizens divide immigrants from themselves, relegating them to inferior social, political, and economic positions and attempting to keep them out or forcibly extrude them. If, as the philosopher Jacques Derrida argues, ethics and culture *are* hospitality, then citizens are but a shadow of their lost humanity in passively or actively sustaining the walls between themselves and migrants.

Derrida describes how the foreigner or the stranger puts each of us in question, poses a question to us. The foreigner through his or her very being asks what kind of neighbor we are. The stranger's presence holds a mirror up to us, showing us our own faces of disregard, of scorn, of fear, of interest or ignorance, of hospitality. He stresses that the essence of hospitality is its unconditional nature. It does not ask the stranger to speak our language, to visit only on our terms, or to be only the wealthy.

> Absolute hospitality[1] requires that I open up my home and that I give not
> only to the foreigner (provided with a family name, with the social status
> of being a foreigner, etc.), but to the absolute, unknown, anonymous other,
> and that I *give place* to them, that I let them come, that I let them arrive,
> and take place in the place I offer them, without asking of them either reci-
> procity (entering into a pact) or even their names. The law of absolute hos-
> pitality commands a break with hospitality by right. (Derrida 2000, 25)

While political policy cannot be directly drawn from such an unconditional proposition, ought not its spirit be somewhere visible in the way we live our relations and craft our laws? Divided by nationality, are we not united, as Kant pointed out, by being citizens of our one common world?

Derrida underscores a psychological fact: we are only truly at home with ourselves when we are open to receiving the other. Is a home a home when it keeps the stranger out? The paradox he is working to unveil is that without welcoming the stranger, the host is a hostage in his own home. While the host is inside, without inviting the guest, he is on the outside of the inside. *Only the invited guest can invite him into the inside of his own home.*

As Derrida urges us, "Let us say yes to who or what turns up, before any determination, before any anticipation, before any identification[,] whether or not it has to do with a foreigner, an immigrant, an invited guest, or an unexpected visitor, whether or not the new arrival is the citizen of another country—a human, animal, or divine creature, a living or dead thing, male or female" (2000, 77).

We must heed a caution regarding the language of hospitality.[2] If we use it, we must reflect on the shadow of this way of naming the situation, a shadow that introduces crucial and critical complexity. If one people invades and occupies another people's land, is it hospitality if the descendants of the original inhabitants are allowed to come back to visit or to live? If one people enjoys wealth, and advanced education and health care partly from the profits gained from the exploitation of another people, is it hospitality when these benefits are shared? When people work very hard for small reward, enabling others to grossly profit; when they are separated from their loved ones and their community; when they have risked their lives to provide for their families; when they suffer the loneliness of separation from their homeland, their families, and communities—should they be dependent on hospitality, instead of enjoying the rights of refuge?

Hospitality is not just something to be extended by the citizen only for the sake of the migrant. It is extended by the citizen also for the sake of his or her own soul. The one who could offer hospitality, but does not, symbolically loses the heart of his or her own home. The one who might be hospitable needs the stranger in order to come home to himself, to live within his humanity, and to reclaim his own shadow. Chicana writer Gloria Anzaldúa (2007) advises Anglos: "Admit that Mexico is your double, that she exists in the shadow of this country, that we are irrevocably tied to her. Gringo[a], accept the doppelganger in your psyche. By taking back your shadow the intracultural split will heal" (384).

In her book *Dignity: The Essential Role It Plays in Resolving Conflict* (2011), Donna Hicks describes our human desires for dignity: our desire to be understood, for our suffering to be seen and acknowledged, to feel "free from domination so that a sense of hope and possibility [can] blossom," to be given the benefit of the doubt, and to be apologized to when wronged. A welcoming community is one where all members' desires for dignity are affirmed in their interactions with others.

Dignity—our inherent value and vulnerability as human beings—is a birthright, a birthright that is essential to each of us our entire life, regardless of the nation we reside in. Dignity travels with us across international borders. Each of us is called to acknowledge, honor, and uphold the sacred dignity of each person, citizen or noncitizen.

Dignity is indivisible: the dignity of the citizen depends on the dignity of the immigrant.

From Standing in the Shadows of Walls to Imagining Them Otherwise

> Borders are scratched across the hearts of men,
> By strangers with a calm, judicial pen,
> And when the borders bleed, we watch with dread
> The lines of ink across the map turn red.
>
> Marya Mannes, *Subverse: Rhymes for Our Times* (1959)

WALLS BEGET WALLS, WALLS BEGET "BETTER" WALLS

What have we learned from our decade of sustained reflection on the U.S. wall at the U.S.-Mexico border? First, walls beget walls. In societies that are still marred by ethnoracism and that tightly cling to economic advantages over the rest of the world, the possibility of resorting to walls as a response to forced migration is grave. Over the last two decades, not only has U.S. society suffered a proliferation of walls, literal and metaphorical; in addition, we have seen separation barriers embraced around the earth as a means to stem the tide of forcibly displaced and resource-poor peoples.

Also, walls beget supposedly "better" walls. In the course of our research, we have learned an alarming fact about literally walling out others. If the purported aim is exclusion, those whose task it is to orchestrate the walling effort will move to ever more complex and sophisticated elaborations to succeed at their job. The simple border fence we encountered at Friendship Park in 2002, where people on both sides could still talk with one another and touch each other's hands, where children could ease their bodies halfway through the slats to be in two countries at once, has given way to a network of triple walls, roadways, helicopters, drones, surveillance towers, and ground and heat sensors. Now electronic "virtual walls" are being researched and proposed.

Wall building takes on a life of its own, attempting over time to plug all gaps and prevent all movement across what was once only a line created on a map. Wall building falls into line with other tragic situations, where the goal of efficiency in accomplishing a task becomes detached from any serious questioning about that end. Hannah Arendt's analysis of the banality of evil needs to be remembered in this regard. While addressing the Nazis' bureaucratic efforts to ever more efficiently engineer genocide, she draws our attention to the deep dissociative tendencies that human beings can exhibit while pursuing the work assigned to them.

Once set into motion by a society, wall building takes on a life of its own that is extremely difficult to interrupt; it strives for perfection. This pursuit in the United States has yielded tragic consequences for millions of families, for women separated from their children, for children growing up without their parents, for men marooned from all of the people they love and who care about them, for migrants who have died before they even have the opportunity to pull their families up from hunger and destitution, for women raped in the desert as they struggle to find their way north, for those caught in a vast deportation net and separated from their families (Kanstroom 2012). To these displaced people—the absent ones, *los ausentes*—and to their families, we dedicate this book.

We have learned that a society should take a profound pause before embarking on building a wall, lest the very activity of that building take on a life of its own, perilously inscribing in concrete and metal a divide between peoples. Taken to its end logic, the management of forced migration through wall building would lead to a multitude of walled countries at the very moment that globalization has reached a new zenith, a seeming paradox worthy of reflection. The countries and regions walling themselves off are, of course, those with assets that are prized by the rest of the world. In many cases, these resources have been enhanced by exploiting those parts of the world from which migrants are now forced to depart.

WALLING OFF THE POOR

We are moving toward a world ever more divided between the excessively rich and the desperately poor. To re-imagine the U.S.-Mexico border, it is this staggering and unconscionable division that we must grapple with, that must affect our hearts and actions vis-à-vis ourselves and our earthly neighbors (both human and animal).

We have learned that building a wall on the outer border of a nation-state is a naive and misguided approach to sustaining economic divides. For the reality is that the same centrifugal dynamics of globalization that have created the exodus of people from their homelands exist within the United States as well (and within the cities of Western Europe). In the United States, people in cities like Camden, New Jersey, no longer have city services, except those provided for securitization, police (Hedges and Sacco 2012). Citizens are forced to dismantle their own buildings to get meager proceeds from selling scrap metal to Asia. Desperation has given rise to escalating drug use, as a population finds itself abandoned and sinking.

Deep economic divides fuel a pernicious and destructive autoimmune process in societies. The journalist Chris Hedges (2010) argues that when a society no longer recognizes that nature and human beings have a sacred dimension, the society will cannibalize itself until it dies. The walling off of those who are left in need undermines the integrity and well-being of the whole of a city, state, or nation.

The ethnoracialized underclass created in the United States desperately struggles to keep its children off the streets, lest they join the steady flow of poor young people of color who are used to fuel the profits of the prison-industrial complex. The walls of prison complexes and the immigrant detention facilities—often one and the same—are the interior physical ana-logues to the exterior wall at the border. Indeed, any country that is walling itself at its borders will possess a network of walls arising, or already in place, inside its borders. It has inflicted on itself the same strategy it follows on its outer edges. The grim logic of wall building applies within as well as without.

In this volume, we have outlined a different logic, calling for a differ-ent set of actions and for a distinctly "other" manner of being in relation to others. This logic requires us to step back from forced migration as only an issue of management and instead to inquire into its root causes and our affective and moral responses to these. Without this inquiry and the appropriate restorative actions that need to arise from it, the current practices of globalized capital that are making whole regions unsustainable will continue apace. To undertake such an inquiry, citizens need to wake up from the historical amnesia that has been intentionally induced by media, corporations, and government. We need to begin to metabolize national shame and to undertake reparative actions. We will not be able to begin to set things straight until we face our own shadow with respect to the injustices we have done to Mexico, to Mexicans, and to those of Mexican descent: the original theft of land and of economic and political power in the nineteenth century, the creation and exploitation of a Mexican under-class, the expulsion of U.S. citizens of Mexican descent, the criminalization of migrants, the detention (often within jails and prisons) and deportation of innocent people without representation, the recent imposition of eco-nomic policies that have made it impossible for many Mexicans to sustain themselves on their ancestral lands, the unrelenting pursuit of a drug war that has caused many Mexicans to flee deadly violence in their midst, and the use of Mexican migrants as scapegoats at a number of points in our national history. In lieu of funding the continuing maintenance of a brute wall, we must address these issues.[1]

The political scientist Wendy Brown (2010), author of *Walled States, Waning Sovereignty*, interprets the current rash of wall building between states as a symptom of the erosion of nation-state sovereignty in an age of globalization. She proposes that separation walls "function theatrically, projecting power and efficaciousness that they do not and cannot actually exercise and that they also performatively contradict" (Brown 2010, 25). They express desires for "potency, protection, containment, and even innocence" (ibid., 114), and, of course, often for purity of culture and the warding off of victims of "uneven development." Brown also argues that walls function as "national psychic defenses, as prophylactics against confrontation with our own ills or as projections onto others" (ibid., 114–115). They apply a "political-economic logic" that converts the "poor, the colonized, and the exploited" into aggressors. To place obsessive attention on the supposed dangers at its borders diverts attention from the dangers within a society. In addition, such walls act to undermine a sense of being at home in the world. For the migrant, anxieties arise from displacement, exclusion, and insecurity, from being seen as a criminal intruder; for the citizen, the mentality of walls feeds a sense of oneself as in need of protection from external and internal threats, fostering "a subjectivity that is defensive, parochial, nationalistic, and militarized" (ibid., 40).

IMAGINING BORDERS INTO BOUNDARIES

Walling in and walling out are two directional vectors within one and the same basic action: that of *closure*, rendering movement across a border difficult and unlikely.

Walls of the magnitude of La Frontera close in citizens with documentation, even as they close out those without it. The other main use of a wall is to provide shelter (as in a home) or peaceful retreat (as in a garden wall). Such walls almost always feature doors and/or windows, that is, openings onto the surrounding world. They are *boundaries*, in our sense of the term—edges that favor movement across them. As an ideal, this is beautifully illustrated by the painting of an open door affixed to the U.S. border wall in Tijuana.

Wall—one and the same word—signifies these two very different ways of structuring space and creating place. One is inhibitive and exclusive; the other is welcoming and inclusive. These spell out two ways of being in the place-world. Our book can be seen as telling the tale of the imposition of

Figure 27. Painting of an open door, affixed to the U.S. border wall, Playas de Tijuana, Tijuana, Mexico, 2004. Photo by Mary Watkins.

an inhibitory and exclusionary wall onto the border, as well as tracking the ways in which the border could be treated more as a boundary, with "windows" and "doors"—both metaphorical and real.

In pursuing the latter path, we have turned to the protective "walls" that shelter immigrants as they gather to celebrate their culture and to advance their rights. We have described the protective spaces that are needed for citizen and migrant to come to know each other, to share neighborship. And, finally, we have advocated for seeking out spaces that would provide an aegis for more formal efforts of reconciliation between Anglos and those of Mexican descent.

Whether or not a border is reinforced by a physical wall, it is important to recognize that, once established—whether by fiat or by common agreement—borders are *there*, if only as pinpointed on an official map. And being there, *just there* at a definite locus in a surrounding landscape, they are subject to contestation and subversion.

No thoughtful treatment of forced migration can fail to address the present collision of a nation's right to legislate who can cross its borders with the human rights of migrants who are forced to leave their homeland. To assert the rights of the nation without taking into account the plight of forced migrants is itself an example of "walled-in" thinking, a thinking that so oversimplifies the human situation that it does indeed require the brute strength of metal to enforce its partial logic. What happens at borders defies this logic. The edge that borders embody often possesses a rare fertility in which different cultures and languages meet and generate hybrid forms. There is no steel wall that can undo the diversity of southwestern border cultures that defy national borders. We need to shift our thinking back from a border as an impenetrable barrier to the idea and lived reality of *borderlands*—where people on both sides of an international border create and share a finely woven and distinctive tapestry of languages, traditions, histories, shared commerce, and cultural arts.

During a period when our research on the wall was particularly disheartening, as state legislatures were creating immigration laws injected with racism, we took an opportunity to visit the site of a toppled wall: the Berlin Wall.

The day the Berlin Wall fell should be remembered by all those who wish to live without separation barriers. On November 9, 1989, the East German Politburo member Günter Schabowski gave a press conference during which he announced that there were to be new regulations regarding travel to the West. When asked by a journalist when these regulations were to go into effect, Schabowski responded, "Immediately." Very quickly, thousands of East Berliners heard the announcement about the fall of the wall. They swarmed out of their houses and approached the wall as a moving mass. The border guards themselves, still in their watchtowers and at their sentry posts, had not been informed of the change. Rather than shoot into the approaching crowds, they stood aside as people climbed over the wall, took hammers to it, and created large openings through which people could finally walk freely to the other side.

We are left to wonder what might have happened if people had much earlier challenged the walling off of their city and country, reversing the pernicious process of militarized separation. We will never know if a show of resistance of massive proportions might have been successful in destroying the wall and the societal and political structures on which it was premised.

In Berlin, we walked the path where the wall once stood. To build this wall, everything in the wall's way was obliterated, including a massive church. The ground was deprived of all growth. Now, decades later, in its place is a peaceful, green beltway. In one area, there is a cascading arch of cherry trees, given by the Japanese. They curve over the pathway, meeting in the middle, a gentle reminder of the reconciliation between two parts of the city, once so brutally divided. The scar on the earth that the wall once inflicted now exists only in traces, even if the intersocietal injuries induced by this same wall will require a longer span of time to heal fully. This metamorphosis gave us hope to return to our labors.

The wall at La Frontera runs through our hearts. It proceeds through our local communities, placing some children in inferior schools and others in schools with every possible advantage; separating those with health care from those without; forcing many into backbreaking labor for wages that fail to repay their toil; denying adequate housing and the rights to political participation to people who are fully contributing to their community. This deep vein of division, like that formerly in Berlin, must one day be replaced by a boundary graced by interconnection and verdant vitality. To such reimagining of the border and the actions it inspires in our towns, cities, and nation, we have devoted this work.

Notes

INTRODUCTION

1. Twenty-four percent of the world's population (1.7 billion people) live in absolute poverty; one in four human beings lacks an adequate daily caloric intake and access to clean water. People in this segment have no hope of improving their situations or those of their loved ones through education or employment.

2. According to the 2010 U.S. Census, Latinos constitute 16 percent of the American population; 63 percent of those are of Mexican descent. Three-quarters of the eleven million immigrants without documents in the United States are Mexican.

3. "Liberation psychology" (Watkins and Shulman 2008) was initially named by the Jesuit and social psychologist Ignacio Martín-Baró (1994), who confronted North American psychology with liberation theology's commitment to giving preference to poor and oppressed majorities. Liberation psychology serves both as a critique of the goals of mainstream European and American psychologies and as a set of theories and practices to assist in building more just, peaceful, and sustainable communities, where the needs of the many are not compromised by the greed of the few. Martín-Baró was assassinated in El Salvador in 1989 by paramilitaries trained by U.S. armed forces in collaboration with the CIA.

CHAPTER 1: LA FRONTERA AS BORDER AND BOUNDARY

1. In the latter capacity, edges may indicate still deeper structures that are themselves hidden from view; think of the way that the outlines of the rib cage in the chest area of higher vertebrates disclose bone structures otherwise concealed under the skin.

2. Different types of edge are described in detail in *The World on Edge* (Casey, forthcoming).

3. It is telling that a border marker in El Paso, Texas, sports these two inscriptions side by side: "Limite de los estados unidos mexicanos" (on left) and "Boundary of the United States of America" (on right). If we allow for the common confusion between "border" and "boundary" in English, here "boundary [read: border]" is assimilated to "limit"—a most revealing equivalence and highly pertinent to the discussion at this point in our text.

4. A given limit, such as that provided by a border, can be ideal as well as material. For a more detailed account of the concept of limit, see the section titled "Limit and Edge" in Casey's *The World on Edge* (forthcoming). By speaking of the border as "ideal," we mean not that it is a good or desirable thing—as on a Platonic model of ideality (e.g., the Form of the Good)—but that it is projected as an entity *at the limit*, notably, a limit that marks the exact extent of national territory. Whereas a border literally *delimits* the territory in question and *contains* those held within it (and *excludes* those outside it), the Form of the Good *liberates* those who come into its presence (e.g., the prisoners in the allegory of the cave, in Plato's *Republic*). (This last observation was offered by Drew Leder.)

5. Mark Clark, an artist-provocateur, organized a border-art show, *Art Against the Wall*, at the wall in Brownsville in February 2010, in which this thirty-one-foot-tall ladder, constructed from bamboo by David Freeman, figured prominently. It was tied to the wall because the high winds kept blowing it down. No one attempted to climb over the wall by means of this ladder—given that the wall, as Clark observes, "is easy enough to climb [even] without a ladder" (personal communication, April 29, 2011). Remarkably, the Border Patrol stood back and let the show go up without interference (the winds forced Clark to call a halt several hours later). The show featured a number of artworks overtly critical of the wall, including Clark's own *Montezuma's Revenge* and Susan Harbage Page's corona wreath made of ribbons that commemorated those who lost their lives crossing.

6. For residents of the region and for all those who care about the fate of migrants, it highlights the plight of those whom it holds back, thereby eliciting empathy for them; it may even invite the glorification of their suffering. These feelings are themselves transgressive of the wall's stated purpose to exclude those who do not have the "right" to enter.

7. Our conversations with migrants in Nogales and Tijuana in the last few years included many such testimonies.

8. David Spener (2003) offers an excellent discussion of the manifest failure to stem migration in the Laredo/San Juan area in an essay on this topic, "Controlling the Border in El Paso del Norte: Operation Blockade or Operation Charade?"

9. An exemplary boundary is found in the Rio Grande, which serves as the basis for the U.S.-Mexico border for two-thirds of its entire length yet is itself easily traversable at many junctures. Any attempt to regard the Rio Grande as a precisely determinable edge or limit is foredoomed. We will return to this paradoxical circumstance in chapter 4.

10. A telling instance of this fact is at play in the last scene of Jean Renoir's film *The Grand Illusion*, when German soldiers stop shooting at French soldiers who flee to safety over the Swiss border even though they could easily have killed them and even though *the border is hidden under the snow*. Here the border's literal invisibility stands metaphorically for its intrinsic invisibility. (I owe this example to John Protevi.)

11. In Husserl's original usage in section 88 of his *Ideas I*, the term *irreal* names the status of the noematic content (*Gehalt*) of an intentional act. Though not immanent to the act of consciousness, this content is a configuration intended by this act. This configuration is a theme whose core is a meaning or sense (*Sinn*) that can be repeated and realized in many concrete contexts. The irreal noematic content is thus independent of the physically or historically real (e.g., a material wall), whose core sense is nevertheless irreal. In the foregoing discussion, I use "ideal" and "abstract" to refer to meaning constituted in the conscious intentional acts of geographers and politicians (and ourselves insofar as we subscribe to what they have posited). Thanks to their noematic sense, borders exist apart from the particularities of walls that embody them and from the borderlines that demarcate them. (I owe this elucidation of Husserl to discussions with my colleague Donn Welton.)

12. At a deeper level, this is because an international border reflects the changing ratio between what counts as bare life and the law that is determined by a sovereign state: a bare life that is stateless and without basic rights and a law whose entire interest is that of maintaining or extending power. The relationship between bare life and state law is taken up by Giorgio Agamben (1998) in *Homo Sacer: Sovereign Power and Bare Life*.

13. Jessica Sims points out that the leaking to which I refer involves far more than just the wall at La Frontera, for it serves as the justification for implementing anything that is designed to plug up existing "holes" in matters of immigration or drugs: "It is a matter of making the need for the wall appear self-evident, while simultaneously covering over the fact that the problems at the border are themselves the result of the artificial construct that has been put in place to protect certain vested interests" (J. Sims, personal communication, March 15, 2012).

14. Moreover, the wall is only imperfectly effective for preventing terrorists from entering the United States from Mexico (an early fantasy of the Department of Homeland Security): such was the intention, the promise, especially in the wake of 9/11. If the current wall does not undercut the transfer of pistols and rifles across it, how can it prevent the transmission of components for bombs?

15. Approximately 400,000 deportations a year have occurred in 2010, 2011, and 2012.

CHAPTER 2: AMBOS NOGALES

1. These others include Douglas/Aqua Prieta, San Diego/Tijuana, El Paso/Ciudad Juárez, Presidio/Ojinaga, Del Rio/Ciudad Acuña, Eagle Pass/Piedras Negras, Columbus/Puerto Palomas, Laredo/Nuevo Laredo, McAllen/Reynosa, Brownsville/Matamoros, Naco/Naco, and Calexico/Mexicali.

2. The paucity of twin cities on the U.S.-Canadian border is striking: Niagara Falls, Ontario/Niagara Falls, New York; Superior, Wisconsin/Duluth, Minnesota; and International Falls, Minnesota/Fort Frances, Ontario, are the only instances of paired cities of any significant size along this border.

3. In trips to the region, we have heard abundant testimony to this effect from inhabitants of both Nogaleses, as well as from inhabitants of Douglas/Agua Prieta.

4. For a more detailed account of the colorful history of Ambos Nogales than we can offer here, see Ingram, Laney, and Gillilan 1995; and Davidson 2000. Davidson's overall assessment is notable: "Ambos Nogales is a place of both opportunity and despair, new beginnings and the death of dreams" (2000, 7).

5. Heidegger has linked pole and *polis*, as in this statement: "Perhaps the polis is that realm and locale around which everything question-worthy and uncanny turns in an exceptional sense. The polis is *polos*, that is, the pole, the swirl [*Wirbel*] in which and around which everything turns" (Heidegger 1984, 81). In the current context, the single pole around which the *polis* of the two Nogaleses turns is the border at La Frontera. What Heidegger here terms "pole" I am calling "hinge," "axis," or "pivot."

6. Alicia Enciso, a native of Nogales, Arizona, assures us that there is a dynamic life in this city and that it is simply less evident as one passes through it. Its downtown region in particular is less lively than that of its sister city. Part of this difference is due to the fact it has a population of only 20,000 in contrast with that of ca. 400,000 people in Nogales, Sonora. Another, more significant part bears on the cultural differences between the inhabitants of these two cities.

7. As we learned from two women who have instructed residents of the colonia of Flores Magón of their rights on a wholly informal basis. In an unjust system where being a few minutes late to work means the cancellation of the "bonuses" earned from working overtime and women are routinely given pregnancy tests, women are not permitted to discuss these matters in the factories—factors that, according to one informant who wants to remain anonymous, restrict these two advocates of human rights to intentionally informal gatherings and door-to-door visits.

8. Mexico has a complicated system of land ownership. Squatting on a piece of unoccupied land for a certain amount of time—typically, one year or more—used to entitle one to continue to live on this land indefinitely. This has changed in the wake of NAFTA (to be discussed in the prelude to Part 2). Even so, one must begin to make payments after a certain amount of time; these go to the landlord or manager, who in effect "owns" the whole tract. These payments are supposed to go toward eventual legal ownership on the part of the squatter, but they often serve merely as "rent" that does not build up equity in one's plot. The landlord "allows" the squatting to happen, on the understanding that he/she does not have to supply electricity or water for the area of the colonia he/she oversees.

9. To be irregular or vague is not to be ineffective as a border. Even if the exact perimeter of one's plot in a colonia does not have fully legal status and is not listed in any land register, the assumed limit of the plot serves no less to demarcate one family's immediate dwelling area from another's; it is known to be present thanks to a tacit agreement between neighbors. As we have shown in the case of the border itself, its lack of literal delineation is not a lack of force or effect in the place-world it traverses.

10. Bassett often counsels migrants not to cross the border during the hottest times, when the heat on the floor of the desert can rise to 120 degrees during the day. His effort is to save as many lives as possible, in keeping with comparable goals of other groups, such as Humane Borders and No More Deaths, both of which are based on the Arizona side of the border and which regularly set out kegs of fresh water at marked locations through which migrants are likely to pass under conditions of imminent dehydration. These kegs are just as regularly slashed by vigilantes and others, depriving migrants of what may well be the difference between life and death.

11. In fact, as noted in chapter 1, surveillance cameras are stationed on high: their remote positioning induces a sense of being seen by more than human eyes. The images in which these cameras capture suspicious movements at or near the wall are monitored continuously by personnel hired expressly to detect such movements; human eyes collude with the wholly mechanical eyes of the cameras.

12. For the full discussion of striated vs. smooth space, see Deleuze and Guattari 1987 (447–501).

13. In fact, many members of the Border Patrol live in Rio Rico, a small upscale town north of Nogales, Arizona.

14. *Border Dynamics* is the title of a remarkable sculpture created by Alberto Morackis and Guadalupe Serrano that will be discussed in chapter 8.

15. Peter Warnek, of the University of Oregon, proposes suggestively that the verb *trespass* means, in origin, to go along a third way or to split one's way along a third path. Those who trespass in the present situation are in effect transgressing onto a third path of improvisation.

16. Whether they are in fact equally justified is another issue, one whose outcome depends on whether the requirements of vital needs are on a par with those of protecting private property. We are here speaking at the level of feeling or personal conviction, not that of ultimate validity or ability to justify. (In our own view, the migrants possess the right to seek employment wherever they can find it. If this means traveling over private property to reach gainful work located elsewhere, we see this as justified as long as no willful destruction of the property itself occurs.)

17. Tim Johnston points out the parallel to the perception of the human face regarded as a wall of flesh; the wall at La Frontera "seems to function as a kind of visual Gestalt that functions in the same way facial features do. It allows for the immediate structuring of here/there and us/them . . . that mark and demarcate us daily" (T. Johnston, personal communication, July 21, 2012).

18. Since the timing of my (EC) first visit to Nogales in 2005, the passage of Arizona law SB 1070 in early 2010 extends the right of stopping any person and asking for proper documentation, even if this person is not engaged in any suspicious or objectionable behavior. Clearly, such a law permits, indeed encourages, racial profiling.

19. We put the term "illegal immigrants" into quotation marks here and elsewhere to indicate its status as a politically loaded shibboleth in current discussions of the situation at La Frontera. The term bears a distinctly negative connotation, as if to say that such people have no right to live and work on American soil. Hence we use the basic word "migrants" to signify all those who seek employment or political asylum in another country, irrespective of their exact legal standing when in that country. This term also conveys the sense of

forced migration that is required of those who must change their location if they are to satisfy their basic human rights.

20. Even in Nogales, Arizona, most people (94 percent) are Hispanic or Latino. Indeed, the town is so well known for its population of Mexican origin that it is often referred to derogatorily in such racially charged epithets as "Noghetto" and "Drogales" (A. Enciso, personal communication, June 1, 2008).

21. Not that an expensive and elaborate wall is required to keep people apart; as one can see at the encampment near Agua Prieta, strife can be generated even when the border itself is marked by nothing but a bare barbed-wire fence or a plain dirt road. On the other hand, the literal removal of a wall does not solve all problems at the border, especially those stemming from economic disparities.

CHAPTER 3: TIJUANA

1. Much the same is true of the other border towns we have considered, from Brownsville in the extreme east to Nogales. But where Brownsville is located on the American side and Nogales on both sides, Tijuana is found on the south side alone. Despite these differences in location, each place reflects the nearby presence of the border, depending on it (though in differing degrees) for its very identity and for its well-being.

2. I still remember the sketch portrait my cousin Robert Johntz purchased when he visited Tijuana as a high school student in the late 1950s: it showed him dancing to a salsa beat and holding a flask of tequila behind his back.

3. Mike McCoy, naturalist and environmental activist in the region, tells me that plans for channelization were first discussed in the 1940s, then realized in the 1970s. By 1976, U.S. Senator Pete Wilson, advised by McCoy and the United States Army Corps of Engineers, approved a dissipation system that diverted, absorbed, and redirected flows by constructing dikes and engineered levees. McCoy adds: "The Tijuana River in its natural state is an ephemeral river, but today it flows all year, due to development. Sewage is a real problem because of this, and contaminates beaches and the ocean on both sides of the border, which causes public health problems and destroys tourism and the economy" (personal communication, May 10, 2007).

4. Frantz Fanon, in *Black Skin, White Masks* (1967), describes how racism epidermalizes the black subject, reducing him or her through the white gaze to the color of the skin. The border wall—conveying a plethora of racist messages to the brown body—can be experienced as cutting through the body, even dividing the heart, separating loved ones into two countries that can seem unreachable to each other.

5. McCoy observes, "It is interesting to compare the sinuous natural flow of a river or an old braided river that appears contained but is never contained under natural circumstances unless forced by dikes and levees (and even these are temporary over time). A case in point is the Tijuana River and delta. A river and a flood plain are integral parts of the whole where the river is never contained but evolves as part of a natural system" (personal communication, June 22, 2007).

6. For a more complete account, see Tierra Environmental Services (2004). This account makes it clear that three habitats were at stake: the marsh area described above, a mudflat near the main tidal channel, and a higher marsh plain that was left unplanted in order to encourage natural growth to occur. Each of these areas involved their own characteristic edges. See also J. Karnik 2002. These efforts were elicited by earlier neglect and pollution in the Tijuana watershed as a whole; it took constructive human intervention to correct the baneful effects of previous human interventions.

7. Other such efforts are those of the Oneonta Tidal Linkage in the northern part of the estuary (winter of 1997), the Goat Canyon Quarry restoration and enhancement (fall

of 2000 through 2003), and the currently envisioned Tijuana Estuary Tidal Restoration Program, Phase II. The environmental risk ensuing on the building of a second and third reinforcement wall comes from the displacement of massive amounts of earth taken from the leveling of whole mesas in the southern part of the Tijuana Estuary region. This displacement "destabilized the structure of this [eco]system which leads to erosion after heavy rains" (M. McCoy, personal communication, May 2, 2011).

8. Congressman Duncan Hunter, of Southern California, was the driving force behind the initial erection and recent reinforcement of the wall in this area; he took this initiative without consulting local residents and without any consideration of the predictable damage to the estuary region on its immediate north side. In this move, he joined forces with Michael Chertoff, secretary of the Department of Homeland Security, who waived recognition of existing environmental protection laws here as well as elsewhere along La Frontera.

9. By "environment," McCoy means "natural environment." McCoy adds: "Nature does not recognize artificial borders like political lines drawn in the sand. Power, corruption, wealth, deception, fear, and fraud love political [borders]" (personal communication, May 10, 2007). Compare this statement as well: "Nature works without borders. It doesn't recognize the line between two countries" (Karnik 2002). To McCoy's claim we need only add that human beings don't have intrinsic borders either—for they, too, are part of the natural order (A. Cruz, personal communication, November 1, 2007).

10. Certain nonhuman animals create borders in order to claim and maintain territoriality, establishing a safe space into which other species are forbidden entry. I refer, for example, to the use of the scent of urine to announce "no trespassing." Human beings follow suit in their own distinctive claims to territory, but they often articulate the border in verbal or other symbolic terms. Walls are in this respect an intermediate case, situated uneasily between something wholly physical and something purely symbolic.

11. Even the edges of places that are specifiable in geometric terms may be porous—for example, the fractal formations of coastlines and other natural phenomena. Despite the formality of the geometrical determination, such edges are boundaries in the sense we have just outlined.

12. This is not to deny that on the U.S. side of La Frontera the environment is also given short shrift—for instance, by home construction that is expanding southward from nearby San Diego. In the face of these unfortunate trends, the effort to preserve and strengthen the Tijuana Estuary is all the more admirable—and all the more desperately needed.

13. I am thinking of the assiduous efforts of Oscar Roma in reaching agreement on environmental concerns between those in charge of the Tijuana Reserve on the American side and the mayors of Tijuana and Tecate. I rely here on the account given by Mike McCoy in the manuscript "Script for Border Fence Film" (5).

14. The term *ecotone* covers much of the semantic range of *borderland* and of *boundary*, but in this book we employ the latter two terms in the semitechnical ways set out in chapter 1, and we here adopt this new term because of its widespread use in the emerging science of ecology. It is especially apt as a description of the situation of the Tijuana Estuary and, as we shall see, of the surrounding cultural circumstance.

15. As if in recognition of the value of supporting such ongoing biodiversity in the Tijuana Estuary, the Tijuana River National Estuarine Research Reserve is one of only twenty-eight estuarine reserves in the United States that are dedicated to education and research. In 1980 it became a national wildlife refuge, and in 1982 it was named a national estuarine research reserve. It was designated in 2005 as a Ramsar site—a wetland of international significance. In 2010 it became a California state marine conservation area.

16. Mike McCoy suggests this related thought: "If you want to draw in one other component I will suggest you can take structure and content and define it with function. Structure defines the anatomy of a biological organism and function defines its physiology.

The same is true with larger systems of life where function is defined ecologically rather than physiologically. This concept . . . might further define interrelationships within and between complex biological, social and ecological systems" (personal communication, June 22, 2007).

17. I am mindful of the admonitory remark by Florence Krall, who said, "Underlying the familiar culture/Nature dichotomy is instead a webbing of gender, race, politics, economics, and spirituality that preoccupies wayfaring humans on this planet" (1994, 6). By "cultural" in this phase of my discussion, I am referring to anything artificially produced (i.e., to what is humanly made), as this belongs to an encompassing historical and traditional context.

18. Mike McCoy remarks, "This wall is antithetical to an ecotone. [It] is a true dead zone. It is designed to prohibit intermingling at all levels, biological, social and ecological. Those who build walls and borders are disconnected from the reality of life. They prefer a sterile environment" (personal communication, June 22, 2007). McCoy's remark rests on the assumption that ecotones belong to natural circumstances in the paradigm case. With hints from Krall and from McCoy himself, I prefer to broaden the semantic scope of the term "ecotone" and especially to regard the wall as radically anti-ecotonal.

19. Irigaray's description of the interval created by sexual differences provides pertinent terms for the otherwise very different situation discussed in this chapter. In this situation, the differences that matter most are those that structure the natural and cultural dimensions of this situation: interspecies, meteorological, and ecological on one side; racial, linguistic, and historical on the other. Moreover, these differences dynamize the intervening space between city and estuary, a space that is the *place* of their interaction.

20. Kerosote (2007) writes, "Unfortunately, since the fence along the United States-Mexico border is designed to keep people out, it can't be outfitted with features that allow wildlife to migrate over and under livestock fences and highways. . . . There are better ways to protect our borders than building a wall that people will inevitably find ways around but wildlife won't." In the same article, Nancy Brown, an outreach manager at the Santa Ana National Wildlife Refuge, is quoted as saying, "If you have a fence that runs several miles long, if you are a tortoise or any animal that can't fly over or go through it, then you have a pretty long distance that you have to go to get water."

Chapter 4: Wall and River in the Lower Rio Grande Valley

1. Dr. Taméz is an associate professor and the director of the M.S. Program in Nursing at the University of Texas at Brownsville. For the account here given, I am indebted to her reconstruction of the situation that preoccupied her from 2007 to the present moment. The remark cited in this sentence is from a conversation of May 30, 2009.

2. Scott Nicol comments, "This was part of the Environmental Impact Statement (EIS) preparation process, and there were similar meetings in McAllen and Rio Grande City. The McAllen meeting was well attended, because No Border Wall and the McAllen Economic Development Council teamed up to stage a protest in the same convention center at the same time, and the protesters then walked down the hall and offered comments. But [these meetings] were all farces (I attended them), with no opportunity for back-and-forth discussion or presentations of the merits of various options. When [Michael] Chertoff waived the National Environmental Policy Act in 2008, the EIS process ended and they became moot" (personal communication, June 7, 2001).

3. The University of Texas at Brownsville website (www.utb.edu) contains an archive on the history of the special campus wall. Anthony Zavaleta describes the valiant efforts of the university's president, Juliet V. García, and others at the institution (including himself) to defy the Department of Homeland Security (DHS) in its efforts to build a wall that would have divided the campus. Andrew Hanen, a federal judge, ordered the university and the

DHS to reach agreement after mutual discussions as to the kind of wall to build and its location. Eventually the two sides agreed on July 31, 2008, that if the university were to increase the height of an existing wall on the southern edge of the campus to ten feet, it would count as the official wall, but the university would retain the right to determine the exact type of wall and its appearance. The result was a beige brick structure "indistinguishable from any regular university or institutional fence . . . [that] complements the natural landscape on the campus' southern edge" (Zavaleta 2010, 292–293). Concerning the impact of the wall on the concrete lives of individuals such as Eloisa Taméz, see Garrett 2010.

4. Anthony Zavaleta put it this way: "We live between two armies" (personal communication, April 11, 2011). Braune's comment came from a conversation in McAllen, Texas, May 30, 2009. Braune teaches philosophy at Texas Southmost College, Mid-Valley campus. Much of the material in this section stems from this conversation and a later talk of April 12, 2011. See also Braune's articles on the website www.texascivilrightsreview.org.

5. At the University of Texas–Pan American, at nearby Edinburg, the CIA maintains a program to recruit undergraduates and to encourage these same undergraduates to convince high school students to join the CIA directly after their graduation, while summer youth camps in the area stimulate young people's interest in careers as police officers. With the immigration situation far from resolved, and with the drug cartels (and the closely associated arms trade) flourishing, the future prospects of employment in law enforcement look increasingly promising, if not irresistible, to young people caught in the midst of a major economic recession and living in a region high in unemployment.

6. Neither the detention centers nor the government provides legal counsel for immigration cases; detainees must pay for it themselves, a remote possibility for this mostly indigent population. Typically, detainees, who are picked up on a variety of charges, must wait several weeks or even months to get a hearing. They are often tried by judges who are former prosecutors, resulting in a kangaroo-court situation. Several years ago, Jodi Goodwin and several other lawyers associated with her attempted to inform detainees at the Willacy detention center in Raymondville of their right to hire counsel while awaiting the hearing (and their right to court-appointed representation if they were formally charged with a crime at the hearing itself). Such counsel was provided through the Legal Orientation Program ("LOP"). But the lawyers soon found themselves besieged by claims of mistreatment in the detention center at Raymondville, some of which they felt obliged to report. At that point, the center forced Goodwin and her colleagues to talk with detainees in small groups of ten or fewer, undermining their effectiveness and increasing the time necessary to accomplish the task of informing detainees, which forced the attorneys to discontinue their pro-bono work and left the detainees in a legal limbo. The lawyers could no longer find the time to help out those who needed legal advice, and the program had to be discontinued. The LOP program did continue at the detention center near Port Isabel, however, and more recently, thanks to a special grant to the Texas Rio Grande Legal Aid office, LOP was reinstated in Raymondville (J. Goodwin, personal communication, April 12, 2011).

7. Still other problems arise from the North American Super Corridor Coalition, which aims to build a superhighway from Canada to Mexico that will pass through this part of the world. Problems also arise with the TransTexas Corridor, which will link the United States with ports of entry on the west coast of Mexico. These ambitious projects take money and resources (e.g., waters from underground aquifers) out of the region and place them in the hands of the corporations behind such projects.

8. Braune writes: "Instituted during the war years when labor was in short supply, the *bracero* program is arguably the start of the 'Mexican immigration problem,' which mainly reflected concerns about Mexicans taking factory jobs from U.S. workers." Not all Mexican workers came as braceros; others came on their own. Braune adds: "'Operation Wetback,' a successful military-style action of 1954 under President Eisenhower, forced between

500,000 and one million Mexican workers and family members to leave the United States" (Braune, personal communication, May 19, 2011). Now the wall is discouraging the children and grandchildren of the braceros from coming back to the United States.

9. Eloisa Taméz remarked that such leveling at the top decreased the effectiveness of the levee as a protection against serious flooding, which is presumably the primary purpose for building the levees (personal communication, May 30, 2009).

10. In recent constructions, including one at Nuevo Progreso, the checkpoints now include a separate bridge with its own open lane for Border Patrol cars.

11. Jodi Goodwin said this in our conversation of April 12, 2011, but words close to this came continually to people's lips as we spoke to them on recent trips to the region. Jay Johnson-Castro Sr. says, "The Wall is a military decoy . . . used by the military-industrial complex to siphon billions of our dollars on our own soil" (personal communication, June 19, 2011). We thank Tim Johnston for pressing us to clarify our construal of the wall's complexity as effecting a deconstruction of the dyad of presence/absence (personal communication, August 20, 2010).

12. Nicol writes: "During the summer of 2006 the US House and Senate passed differing versions of immigration reform, each of which contained walls to mollify conservatives. The two bills were not reconciled, so they died, and only the wall portions were resurrected in the Secure Fence Act of 2006" (personal communication, June 7, 2011). Scott has tracked the construction of the border wall in the Lower Rio Grande Valley region. See www.no-border-wall.com, www.texasbordercoalition.com, and www.Sierraclub.org/borderlands.

13. This joke has been attributed to Janet Napolitano when she was governor of Arizona, before she became the secretary of homeland security in the Obama administration. Many in the region repeat the joke without attribution.

14. As a vehicle for governmental debate and an excuse for ongoing stalemate, the dialectic between the sheer materiality of the wall and its literal absence in the gaps to which we have been pointing is transfigured into something distinctly hybrid, neither simply present nor altogether absent: a "third thing," to invoke Kantian parlance. This deconstruction of the binary of sheer presence/absence into a mere bargaining chip, an item of political debate—in short, a symbolic gesture—provides a dark contrast to the more felicitous role of the former bridge at Candelaria. This bridge was a very different third thing that, before its destruction, served as a vital link between human beings separated by a river.

15. Efforts to create a virtual wall, though heralded with much fanfare, have so far come to naught. A billion-dollar-plus contract with Boeing was canceled by the U.S. government in February 2011 for lack of significant progress. The director of the electronic fence program at the Department of Homeland Security, Mark Borkowski, said, "It was a great idea, but it didn't work" (quoted in S. Nicol 2011).

16. This happened even though the Mexican team had made more progress than their American counterparts at that same time: "Following the course and sinuosities of the river as closely as possible, the [Mexican] surveying party made a more detailed survey on the Mexican side of the Rio Grande [than did their American counterparts]" (Werne 2007, 124). The Mexican maps were especially notable for their extensive topographic representations.

17. One observer put it this way: "Frequently hundreds of acres would be passed in a single day by a cut-off in the bend of one channel, and sometimes the bed would change from one firm bank to the other, a distance of perhaps 20 miles in length by 6 [miles] in width" (quoted in Rebert 2001, 175). One can still see today the traces of earlier channels, long since bypassed, in the Rio Bosque Wetlands Park east of El Paso.

18. The Boundary Survey reopened on both sides in 1853 and continued, with ongoing interruptions, until it was officially "completed" in 1857. The Mexican team claimed to be

finished with their work as early as 1854, but they were never able to cover the stretch of the river between San Carlos and Laredo. This stretch was later surveyed by the U.S. team. Nevertheless, the survey of the Rio Grande undertaken at that time can hardly be considered fully complete. Not only was it the case that "U.S. topographical work on the lower Rio Grande was not well documented," as Rebert (2001, 173) comments; more generally, "the river's survey [could not] ever be considered finished, as the Rio Grande irritatingly shifted its channel from time to time, transferring land from one nation to another" (Werne 2007, 151–152). It took the International Boundary Commission of 1889 to adjudicate the outcome of many of these shifts; even so, many uncertainties remained, including the disputed land abutting the river at El Chamizal, near El Paso, which was not settled until 1963 (Rebert 2001, 2002–2006). Reflecting the mutating fate of the submerged channels, in 1884 the International Boundary Commission decided to distinguish between river channels that moved relatively slowly with erosion and ones that changed quickly because of rapid water movement. In the former case, the border moved with the change of channels; in the latter (called "avulsions"), it remains in its original location. But what of intermediate instances, channels that changed neither very slowly nor very rapidly? Where is the exact locus of the border in their case?

19. *"Panta rhei,"* as Heraclitus says in fragment 20 (1959, 28): "everything flows and nothing abides."

20. Protestors in recent times have also called it a *muro de odio* (wall of hatred) and a *muro de vergüenza* (wall of shame).

Prelude to Part 2: Friendship Park

1. Quakers use the phrase "friendly adult presence" to describe adults accompanying youth.

Chapter 5: The Creation of an Internal Colony

1. FAFSA stands for Free Application for Federal Student Aid.

2. The pueblo was located in an area now bounded by De la Guerra Street, Canon Perdido Street, Garden Street, and Anacapa Street.

3. Charles Nordhoff also contributed to the tourist boom. The city's reputation as a salubrious locale was so great that, it is said, police in San Francisco had to regulate crowds trying to get on the boats to Santa Barbara. Tuberculosis patients vied for hotel rooms.

4. Anglo labor unions disregarded Mexicans for the first three decades of the 1900s, but Mexicans were able to join with others, such as Japanese, in the 1903 Sugar Beet Strike in Oxnard, fighting against oppressive working conditions. In Santa Barbara in 1903, striking lemon workers sought a reduction in the workday, from ten to nine hours, and increased wages.

5. Between 1910 and 1920, when Japanese agricultural workers protested their wages in Carpinteria, they were replaced by Chicanos and Mexican migrants who were willing to work for lower wages. The "Mexicans"—who included U.S. citizens—lived on the west side of Carpinteria, in what was variously named "Old Town," "Mexican Colony," and "Mexican Town." Many also lived in the Cramer tract, which is now directly across from Highway 101. It consisted of minimally constructed houses without plumbing. During rains, this tract flooded, and the dirt streets became mud holes. The parents petitioned for the addition of bathing facilities in the school building, since their children did not have them in their slum-like housing.

6. Once the Aliso School began admitting Anglo students, repairs and adjustments were made to the facilities, which had otherwise languished for years. These improvements

included replanting grass on the playground. Now the events of the school were publicized in the newspaper, as they had been for the Anglo students in Main school. Mexicans still could not rent or buy houses wherever they liked in Carpinteria.

7. Using a single day as an example, Chief Deputy Don Patterson, of the Santa Barbara Sheriff's Office, said that on April 6, 2011, there were 243 foreign-born people in the Santa Barbara County jail, and 95 had Immigration Customs Enforcement holds on them.

8. See Immigration and Customs Enforcement, National Interoperability Statistics, by Jurisdiction, ICE FOIA 10-2674.000087_ICE FOIA 10-2674.000094.

9. Romero made this comment at the Community Forum on Gang Injunctions, held at Santa Barbara's Westside Community Center, March 3, 2011.

CHAPTER 6: JUAN CROW

1. Copycat laws, inspired by Arizona's legislation, have been drafted in various states by Kris Koback of FAIR (Federation for American Immigration Reform), an organization named a "hate group" by the Southern Poverty Law Center in 2007. Those who are concerned about immigrants' using government benefits that empty local coffers need to address their energy to the redistribution of tax and social security funds that undocumented immigrants pay into the system. Undocumented immigrants are estimated to pay $7 to $12 billion a year into Social Security and Medicare annually, despite their not being able to claim any of this at retirement age. While estimates vary, they pay between $90 and $140 billion in federal, state, and local taxes each year but receive only $5 billion in public benefits a year.

The Congressional Budget Office estimates that if E-Verify were mandated universally, federal tax revenues would decrease by $17.3 billion between 2009 and 2018. While anti-immigrant groups argue for detention and deportation on economic grounds, their logic fails. A study from the Center for American Progress and the Immigration Policy Center shows that creating more flexible immigration channels and legalizing undocumented immigrants would expand the economy by $1.5 trillion in gross domestic product over ten years, through such things as increased consumer spending and higher tax receipts. A deportation approach shrinks the economy by $2.5 trillion over the same ten-year period (Fitz, Martinez, and Wijewardena 2010).

2. If we peel back the rhetoric and ask about the "criminality" of Mexican immigrants in terms of our usual ideas of criminality, we find, for instance, that Mexican men in California are eight times less likely than their U.S.-born counterparts to be imprisoned (Service Employees International Union, n.d.). Indeed, according to conservative Americas Majority Foundation (Service Employees International Union, n.d.), crime rates are lowest in states with the highest immigration growth rates. From 1999 to 2006, the total crime rate declined 13.6 percent in the nineteen highest-immigration states, nearly twice the 7.1 percent decline in the other thirty-two states.

3. Steven Logan, CEO of Cornell Industries, spoke openly in 2011 about his intention to capitalize on post-9/11 enforcement fever: "It's clear that since Sept. 11 there's a heightened focus on detention . . . more people are gonna get caught. So I would say that's positive . . . with the focus on people that are illegal and also from Middle Eastern descent in the United States there are over 900,000 undocumented individuals from Middle Eastern descent . . . that is a population, for lots of reasons that is being targeted. . . . The Federal business is the best business for us and . . . Sept. 11 is increasing that business" (quoted in Kirkhan 2011).

4. The same corporations responsible for building these inhumane prisons, which punish and control through isolation, have found a new market niche: the detention of immigrants, overwhelmingly Mexicans. In 1983 Corrections Corporation of America signed a contract with the INS for immigrant detention, thus giving birth to the private for-profit

detention industry. Companies such as the Corrections Corporation of America (sometimes called the Corruption Corporation of America) and Management and Training Corporation are building detention facilities all over America. They enjoy considerable corporate profits as they create the deportation pipeline that eliminates from our communities those we have now defined as criminals, the majority of whom have never committed what we would ordinarily think of as a crime.

5. While house raids are purportedly mounted to apprehend "violent gang members," innocent bystanders get swept into the deportation pipeline (Kanstroom and Rosenbloom 2009).

6. According to the Center for Constitutional Rights (2010), from October 2008 to June 2010, "79% of those deported due to S-Comm are non-criminals or were picked up for lower level offenses, such as traffic offenses or petty juvenile mischief."

7. G. Gordon Liddy used this term to describe Mexicans during his radio broadcast on July 6, 2010.

8. In the United States, African American men are disproportionately charged and prosecuted; in addition, they receive longer sentences than do their white counterparts, who are also more likely to receive parole. When asked to close their eyes and imagine a drug user, 95 percent of U.S. respondents imagine a black male, even though African Americans are only responsible for 15 percent of the drug abuse in the United States (Alexander 2010, 103). The black male body is too often imagined as armed and using and dealing drugs, and most who imagine this are unaware of the racial bias carried by their imagination. Alexander details how the media helped to construct this image of the young black man, allowing the white imagination to proceed according to a logic different from the one whites deploy in their conscious attitudes. The same negative images of the brown male body, and the Mexican body generally, are being forged today as Mexicans find themselves internalizing Anglo projections of themselves as uneducated, drug peddlers, gang members, criminals, and even terrorists.

CHAPTER 7: THE SOULS OF ANGLOS

1. In 2010, Arizona banned ethnic studies from its public school curriculum, eventually limiting the ban to Chicano studies. It was a forceful effort to amputate the history and narratives of the dispossessed. Proponents argued that the students who took these classes not only deepened their understanding of justice but did better academically and that learning the history of one's ethnic group contributes to pride and increased self-esteem (research bore out the second claim, showing that students who participated in Arizona's ethnic studies classes were more engaged in their overall education and did better in their schoolwork [SaveEthnicStudies.org, n.d.]). Opponents called the classes propaganda and argued that calls to cede portions of the Southwest back to Mexico, which originally included them, were equivalent to promoting the overthrow of the U.S. government (Lacey 2011). Further, they argued that any program advocating ethnic solidarity instead of individuality should be banned. Texts deemed objectionable had references to white people as "gringos" and described privilege as being related to one's color and other racial characteristics.

CHAPTER 8: BORDER-WALL ART AS LIMIT ACTS

1. The transborder feature of their collaboration is common to other groups, such as the Border Art Workshop/Taller de Arte Fronterizo (BAW/TAF), that have striven to embody in their collaboration the hybridity they value at the border. The Border Art Workshop was founded in 1984 under the sponsorship of Centro Cultural de la Raza (San Diego) to address "the social tensions the Mexican-American border creates, while asking us to imagine a world in which this international boundary has been erased" (quoted in Chavéz,

Grynsztejn, and Kanjo 1993, 25). It was among the first groups to use conceptual art to highlight the politics of the border that exclude migrants while inviting the free flow of capital (Prieto 1999).

2. Quiroz's work was funded by an Artist Project grant from the Arizona Commission on the Arts. Unfortunately, given increased security concerns at the border, the entire installation was removed in 2010 to protect it from theft.

3. Magón was an anarchosyndicalist theorist and activist who helped the Mexican revolution.

4. In 2011 it was taken down, one hopes temporarily, to allow the United States to put in a new border fence that will allow the border patrol to see into Nogales. Whether or not art that obscures U.S. Border Patrol's vision to the other side will be allowed is uncertain.

5. In West Berlin, the desire to express thoughts and reactions on the East Berlin side of the wall was so great that the artist Peter Unsicker threw a cloth with red paint over the section of the wall in front of his window, intending to make a mark there. A forbidding and impassable wall invites such transgression and free expression (personal communication, 2007).

CHAPTER 9: CREATING COMMUNITIES OF HOSPITALITY

1. Sanctuary Cities include Washington, D.C.; New York City; Los Angeles; Chicago; San Francisco; Santa Ana; San Diego; San Jose; Salt Lake City; El Paso; Houston; Detroit; Jersey City; Minneapolis; Miami; Denver; Baltimore; Seattle; Portland; New Haven, Connecticut; Somerville and Cambridge, Massachusetts; and Portland, Maine.

2. In 1971, the Berkeley City Council declared Berkeley to be a City of Refuge, and in 2008 it reaffirmed this status and passed a resolution that requires that "no department, agency, commission, officer or employee of the City of Berkeley shall use any city funds or resources to assist in the enforcement of Federal immigration law or to gather and disseminate information on the status of individuals in the City of Berkeley."

3. "Officers shall not initiate police action with the objective of discovering the alien status of a person. Officers shall not arrest nor book persons for violation of title 8, section 1325 of the United States Immigration code (Illegal Entry)."

4. For more, see www.greensborotrc.org.

5. In 1979, during a demonstration, white Klan and neo-Nazi members killed five members of the Communist Workers' Party, and injured ten others. Aware of the potential for violence at the rally, the police decided to be absent, colluding with the violence that erupted. As many white city officials distanced themselves from the event, and never inquired into the underlying issues, these issues continued to fester and create distrust and enmity between white and black communities. The TRC proceedings offered public space for many to come forward from various sectors of the community to give testimony regarding what happened in 1979. The commissioners hoped that increased public acknowledgment would lead to institutional reforms and citizen engagement and transformation. Recommendations that arose from the TRC included the establishment of living wages, antiracism training, citizen review committees to ensure police accountability, and the creation of a community justice center.

POSTLUDE 2: GAINING ACCESS TO THE HEART OF OUR HOME

1. The "guest" worker proposals before the Senate and Congress bear no relation to hospitality, despite their name. These proposals give all power to employers regarding the coming and going of employees within strict time limits set by the federal government. Workers must accept whatever work conditions they find themselves in, or else they must leave the United States. The "guest" proposals separate families, deny migrants sufficient

long-term security to enable them to develop roots in their communities, and deny them the dignity of being able to claim basic human rights in the workplace. A child of the bracero program of the 1950s, the guest-worker program should be named the "exploited worker" program.

2. In acknowledgment of this shadow, some communities prefer to refer to themselves as "receiving" or "welcoming" communities.

Epilogue: From Standing in the Shadows of Walls to Imagining Them Otherwise

1. Population predictions (Dowd 2005) suggest that in several decades, given the dramatic decrease in birth rates in Mexican families (from 6.9 children per woman in 1955 to 2.5 in 2005), Mexico will need most of its own workers. Efforts to prevent the flow of migration may then seem silly indeed, when the U.S. need for Mexican workers exceeds these workers' own desires for jobs in the United States.

Bibliography

Acuña, R. 2010. *Occupied America: A History of Chicanos*. 7th ed. New York: Prentice-Hall.

Addams, J. 1912. *Twenty Years at Hull-House: With Autobiographical Notes*. New York: Macmillan.

Agamben, G. 1998. *Homo Sacer: Sovereign Power and Bare Life*. Translated by D. Heller-Roazen. Stanford, CA: Stanford University Press.

———. 2005. *State of Exception*. Translated by K. Attell. Chicago: University of Chicago Press.

Ahmed, S. 2004. *Cultural Politics of Emotions*. New York: Routledge.

Alcoff, L. 2009. "Latinos beyond the Binary." *Southern Journal of Philosophy* 47 (S1): 112–128. http://www.alcoff.com/content/beyondbinary.html.

Alexander, M. 2010. *The New Jim Crow: Mass Incarceration in the Age of Colorblindness*. New York: New Press.

———. 2012. "End Mass Incarceration: Close Attica." Panel presentation, Riverside Church, New York, September 14.

Ali, S., ed. 2007. *Peace Parks: Conservation and Conflict Resolution*. Cambridge, MA: MIT Press.

Allen, R. 2005. "Reassessing the Internal (Neo)Colonialism Theory." *The Black Scholar* 35 (1): 2–11.

Alvarez, M. 2008. "La Pared Que Habla: A Photo Essay about Art and Graffiti at the Border Fence in Nogales, Sonora." *Journal of the Southwest* 50 (3): 305–334.

Amnesty International. 2009. "Jailed without Justice: Immigration Detention in the US." http://www.amnestyusa.org/uploads/JailedWithoutJustice.pdf.

"An Invitation to Abuse and Chaos." 2012. *New York Times*, April 22. http://www.nytimes.com/2012/04/22/opinion/sunday/an-invitation-to-abuse-and-chaos.html.

Anzaldúa, G. 1999. *Borderlands/La Frontera: The New Mestiza*. San Francisco: Aunt Lute.

Archibold, R. C. 2009. "Hired by Customs, but Working for the Cartels." *New York Times*, December 18.

Arendt, H. 2003. "Organized Guilt and Human Responsibility." In *The Portable Arendt*, edited by P. Baehr, 146–156. New York: Penguin.

———. 2005. *Essays in Understanding, 1930–1954: Formation, Exile, Totalitarianism*. New York: Schocken.

Aristotle. 2000. *Politics*. Translated by B. Jowett. Mineola, NY: Dover.

Bacon, D. 2005. "Communities without Borders." *The Nation*, October 24. http://archive.truthout.org/article/david-bacon-communities-without-borders.

Bada, X., J. Fox, and A. Selee. 2007. *Invisible No More: Mexican Migrant Civic Participation in the U.S.* Wilson Center and University of California, Santa Cruz. http://

www.wilsoncenter.org/publication/invisible-no-more-mexican-migrant-civic
-participation-the-united-states.

Baldwin, J. 1961. *Nobody Knows My Name.* New York: Dell.

———. 1965. "White Man's Guilt." *Ebony,* August, 47–54.

Battle, M. 1997. *Reconciliation: The Ubuntu Theology of Desmond Tutu.* Cleveland: Pilgrim.

Beirich, H. 2011. "The Year in Nativism." *Southern Poverty Law Center Intelligence Report,* 141:35–37.

Belarmino, V. 2007. "Artists to Take Over the Separation Wall in Israel and Palestine." July 1. http://www.labforculture.org/en/groups/public/labforculture/events-and -news/55227.

Bender, S. W. 2003. *Greasers and Gringos: Latinos, Law, and the American Imagination.* New York: New York University Press.

Benhabib, S. 2004. *The Rights of Others: Aliens, Residents, and Citizens.* Cambridge: Cambridge University Press.

Bergson, H. 1988. *Matter and Memory.* Translated by N. M. Paul and W. S. Palmer. New York: Zone.

Bernstein, N. 2011. "Immigrant Crackdowns Turn into Big Business." *New York Times,* September 29, A11.

Bevans, C. I., comp. 1974. *Treaties and Other International Agreements of the United States of America, 1776–1949.* Washington, DC: GPO, 1968–1976.

Blackmon, D. 2009. *Slavery by Another Name: The Re-Enslavement of Black Americans from the Civil War to World War II.* New York: Anchor.

Blauner, B. 2001. *Still the Big News: Racial Oppression in America.* Philadelphia: Temple University Press.

BorderLinks. 2012. "A Sit Down with One of the Many Minds Behind BorderLinks." http://www.borderbeat.net/people/2018-borderlinks-article.

Brabeck, K. M., M. B. Lykes, and R. Hershberg. 2011. "Framing Immigration to and Deportation from the United States: Guatemalan and Salvadoran Families Make Meaning of Their Experiences." *Community, Work, and Family* 14 (3): 275–296. doi: 10/1080/13668803.2010.520840.

Bracamontes, A. 2012. "Director of El Paso's Annunciation House Receives Teacher of Peace Award." *El Paso Times,* April 18. http://www.elpasotimes.com/news /ci_20424411/annunciation-house-director-receives-teacher-peace-award-work?source=rss.

Braithwaite, J. 1989. *Crime, Shame, and Reintegration.* Cambridge: Cambridge University Press.

"Brief Background of Metales y Derivados." n.d. In *U.S./Mexico Border Reader.* San Francisco, CA: Global Exchange.

Brown, W. 2010. *Walled States, Waning Sovereignty.* New York: Zone.

Butler, J. 2006. *Precarious Life: The Powers of Mourning and Violence.* New York: Verso.

Byrd, B., J. W. Byrd, and L. Crosthwaite, eds. 2002. *Puro Border: Dispatches, Snapshots and Graffiti from La Frontera.* El Paso, TX: Cinco Puntos.

Cabranes-Grant, L. 2004. In "Director's Notes for *Bordertown* and *La Barda* (The Wall)," by J. Velasco, Ensemble Theater Company, Santa Barbara, CA.

Camarillo, A. 1996. *Chicanos in a Changing Society: From Mexican Pueblos to American Barrios in Santa Barbara and Southern California, 1848–1930.* 2nd ed. Cambridge, MA: Harvard University Press.

Carrigan, W. 2003. "The Lynching of Persons of Mexican Origin or Descent in the United States, 1848 to 1928." *Journal of Social History* 37 (2): 411–438.

Casanova, J. P. n.d. "A Brief Comment on the Significance of the Project, 2501 Migrantes." http://www.2501migrants.com/home.html.

Casey, E. S. 1997. *The Fate of Place*. Berkeley: University of California Press.

———. 2002. "Rectangularity and Truth." In *Representing Place: Landscape Paintings and Maps*, 213–233. Minneapolis: University of Minnesota Press.

———. 2009. *Getting Back into Place: Toward a Renewed Understanding of the Place-World*. 2nd ed. Bloomington: Indiana University Press.

———. 2012. "At the Edges of My Body." In *The Oxford Handbook of Contemporary Phenomenology*, edited by D. Zahavi, 243–261. Oxford: Oxford University Press.

———. Forthcoming. *The World on Edge*. Bloomington: Indiana University Press.

Cave, D. 2012. "American Children, Now Struggling to Adjust to Life in Mexico." *New York Times*, June 18. http://www.nytimes.com/2012/06/19/world/americas/american-born-children-struggle-to-adjust-in-mexico.html?pagewanted=all&_r=0.

Center for Constitutional Rights. 2010. Briefing guide to "Secure Communities," 1–4. http://www.ccrjustice.org/files/Secure Communities Fact Sheet Briefing guide 8-2-2010 Production.pdf.

Center for Global Justice. 2011. http://www.globaljusticecenter.org/2011/11/policyoninvolvement.

Chalquist, C. 2008. *Deep California: Images and Ironies of Cross and Sword on El Camino Real*. Bloomington, IN: iUniverse.

Chavéz, P., M. Grynsztejn, and K. Kanjo. 1993. *La Frontera/The Border: Art about the Mexico/United States Border Experience*. San Diego, CA: Centro Cultural de la Raza, San Diego Museum of Contemporary Art.

Chertoff, M. 2008. "Why Washington Doesn't Work." Speech at Harvard University, Cambridge, MA, February 7.

Chodorow, J. 2009. "Soul's Body: Emotions and Their Development." Jung Society of Washington, Jung Memorial Lecture, delivered at the Embassy of Switzerland, Washington, DC, June 5.

Clark, K. 1965. *Dark Ghetto: Dilemma of Social Power*. Hanover, NH: Wesleyan University Press.

Clark, P. 2006. "Greensboro Truth and Reconciliation Commission: Seeking Truth, Working for Reconciliation." One by One Conference, Riverdale, NY, November 14.

Clifford, J. 2003. *On the Edges of Anthropology (Interviews)*. Chicago: Prickly Paradigm.

Collingwood, R. G. 1938. *Principles of Art*. Oxford: Oxford University Press.

Costantini, C. 2011. "Municipal ID Cards Given to Undocumented Immigrants in Cities across the U.S. with Varied Success." October 21. http://www.huffingtonpost.com/2011/10/21/municipal-id-cards-undocumented-immigrants_n_1024412.html.

Davidson, M. 2000. *Lives on the Line: Dispatches from the U.S.-Mexico Border*. Tucson: University of Arizona Press.

Deleuze, G. 1992. *The Fold: Leibniz and the Baroque*. Translated by T. Conley. Minneapolis: University of Minnesota Press.

Deleuze, G., and F. Guattari. 1987. *A Thousand Plateaus*. Translated by B. Massumi. Minneapolis: Minnesota University Press.

Derrida, J. 1987. *The Truth in Painting*. Translated by G. Bennington and I. McLeod. Chicago: University of Chicago Press.

———. 2000. *Of Hospitality (Cultural Memory in the Present)*. Palo Alto, CA: Stanford University Press.

———. 2001. *On Cosmopolitanism and Forgiveness*. New York: Routledge.

Descartes, R. 1998. *Meditations on First Philosophy*. Translated by D. C. Cress. Indianapolis: Hackett.

Detention Watch Network. 2011. "The Influence of the Private Prison Industry in Immigration Detention." May 4. http://www.detentionwatchnetwork.org/privateprisons_note2.

Dowd, M. 2005. "The Mexican Evolution." *New York Times*, August 1. http://www
.nytimes.com/2005/08/01/opinion/01dowd.html.

Downes, L. 2010. "The Hunt for American Decency in the Arizona Quicksand." *New York Times*, August 3. http://www.nytimes.com/2010/08/04/opinion/04wed4.html.

Du Bois, W. E. B. (1903) 1989. *The Souls of Black Folk*. New York: Penguin. Citations refer to the 1989 edition.

Eisler, J. 2004. *Slave Reparations: The Final Passage*. CrabTree Pictures.

Eliot, T. S. 1971. "The Dry Salvages." From *The Four Quartets*. Orlando, FL: Harcourt.

Emerson, R. W. 1981. *The Portable Emerson*. New York: Penguin.

Emmott, R. 2009. "A Costly U.S.-Mexico Border Wall, in Both Dollars and Deaths." *Reuters*, October 2. http://blogs.reuters.com/global/2009/10/02/borderwallcosts/.

Emory, W. H. 1851. *Notes on the Survey of the Boundary Line between Mexico and the United States*. Cincinnati: Morgan and Overend.

———. 1857. *Report on the American and Mexican Boundary Survey Made under the Direction of the Secretary of the Interior*. Thirty-fourth Congress, first session, H. Ex. Doc. 135. Washington, DC: C. Wendell, 1857–1859.

Faier, L. 2009. *Intimate Encounters: Filipina Women and the Remaking of Rural Japan*. Berkeley: University of California Press.

Fanon, F. 1967. *Black Skin, White Masks*. New York: Grove Press.

———. 2005. *The Wretched of the Earth*. New York: Grove Press.

Fitz, M., G. Martinez, and M. Wijewardena. 2010. "The Costs of Mass Deportation: Impractical, Expensive, and Ineffective." http://www.centerforamericanprogress.org /issues/immigration/report/2010/03/19/7470/the-costs-of-mass-deportation/.

Flores, L. 2003. "Constructing Rhetorical Borders: Peons, Illegal Aliens, and Competing Narratives of Immigration." *Critical Studies in Communication* 20 (4): 362–387.

Foucault, M. 1998. "A Preface to Transgression." In *Aesthetics, Method, and Epistemology*, edited by J. D. Faubion, 69–89. New York: New Press.

———. 2004. *Security, Territory, Population: Lectures at the Collège de France 1977–1978*. Edited by A. I. Davidson. Translated by G. Burchell. New York: Palgrave.

Freire, P. (1970) 1989. *Pedagogy of the Oppressed*. New York: Seabury. Citations refer to the 1989 edition.

———. 1998. *Pedagogy of the Heart*. New York: Continuum.

Friese, H., and S. Mezzadra. 2007. "Hospitality and Transnational Migration in Europe and the Mediterranean Middle East and North Africa." Robert Schuman Center for Advanced Studies, European University Institute, March 21–25. http://www.eui.eu /Documents/RSCAS/Research/Mediterranean/WS15MRM2007.pdf.

Frost, R. 2002. *Robert Frost's Poems*. New York: St. Martin's.

Fuentes, C. 1985. *The Old Gringo*. New York: Farrar, Straus and Giroux.

Garrett, T. M. 2010. "A Critique of the Department of Homeland Security and the Border Wall in the Rio Grande Valley." *Continuing Studies in Rio Grande Valley History* 9:305–324.

Gibson, J. J. 1986. *An Ecological Approach to Visual Perception*. Hillsdale, NJ: Lawrence Erlbaum Associates.

Gilbert, M. 2001. "Collective Remorse." In *War Crimes and Collective Wrongdoing: A Reader*, edited by A. Jokic and A. Ellis, 216–235. New York: Wiley-Blackwell.

Gilligan, J. 1997. *Violence: Reflections on a National Epidemic*. New York: Vintage.

Gobodo-Madikizela, P. 2003. *A Human Being Died That Night: A South African Woman Confronts the Legacy of Apartheid*. New York: Houghton Mifflin Harcourt.

Griffin, S. 1978. *Woman and Nature: The Roaring inside Her*. New York: Harper and Row.

Grosfoguel, R. 1999. "'Cultural Racism' and Colonial Caribbean Migrants in Core Zones of the Capitalist World-Economy." *Fernand Braudel Center* 22 (4).

Hayduk, R. 2006. *Democracy for All: Restoring Immigrant Voting Rights in the U.S.* New York: Routledge.

Hedges, C. 2010. "We Stand on the Cusp of One of Humanity's Most Dangerous Moments." *Alternet*, March 17. http://www.alternet.org/story/146005/we_stand_on_the_cusp_of_one_of_humanity's_most_dangerous_moments.

Hedges, C., and J. Sacco. 2012. *Days of Destruction, Days of Revolt.* New York: Nation Books.

Heidegger, M. 1962. *Being and Time.* Translated by J. Macquarrie and E. Robinson. New York: Harper and Row.

———. 1971. *Poetry, Language, Thought.* Translated by A. Hofstadter. New York: Harper and Row.

———. 1984. *Hölderlin's Hymn "The Ister."* Translated by J. Davis and W. McNeill. Bloomington: Indiana University Press.

Heraclitus. 1959. *Heraclitus.* Translated by P. Wheelwright. New York: Atheneum.

Heschel, A. J. 1951. *The Sabbath: Its Meaning for Modern Man.* New York: Farrar, Straus and Young.

Heyman, J. 2008. "Constructing a Virtual Wall: Race and Citizenship in U.S.-Mexico Border Policing." *Journal of the Southwest* 50 (3): 305–334.

Hicks, D. 2011. *Dignity: The Essential Role It Plays in Resolving Conflict.* New Haven, CT: Yale University Press.

Hill, S. 2003. "Metaphoric Enrichment and Material Poverty: The Making of Colonias." In *Ethnography at the Border*, edited by P. Vila, 141–165. Minneapolis: University of Minnesota Press.

Hillman, J. 1998. "Abandoning the Child." In *Spring '63: Mom and the Kids.* Woodstock, CT: Spring Publications.

Hochschild, A. 1999. *King Leopold's Ghost: A Story of Greed, Terror, and Heroism in Colonial Africa.* New York: Houghton Mifflin.

hooks, bell. 1990. *Yearning: Race, Gender, and Cultural Politics.* Boston: South End.

Hoy, D. 2004. *Critical Resistance: From Poststructuralism to Post-Critique.* Cambridge, MA: MIT Press.

Iglesias-Prieto, N. 2012. "The U.S.-Mexico Border and Children's Social Imaginary: An Analysis of *Wacha el Border* and *Beyond the Border.*" *American Studies Journal* 57. http://www.asjournal.org/203.html.

Ingram, H. N., N. K. Laney, and D. M. Gillilan, 1995. *Divided Waters: Bridging the U.S.-Mexico Border.* Tucson: University of Arizona Press.

Irigaray, L. 1993. "Place, Interval: A Reading of Aristotle, *Physics* IV." In *An Ethics of Sexual Difference*, translated by C. Burke and G. C. Gill, 31–49. Ithaca, NY: Cornell University Press.

Isacson, R., and M. Meyer. 2012. *Beyond the Border Buildup.* Washington, DC: Washington Office on Latin America. http://www.wola.org/files/Beyond_the_Border_Buildup_FINAL.pdf.

"It Gets Even Worse: New Anti-Immigrant Laws are Cruel, Racist and Counterproductive." 2011. *New York Times*, July 3. http://www.nytimes.com/2011/07/04/opinion/04mon1.html.

Johnson, R. 2006. "A Human Parade of Loss: Mexico's Alejandro Santiago Evokes the Toll of Immigration with His Growing Population of Clay Figures." *Los Angeles Times*, April 7. http://articles.latimes.com/2006/apr/07/entertainment/et-migrantes7.

Johnson-Castro, J. 2008. "Inside the Checkpoints: The 51st State." January 4. http://censored-news.blogspot.com/2008/01/inside-checkpoints-51st-state.html.

Kanstroom, D. 2007. *Deportation Nation: Outsiders in American History.* Cambridge, MA: Harvard University Press.

———. 2012. *Aftermath: Deportation Law and the New American Diaspora.* New York: Oxford University Press.

Kanstroom, D., and R. Rosenbloom. 2009. "Restoring Justice and Fairness to Our Deportation Laws." Post-Deportation Human Rights Project, 4–5. Boston, MA: Center for Human Rights and International Justice, Boston College.

Karnik, J., prod. 2002. *A Natural Transformation: Tijuana Estuary Model Marsh Project.* Film. Encinitas, CA: Jim Karnik Productions.

Kerosote, T. 2007. "Borders without Fences." *New York Times,* February 24.

King, M. L., Jr. 2002. "Address at the Conclusion of the Selma to Montgomery March." In *A Call to Conscience: The Landmark Speeches of Dr. Martin Luther King, Jr.,* edited by C. Carson and S. K. Shepard, 111–133. New York: Warner.

Kirkhan, C. 2011. "After 9/11, A New Era in the Business of Detaining Immigrants." http://www.huffingtonpost.com/2011/09/09/911-immigrant-detention-business-for-profit-prism_n_951639.html.

Kleinman, A. 1988. *Rethinking Psychiatry: From Cultural Category to Personal Experience.* New York: Free Press.

Kolb, J. J. 2012. "Federal Immigration Agency Turns to El Paso Migrants' Shelter for Help." Catholic News Service/U.S. Conference of Bishops, February 16. http://www.catholicfreepress.org/national/2012/02/16/federal-immigration-agency-turns-to-el-paso-migrants-shelter-for-help/.

Krall [Shepard], F. R. 1994. *Ecotone: Wayfaring on the Margins.* Albany, NY: SUNY Press.

Kristeva, J. 1987. "Stabat Mater." In *Tales of Love,* translated by L. S. Roudiez, 234–265. New York: Columbia University Press.

Lacey, M. 2011a. "Rift in Arizona as Latino Class Is Found Illegal." *New York Times,* January 9. http://www.nytimes.com/2011/01/08/us/08ethnic.html.

———. 2011b. "Smugglers Guide Illegal Immigrants with Cues via Cellphone." *New York Times,* May 9. http://www.nytimes.com/2011/05/09/us/09coyotes.html.

Lakoff, G., and S. Ferguson. 2006. "The Framing of Immigration." *Huffington Post,* May 19. http://www.huffingtonpost.com/george-lakoff-and-sam-ferguson/the-framing-of-immigratio_b_21320.html.

Leskiw, T. 2009. "A Region of Wounds: Severing the U.S.-Mexico Borderlands." *Terrain. org: A Journal of the Built and Natural Environments.* http://www.terrain.org/articles/24/Leskiw.htm.

Mannes, M. 1959. *Subverse: Rhymes for Our Times.* New York: George Braziller.

Martín-Baró, I. 1994. *Writings for a Liberation Psychology.* Cambridge, MA: Harvard University Press.

Massey, D. 2011. "Isolated, Vulnerable and Broke." *New York Times,* August 4. http://www.nytimes.com/2011/08/05/opinion/hispanic-families-isolated-and-broke.html.

McCafferty, J. D. 2003. *Aliso School: "For the Mexican Children."* Santa Barbara, CA: McSeas.

McCoy, M. n.d. "Border Fence Film." Unpublished typescript.

McCoy, M., and O. Roma, dirs. 2008. *Where Is the Security?* Film. USA.

McKinley, J. C., Jr., and M. Lacey. 2009. "Torrent of Illicit Cash Flows Where U.S. and Mexico Meet." *New York Times,* December 26. http://www.newyorktimes/2009/12/26/world/americas/26laredo.html.

McSwain, R. 2008. "Out Yonder: Rio Grande Foot Bridge Now a Memory." *San Angelo Standard-Times,* July 6. http://www.gosanangelo.com/news/2008/jul/06/out-yonder-rio-grande-foot-bridge-now-a-memory/.

McWhorter, D. 2012. "The Strange Career of Juan Crow." *New York Times,* June 17. http://www.nytimes.com/2012/06/17/opinion/sunday/no-sweet-home-alabama.html.

Memmi, A. 1991. *The Colonizer and the Colonized.* Boston: Beacon Press.

Merleau-Ponty, M. 1964. "Eye and Mind." Translated by C. Dallery. In *The Primacy of Perception*, edited by J. Edie, 160–192. Evanston, IL: Northwestern University Press.

———. 1968. *The Visible and the Invisible.* Translated by A. Lingis. Evanston, IL: Northwestern University Press.

———. 2012. *Phenomenology of Perception.* Translated by D. Landes. New York: Routledge.

Metz, L. C. 2007. *Border: The U.S.-Mexico Line.* El Paso, TX: Mangan.

Morales, A. L. 1999. *Medicine Stories: History, Culture, and the Politics of Integrity.* Boston: South End.

Mostov, J. 2008. *Soft Borders: Rethinking Sovereignty and Democracy.* London: Palgrave Macmillan.

Nicol, S. 2011. "Costly Fence on U.S.-Mexico Border Is Effective—Only in Hurting Nature." *Christian Science Monitor*, February 27. http://www.csmonitor.com/Com
-mentary/Opinion/2011/0227/Costly-fence-on-US-Mexico-border-is-effective-only-in
-hurting-nature.

Nietzsche, F. 2012. *Human, All Too Human.* New York: CreateSpace.

"On the Rise in Alabama." 2011. *New York Times*, November 14, A28.

Peace Parks Foundation. n.d. http://www.peaceparks.org.

Phelan, S. 2011. "Illinois Pulls Out of Secure Communities." *San Francisco Bay Guardian*, May 4. http://www.sfbg.com/politics/2011/05/04/Illinois-pulls-out-secure
-communities.

Pipher, M. 2003. *The Middle of Everywhere: Helping Refugees Enter the American Community.* New York: Mariner.

Pitt, L. 1970. *The Decline of the Californios: A Social History of the Spanish-Speaking Californians, 1846–1890.* Berkeley: University of California Press.

Preston, J. 2011a. "Latinos Said to Bear Weight of a Deportation Program." *New York Times*, October 19. http://www.nytimes.com/2011/10/19/us/latinos-said-to-bear
-weight-of-deportation-program.

———. 2011b. "Some Cheer Border Fence as Others Ponder the Cost." *New York Times*, October 19. http://www.nytimes.com/2011/10/20/us/politics/border-fence-raises-cost
-questions.

Prieto, A. 1999. "Border Art as a Political Strategy." *ISLA: Information Services Latin America.* http://isla.igc.org/Features/Border/mex6.html.

Pueblo Education Fund. 2008. *In the Shadows of Paradise: Testaments from the Undocumented Community in Santa Barbara.* Santa Barbara, CA: Pueblo Education Fund.

Putnam, R. D. 2001. *Bowling Alone: The Collapse and Revival of American Community.* New York: Touchstone Books.

Quijano, A. 2000. "Coloniality of Power, Eurocentrism, and Latin America." *Nepantla: Views from the South* 1 (3): 533–580.

Rabin, N. 2011. *Disappearing Parents: A Report on Immigration Enforcement and the Child Welfare System.* University of Arizona. http://www.law.arizona.edu/depts
/bacon_program/pdf/disappearing_parents_report_final.pdf.

Rainoff, G., dir. 2010. *El muro.* Film. Frontera Filmmakers.

Ramshaw, E. 2011. "Major Health Problems Linked to Poverty." *New York Times*, July 9. http://www.nytimes.com/2011/07/10/us/10tthealth.html.

Rebert, P. 2001. *La Gran Línea: Mapping the United States–Mexico Boundary, 1849–1857.* Austin: University of Texas Press.

Regan, M. 2004. "Artistic Warning." *Tucson Weekly*, May 13. http://www.tucsonweekly
.com/tucson/artistic-warning/Content?oid=1076154.

Robertson, C. 2011. "Critics See the 'Chilling Effect' in Alabama Immigration Law." *New York Times*, October 27. http://www.nytimes.com/2011/10/28/us/alabama -immigration-laws-critics-question-target.html?pagewanted=all.

Robinson, A. R. 2009. "Borderline: Stranded in Nogales: A Reflection on the Lives of New Deportees." *Commonweal Magazine*, May 8. http://commonwealmagazine.org /borderline-0.

Rodriguez, G. 2007. *Mongrels, Bastards, Orphans, and Vagabonds: Mexican Immigration and the Future of Race in America*. New York: Pantheon.

Rodriguez, R. 1992. *Days of Obligation: An Argument with My Mexican Father*. New York: Viking.

Rosas, G. 2012. *Barrio Libre: Criminalizing States and Delinquent Refusals at the New Frontier*. Durham, NC: Duke University Press.

Saillant, K. 2012. "L.A. May Issue Library Cards as a Form of ID." *Los Angeles Times*, September 11. http://articles.latimes.com/2012/sep/11/local/la-me-library-immigrant -card-20120911.

Santner, E. 2001. *On the Psychotheology of Everyday Life: Reflections on Freud and Rosenzweig*. Chicago: University of Chicago Press.

Scheper-Hughes, N. 2007. "The Gray Zone: Small Wars, Peacetime Crimes, and Invisible Genocides." In *The Shadow Side of Fieldwork: Exploring the Blurred Boundaries between Fieldwork and Life*, edited by A. McLean and A. Leibing, 157–184. Malden, MA: Wiley Blackwell.

Schriro, D. 2009. "Immigration Detention Overview and Recommendations." U.S. Immigration and Customs Enforcement. http://www.ice.gov/doclib/about/offices/odpp/pdf /ice-detention-rpt.pdf.

Schultz, K., C. Harris, J. Jackman, and C. Rudolph. 1993. *Santa Barbara Presidio Area: 1840 to Present*. Santa Barbara, CA: Santa Barbara Trust.

Semple, K. 2011. "Illegal Immigrants' Children Suffer Hardships, Study Says." *New York Times*, May 21. http://www.nytimes.com/2011/05/21/nyregion/illegal-immigrants -children-suffer-study-finds.html.

Service Employees International Union. n.d. "'They Take Our Jobs'—Debunking Immigration Myths." http://www.seiu.org/a/immigration/they-take-our-jobs-debunking -immigration-myths.php.

Smith, A. 2010. "One Border, Many Sides." *New York Times*, May 22. http://www .nytimes.com/2010/05/23/opinion/23deavere-smith.html?pagewanted=all.

Snyder, G. 1990. *The Practice of the Wild*. New York: North Point.

Southern Poverty Law Center. 2009. "Climate of Fear: Latino Immigrants in Suffolk County." http://www.splcenter.org/publications/climate-of-fear-latino-immigrants-in -suffolk-county-ny/climate-of-fear.

———. 2011. "SPLC Steps forward to Protect the Human Rights of Immigrants." *Southern Poverty Law Center Report* (Winter).

Spener, D. 2003. "Controlling the Border in El Paso del Norte: Operation Blockade or Operation Charade?" In *Ethnography at the Border*, edited by P. Vila, 187–202. Minneapolis: University of Minnesota Press.

Spener, D., and K. Staudt. 1998. *The U.S.-Mexico Border: Transcending Divisions, Contesting Identities*. Boulder, CO: Lynne Rienner.

Spinoza, Benedictus de. 2000. *Ethics*. Translated by G. H. R. Parkinson. New York: Oxford University Press.

Straus, E. 1966. "The Upright Posture." In *Phenomenological Psychology*, 137–165. New York: Basic Books.

Takaki, R. 1999. *A Different Mirror: A History of Multicultural America*. Boston: Little, Brown.

Theroux, P. 2012. "The Country Just over the Fence." *New York Times*, February 26,

travel section, 6. http://travel.nytimes.com/2012/02/26/travel/nogales-mexico-a-few
-steps-and-a-whole-world-away.html?pagewanted=all.

Thich Nhat Hanh. 2004. *Creating True Peace: Ending Violence in Yourself, Your Family,
Your Community, and the World*. New York: Free Press.

———. 2005. *Being Peace*. Berkeley, CA: Parallax.

Thoreau, H. D. 1991. "Walking." In *Nature Walking*, edited by J. Elder. Boston: Beacon.

Tierra Environmental Services and Southwest Restoration Association for the Tijuana
Estuary. 2004. "Model Marsh." In *Tijuana Estuary Tidal Restoration Program*.

Tutu, D. 2000. *No Future Without Forgiveness*. New York: Random House.

U.S. Congress. 1898. *Report of the Boundary Commission upon the Survey and Re-
marking of the Boundary between the United States and Mexico West of the Rio
Grande, 1891–1896*. Fifty-fifth Congress, second session, S. Doc. 247. Washington,
DC: GPO.

U.S. Immigration and Customs Enforcement. 2010. *Secure Communities: A Modernized
Approach to Identifying and Removing Criminal Aliens*. http://www.ice.gov/doclib
/secure-communities/pdf/sc-brochure.pdf.

Watkins, M., and H. Shulman. 2008. *Toward Psychologies of Liberation*. New York:
Palgrave Macmillan.

"Welcome Dayton: Immigrant Friendly City." n.d. http://www.welcomedayton.org.

Werne, J. R. 2007. *The Imaginary Line: A History of the United States and Mexican
Boundary Survey, 1848–1857*. Fort Worth: Texas Christian University Press.

Whitehead, A. N. 1953. *Science and the Modern World*. New York: Free Press.

Williamson, T. 2000. *Vagueness*. Oxford: Oxford University Press.

Winnicott, D. W. 1989. "Transitional Objects and Transitional Phenomena." In *Playing
and Reality*. New York: Routledge.

Wong, J. 2006. *Democracy's Promise: Immigrants and American Civic Institutions*. Ann
Arbor: University of Michigan Press.

Woolman, J. 1989. *The Journal and Major Essays of John Woolman*. Edited by P. P.
Moulton. Richmond, IN: Friends United.

Yoshikawa, H. 2011. *Immigrants Raising Citizens: Undocumented Parents and Their
Young Children*. New York: Russell Sage Foundation.

Young-Bruehl, E. 2009. *Why Arendt Matters*. New Haven, CT: Yale University Press.

Yun, L. 2009. "21st Century: The Era of the Contract Coolie." Paper presented at American Philosophical Association, Eastern Division Program, Newark, DE.

Zavaleta, A. N. 2010. "The Last Battle of the Mexican-American War: The United States
of America versus the University of Texas at Brownsville and Texas Southmost College." *Continuing Studies in Rio Grande Valley History* 9:259–304.

Index

Index